THE
FELLOWSHIP
OF THE KNITS

THE UNOFFICIAL
LORD OF THE RINGS
KNITTING BOOK

THE
FELLOWSHIP
OF THE KNITS

THE UNOFFICIAL
LORD OF THE RINGS
KNITTING BOOK

By Tanis Gray

REEL INK PRESS

CONTENTS

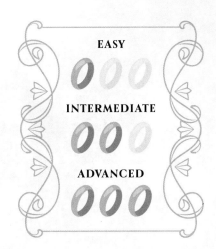

EASY

INTERMEDIATE

ADVANCED

INTRODUCTION

By Tanis Gray

Over twenty years ago, *The Lord of the Rings* trilogy captured the attention of moviegoers across the globe. Never had a sweepingly epic adventure been filmed all at once, then released across three years in theaters. Fans arrived in costume or holding tattered copies of J.R.R. Tolkien's text. Cosplay Elves sat next to popcorn-eating Dwarves; Orcs conversed with Hobbits in hairy rubber feet—it was Middle-earth here on Earth. The lights in the theater dimmed, and we all became part of the Fellowship as we watched.

No matter how you were introduced to Tolkien—via book or film—knitters have long been asking for a book of patterns inspired by the creatures, locations, and events from this fantastic realm. A fan of Gimli? Knit yourself a mosaic Dwarf Helmet on page 11 to keep your head warm while on an adventure of your own. Heading out for brunch with friends? Work up a pair of Second Breakfast Socks on page 161! Chilly while you're out spell casting? A stunning Light of the Two Trees Pullover inspired by Galadriel on page 137 would be a perfect project to cast on next. A superfan? Knit up a clever One Ring Cowl on page 103 with Elvish text. Whether you're Team Fellowship or Team Sauron, there's something for every fan within these pages, whether directly inspired by the trilogy or a costume replica.

With extensive size ranges, yarn choices for all budgets, and a color palette inspired by Middle-earth itself, there are projects for lace, cable, colorwork, double knitting, and brioche knitters across all skill levels. Sprinkled in amongst the garments, accessories, toys, home decor, socks, and shawls are favorite quotes from both the books and the films, as well as information on what inspired the designs.

This is a knitting book by fans, for fans, so grab your needles and yarn, gather your knitting Fellowship, and let's cast on!

CHAPTER ONE

COSTUME REPLICAS

DWARF HELMET

DESIGNED BY ALINA APPASOVA

Known for their lust for gold, stubbornness, and talent for digging for metals and stones in the mines, Dwarves are stocky creatures with a penchant for long beards. With exceedingly long life spans, they choose to spend their time mining and building their great underground halls and cities. While primarily artisans, Dwarves are also excellent warriors. Crafted of leather and precious metals, much of their battle wear and weaponry is adorned with geometric symbols. This knitted Dwarf helmet, inspired by the armor Gimli wears into battle, features an earthy darker-toned palette, reflecting the Dwarves' preference to live most of their lives beneath the mountains in the dark.

With your very own Dwarf helmet, you, too, can feel battle (and cold weather) ready! Knit in garter slip-stitch colorwork, or mosaic knitting, there's no color stranding along the wrong side. First two cheek guard pieces are worked flat. Next the pieces are joined to form the bottom back neck. Additional stitches are then cast on with the remainder of the hat worked in the round. Geometric motifs mimic the beautiful metalwork Dwarves are known for, set on a background of hand-dyed brown to give the appearance of leather.

SIZES

Small (Large)

Designed to fit with little to no ease; choose a size closest to your head circumference for the best fit. Sample modeled is size Small.

FINISHED MEASUREMENTS

Circumference: 20½ (23) in. / 52 (58.5) cm

Back Neck to Crown Height (not including Cheek Guards): 9 (10) in. / 23 (25.5) cm

YARN

Fingering weight yarn, shown in Hazel Knits *Artisan Sock* (90% superwash merino, 10% nylon; 400 yd. / 366 m per 3½ oz. / 100 g hank)

Colorways:

- **Main Color (MC):** Wild Rice, 1 hank
- **Contrast Color (CC):** Nickel, 1 hank

NEEDLES

US 3 / 3.25 mm, 16 in. / 40 cm long circular needle, 24 in. / 60 cm long circular needle and set of 4 or 5 double-pointed needles or size needed to obtain gauge

NOTIONS

Stitch markers (8; 1 unique for BOR)

D-3 / 3.25 mm crochet hook

Tapestry needle

GAUGE

25 sts and 62 rows = 4 in. / 10 cm in 2-color mosaic st worked flat, taken after blocking

Make sure to check your gauge.

PATTERN NOTES

The hat starts with flat knitted cheek guards, worked separately. The cheek guards are then joined to form the back of the neck. After the back is finished, additional stitches are cast on to form the front of the hat, and the remainder of the hat is worked in the round.

Written instructions are provided for the entirety of the pattern. Optional charts are provided. Read carefully through all written instructions before working from the charts to ensure no instructions get missed.

To work from the charts for the flat portions of the hat, read all RS (odd-numbered) rows from right to left and all WS (even-numbered rows) from left to right. When working in the round, read all charted rows from right to left.

When the circumference of the hat becomes too small for the circular needle during the Dome Top Shaping, change to dpns to finish the hat.

On WS rows, when working on top of a kfb, knit both stitches of the kfb.

On WS rows following cast on sts, knit on top of the cast on sts.

On rounds following increases or decreases, purl on top of the increased or decreased stitches.

Instructions are written for size small, with size large in parentheses; when only one number is given, it applies to both sizes.

PATTERN INSTRUCTIONS

LEFT CHEEK GUARD

Using MC and the 16 in. / 40 cm circular needle, CO 14 sts using the Twisted German cast on method. Do not join to work in the rnd.

Join CC.

Follow written instructions below or work from Left Cheek Guard chart.

Row 1 (RS, inc): With CC, kfb, sl1 wyib, k9, sl1 wyib, k2—15 sts.

Row 2 (WS, and all WS rows): With yarn used on previous RS row, knit the knit sts and slip the slipped sts purlwise wyif.

Row 3 (inc): With MC, kfb, k2, sl1 wyib, k5, sl1 wyib, k1, sl1 wyib, k3—16 sts.

Row 5 (inc): With CC, kfb, sl1 wyib, k3, sl1 wyib, k7, sl1 wyib, k2—17 sts.

Row 7 (inc): With MC, kfb, k2, sl1 wyib, k3, (sl1 wyib, k1) 3 times, sl1 wyib, k3—18 sts.

Row 9 (inc): With CC, kfb, sl1 wyib, k3, sl1 wyib, k1, sl1 wyib, k5, sl1 wyib, k1, sl1 wyib, k2—19 sts.

Row 11 (inc): With MC, kfb, k2, sl1 wyib, k5, (sl1 wyib, k1) 3 times, sl1 wyib, k3—20 sts.

Row 13 (inc): With CC, kfb, sl1 wyib, k3, sl1 wyib, k1, sl1 wyib, k7, sl1 wyib, k1, sl1 wyib, k2—21 sts.

Row 15 (inc): With MC, kfb, k2, sl1 wyib, k5, sl1 wyib, k1, sl1 wyib, k5, sl1 wyib, k3—22 sts.

Row 17 (inc): With CC, kfb, sl1 wyib, k3, sl1 wyib, k7, sl1 wyib, k1, sl1 wyib, k3, sl1 wyib, k2—23 sts.

Row 18: With CC, knit the knit sts and slip the slipped sts purlwise wyif.

Break both yarns. Do not bind off; leave live sts on hold on 16 in. / 40 cm circular needle and set piece aside.

RIGHT CHEEK GUARD

Using MC and the 24 in. / 60 cm circular needle, CO 14 sts using the Twisted German cast on method. Do not join to work in the rnd.

Join CC.

Follow written instructions below or work from Right Cheek Guard chart.

Row 1 (RS, inc): With CC, k2, sl1 wyib, k9, sl1 wyib, kfb—15 sts.

Row 2 (WS, and all WS rows): With yarn used on previous RS row, knit the knit sts and slip the slipped sts purlwise wyif.

Row 3 (inc): With MC, k3, sl1 wyib, k1, sl1 wyib, k5, sl1 wyib, k2, kfb—16 sts.

Row 5 (inc): With CC, k2, sl1 wyib, k7, sl1 wyib, k3, sl1 wyib, kfb—17 sts.

Row 7 (inc): With MC, k3, (sl1 wyib, k1) 3 times, sl1 wyib, k3, sl1 wyib, k2, kfb—18 sts.

Row 9 (inc): With CC, k2, sl1 wyib, k1, sl1 wyib, k5, sl1 wyib, k1, sl1 wyib, k3, sl1 wyib, kfb—19 sts.

Row 11 (inc): With MC, k3, (sl1 wyib, k1) 3 times, sl1 wyib, k5, sl1 wyib, k2, kfb—20 sts.

Row 13 (inc): With CC, k2, sl1 wyib, k1, sl1 wyib, k7, sl1 wyib, k1, sl1 wyib, k3, sl1 wyib, kfb—21 sts.

Row 15 (inc): With MC, k3, sl1 wyib, k5, sl1 wyib, k1, sl1 wyib, k5, sl1 wyib, k2, kfb—22 sts.

Row 17 (inc): With CC, k2, sl1 wyib, k3, sl1 wyib, k1, sl1 wyib, k7, sl1 wyib, k3, sl1 wyib, kfb—23 sts.

Row 18: With CC, knit the knit sts and slip the slipped sts purlwise wyif.
Do not break yarns.

BACK NECK— SECTION 1

Follow written instructions below or work from Back Neck—Section 1 chart.

Row 1 (RS, inc): Continuing with the Right Cheek Guard, with MC, (k5, sl1 wyib) 2 times, (k1, sl1 wyib) 2 times, k3, sl1 wyib, k3. Turn work so WS facing and, using the Crochet cast on method, CO 5 sts, pm, CO 60 (84) sts, pm, CO 6 sts. Turn work so RS is facing again. Place the live sts of the Left Cheek Guard on the LHN of the 24 in. / 60 cm needle and, with MC, work across the 23 sts as follows: (k3, sl1 wyib) 2 times, (k1, sl1 wyib) 2 times, k5, sl1 wyib, k5—117 (141) sts. Set the 16 in. / 40 cm circular needle aside; it will be used again later.

Row 2 (WS, and all WS rows): With yarn used on previous RS row, sl1 knitwise wyib, knit the knit sts and slip the slipped sts purlwise wyif to last 2 sts, sl2 wyif.

Row 3 (dec): With CC, k2tog tbl, k2, sl1 wyib, k3, sl1 wyib, k1, sl1 wyib, k5, sl1 wyib, k1, sl1 wyib, k3, sl1 wyib, k5, sm, (sl1 wyib, k5) to M, sm, sl1 wyib, k5, sl1 wyib, k3, sl1 wyib, k1, sl1 wyib, k5, sl1 wyib, k1, sl1 wyib, k3, sl1 wyib, k2, k2tog—2 sts dec.

Row 5 (dec): With MC, k2tog tbl, k4, sl1 wyib, k3, (sl1 wyib, k1) 2 times, (sl1 wyib, k5) 2 times, sl1 wyib, sm, (k1, sl1 wyib, k3, sl1 wyib) to M, sm, k1, (sl1 wyib, k5) 2 times, (sl1 wyib, k1) 2 times, sl1 wyib, k3, sl1 wyib, k4, k2tog—2 sts dec.

Row 7 (dec): With CC, k2tog tbl, k2, sl1 wyib, k3, sl1 wyib, k7, sl1 wyib, k1, sl1 wyib, k3, (sl1 wyib, k1) 2 times, sm, (sl1 wyib, k1) to M, sm, (sl1 wyib, k1) 2 times, sl1 wyib, k3, sl1 wyib, k1, sl1 wyib, k7, sl1 wyib, k3, sl1 wyib, k2, k2tog—2 sts dec.

Row 9 (dec): With MC, k2tog tbl, k4, sl1 wyib, k5, sl1 wyib, k1, sl1 wyib, k5, sl1 wyib, k3, sl1 wyib, sm, (k1, sl1 wyib) to M, sm, k1, sl1 wyib, k3, sl1 wyib, k5, sl1 wyib, k1, sl1 wyib, k5, sl1 wyib, k4, k2tog—2 sts dec.

Row 11 (dec): With CC, k2tog tbl, k2, sl1 wyib, k3, sl1 wyib, k1, sl1 wyib, k7, sl1 wyib, k3, sl1 wyib, k1, sm, (k2, sl1 wyib, k1, sl1 wyib, k1) to M, sm, k2, sl1 wyib, k3, sl1 wyib, k7, sl1 wyib, k1, sl1 wyib, k3, sl1 wyib, k2, k2tog—2 sts dec.

Row 13 (dec): With MC, k2tog tbl, k4, sl1 wyib, k5, (sl1 wyib, k1) 2 times, sl1 wyib, k3, sl1 wyib, k2, rm, k6, pm, knit to 6 sts before M, pm, k6, rm, (k3, sl1 wyib) 2 times, (k1, sl1 wyib) 2 times, k5, sl1 wyib, k4, k2tog—2 sts dec.

Row 14: With MC, sl1 knitwise wyib, knit the knit sts and slip the slipped sts purlwise wyif to last 2 sts, sl2 wyif.

Rep [Rows 3–14] 1 (2) more time(s), working the sts in the red rep box 2 times fewer than the prev rep. Then rep [Rows 3–6] once more.

28 (40) sts dec; 89 (101) sts rem.

BACK NECK— SECTION 2

The st count rem the same throughout this section.

Follow written instructions below or work from Back Neck—Section 2 chart.

Row 1 (RS): With CC, k2, sl1 wyib, k1, sl1 wyib, k3, sl1 wyib, k7, sl1 wyib, k1, sl1 wyib, k3, (sl1 wyib, k1) 2 times, sm, (sl1 wyib, k1) to M, sm, (sl1 wyib, k1) 2 times, sl1 wyib, k3, sl1 wyib, k1, sl1 wyib, k7, sl1 wyib, k3, sl1 wyib, k1, sl1 wyib, k2.

Row 2 (WS, and all WS rows): With yarn used on previous RS row, knit the knit sts and slip the slipped sts purlwise wyif.

Row 3: With MC, (k3, sl1 wyib) 2 times, k5, sl1 wyib, k1, sl1 wyib, k5, sl1 wyib, k3, sl1 wyib, sm, (k1, sl1 wyib) to M, sm, k1, sl1 wyib, k3, sl1 wyib, k5, sl1 wyib, k1, sl1 wyib, k5, (sl1 wyib, k3) 2 times.

Row 5: With CC, k2, (sl1 wyib, k3) 2 times, sl1 wyib, k1, sl1 wyib, k7, sl1 wyib, k3, sl1 wyib, k1, sm, [k2, (sl1 wyib, k1) 2 times] to M, sm, k2, sl1 wyib, k3, sl1 wyib, k7, sl1 wyib, k1, (sl1 wyib, k3) 2 times, sl1 wyib, k2.

Row 7: With MC, k3, sl1 wyib, k1, sl1 wyib, k3, sl1 wyib, k5, (sl1 wyib, k1) 2 times, sl1 wyib, k3, sl1 wyib, k2, rm, k6, pm, knit to 6 sts before M, pm, k6, rm, (k3, sl1 wyib) 2 times, (k1, sl1 wyib) 2 times, k5, sl1 wyib, k3, sl1 wyib, k1, sl1 wyib, k3.

Row 9: With CC, k2, sl1 wyib, k1, (sl1 wyib, k3) 2 times, sl1 wyib, k1, sl1 wyib, k5, sl1 wyib, k1, sl1 wyib, k3, sl1 wyib, k5, sm, (sl1 wyib, k5) to M, sm, sl1 wyib, k5, sl1 wyib, k3, sl1 wyib, k1, sl1 wyib, k5, sl1 wyib, k1, (sl1 wyib, k3) 2 times, sl1 wyib, k1, sl1 wyib, k2.

Row 11: With MC, k3, (sl1 wyib, k1) 2 times, (sl1 wyib, k3) 2 times, (sl1 wyib, k1) 2 times, (sl1 wyib, k5) 2 times, sl1 wyib, sm, (k1, sl1 wyib, k3, sl1 wyib) to M, sm, k1, (sl1 wyib, k5) 2 times, (sl1 wyib, k1) 2 times, (sl1 wyib, k3) 2 times, (sl1 wyib, k1) 2 times, sl1 wyib, k3.

Row 13: With CC, k2, sl1 wyib, k7, sl1 wyib, k3, sl1 wyib, k7, sl1 wyib, k1, sl1 wyib, k3, (sl1 wyib, k1) 2 times, sm, (sl1 wyib, k1) to M, sm, (sl1 wyib, k1) 2 times, sl1 wyib, k3, sl1 wyib, k1, sl1 wyib, k7, sl1 wyib, k3, sl1 wyib, k7, sl1 wyib, k2.

Row 15: With MC, k3, sl1 wyib, k1, (sl1 wyib, k3) 2 times, sl1 wyib, k5, sl1 wyib, k1, sl1 wyib, k5, sl1 wyib, k3, sl1 wyib, sm, (k1, sl1 wyib) to M, sm, k1, sl1 wyib, k3, sl1 wyib, k5, sl1 wyib, k1, sl1 wyib, k5, (sl1 wyib, k3) 2 times, sl1 wyib, k1, sl1 wyib, k3.

Row 17: With CC, k2, sl1 wyib, k9, sl1 wyib, k3, sl1 wyib, k1, sl1 wyib, k7, sl1 wyib, k3, sl1 wyib, k1, sm, [k2, (sl1 wyib, k1) 2 times] to M, sm, k2, sl1 wyib, k3, sl1 wyib, k7, sl1 wyib, k1, sl1 wyib, k3, sl1 wyib, k9, sl1 wyib, k2.

Row 18: With CC, knit the knit sts and slip the slipped sts purlwise wyif, rm as encountered.

Do not break yarns.

LATERAL BAND

On the first setup row, you will work across the existing Back Neck sts, then cast on sts for the front and join to work in the rnd. As you work Setup Row 1, below, knit onto the 16 in. / 40 cm circular needle. The 24 in. / 60 cm needle will not be used again.

Setup Row 1 (RS, inc): With MC, knit to end of row. Turn work so WS facing

and, using the Crochet cast on method, CO 39 (43) sts. Pm for BOR and join to work in the rnd—128 (144) sts.

Setup Rnd 2: With MC, purl to end of rnd.

Break both yarns.

Remove BOR M, slip 49 (56) sts from the LHN to the RHN purlwise. Replace BOR M (the M will be 5 sts to the left of the center back neck). The st count rem the same throughout this section.

Join CC.

Setup Rnd 3: With CC, k55 (63), M1L, pm, k3, s2kp, k3, M1L, pm, knit to end of rnd.

Setup Rnd 4: With CC, purl. Join MC.

Follow written instructions below or work from Lateral Band chart.

Rnd 1: With MC, (k7, sl1 wyib) to M, sm, M1L, sl1 wyib, k1, s2kp, k1, sl1 wyib, M1L, sl1 wyib, sm, (k7, sl1 wyib) to end of rnd.

Rnd 2 (and all even-numbered rnds): With yarn used on previous rnd, purl the knit sts and slip the slipped sts purlwise wyib.

Rnd 3: With CC, (k3, sl1 wyib, k4) to M, sm, k2, sl1 wyib, k1, sl1 wyib, k3, sm, (k3, sl1 wyib, k4) to end of rnd.

Rnd 5: With MC, (sl1 wyib, k1) to M, sm, k3, sl1 wyib, k4, sm, (sl1 wyib, k1) to end of rnd.

Rnd 7: With CC, (k7, sl1 wyib) to end of rnd (sm as encountered).

Rnd 9: With MC, (k3, sl1 wyib, k4) to M, sm, k2, sl1 wyib, k1, sl1 wyib, k3, sm, (k3, sl1 wyib, k4) to end of rnd.

Rnd 11: Work as for Rnd 7.

Rnd 13: Work as for Rnd 5.

Rnd 15: Work as for Rnd 3.

Rnd 17: With MC, (k7, sl1 wyib) to M, rm, k1, sl1 wyib, k3, sl1 wyib, k1, sl1 wyib, rm, (k7, sl1 wyib) to end of rnd.

Rnd 18: With MC, purl the knit sts and slip the slipped sts purlwise wyib.

DOME BOTTOM

The st count rem the same throughout this section.

Setup Rnd 1: With CC, *k23 (27), pm, k9, pm; rep from * to end of rnd (using existing BOR M as final marker).

Setup Rnd 2: With CC, purl to end of rnd.

Follow written instructions below or work from Dome Bottom chart.

Rnd 1 (RS): With MC, *knit to M, sm, sl1 wyib, k1, sl1 wyib, k3, sl1 wyib, k1, sl1 wyib, sm; rep from * to end of rnd.

Rnd 2 (and all even-numbered rnds): With yarn used on previous rnd, purl the knit sts and slip the slipped sts purlwise wyib.

Rnd 3: With CC, *(sl1 wyib, k1) to 1 st before M, sl1 wyib, sm, k3, sl1 wyib, k1, sl1 wyib, k3, sm; rep from * to end of rnd.

Rnd 5: With MC, *knit to M, sm, (sl1 wyib, k3) 2 times, sl1 wyib, sm; rep from * to end of rnd.

Rnd 7: With CC, *(sl1 wyib, k1) to 1 st before M, sl1 wyib, sm, k1, sl1 wyib, k5, sl1 wyib, k1, sm; rep from * to end of rnd.

Rnd 9: With MC, *knit to M, sm, sl1 wyib, k2, sl1 wyib, k1, sl1 wyib, k2, sl1 wyib, sm; rep from * to end of rnd.

Rnd 11: Work as for Rnd 7.

Rnd 13: Work as for Rnd 5.

Rnd 15: Work as for Rnd 3.

Rnd 16: With CC, purl the knit sts and slip the slipped sts purlwise wyib.

Rep [Rnds 1–16] once more.

DOME TOP SHAPING

Follow written instructions below or work from Dome Top Shaping chart for your size.

Both Sizes:

Rnd 1 (dec): With MC, *k1, ssk, knit to 3 sts before M, k2tog, k1, sm, sl1 wyib, k1, sl1 wyib, k3, sl1 wyib, k1, sl1 wyib, sm; rep from * to end of rnd—120 (136) sts rem.

Rnd 2 (and all even-numbered rnds): With yarn used on previous rnd, purl the knit sts and slip the slipped sts purlwise wyib.

Rnd 3 (dec): With CC, *sl1 wyib, ssk, sl1 wyib, (k1, sl1 wyib) to 3 sts before M, k2tog, sl1 wyib, sm, k3, sl1 wyib, k1, sl1 wyib, k3, sm; rep from * to end of rnd—112 (128) sts rem.

Rnd 5 (dec): With MC, *k1, ssk, knit to 3 sts before M, k2tog, k1, sm, (sl1 wyib, k3) 2 times, sl1 wyib, sm; rep from * to end of rnd—104 (120) sts rem.

Rnd 7 (dec): With CC, *sl1 wyib, ssk, sl1 wyib, (k1, sl1 wyib) to 3 sts before M, k2tog, sl1 wyib, sm, k1, sl1 wyib, k5, sl1 wyib, k1, sm; rep from * to end of rnd—96 (112) sts rem.

Rnd 9 (dec): With MC, *k1, ssk, knit to 3 sts before M, k2tog, k1, sm, sl1 wyib, k2, sl1 wyib, k1, sl1 wyib, k2, sl1 wyib, sm; rep from * to end of rnd—88 (104) sts rem.

Rnd 11 (dec): With CC, *sl1 wyib, ssk, sl1 wyib, (k1, sl1 wyib) to 3 sts before M, k2tog, sl1 wyib, sm, k1, sl1 wyib, k5, sl1 wyib, k1, sm; rep from * to end of rnd—80 (96) sts rem.

Rnd 13 (dec): With MC, *k1, ssk, knit to 3 sts before M, k2tog, k1, sm, (sl1 wyib, k3) 2 times, sl1 wyib, sm; rep from * to end of rnd—72 (88) sts rem.

Rnd 15 (dec): With CC, *sl1 wyib, ssk, sl1 wyib, (k1, sl1 wyib) to 3 sts before M, k2tog, sl1 wyib, sm, k3, sl1 wyib, k1, sl1 wyib, k3, sm; rep from * to end of rnd—64 (80) sts rem.

Rnd 17 (dec): With MC, *k1, ssk, knit to 3 sts before M, k2tog, k1, sm, sl1 wyib, k1, sl1 wyib, k3, sl1 wyib, k1, sl1 wyib, sm; rep from * to end of rnd—56 (72) sts rem.

Rnd 18: With MC, purl the knit sts and slip the slipped sts purlwise wyib.

Size Small ONLY:

Rnd 19 (dec): With CC, *sl1 wyib, s2kp, sl1 wyib, rm, k9, sm; rep from * to end of rnd—48 sts rem.

Rnd 21 (dec): With MC, *s2kp, sl1 wyib, (k1, sl1 wyib) to M, sm; rep from * to end of rnd—40 sts rem.

Rnd 22: With MC, purl the

knit sts and slip the slipped sts purlwise wyib.

Break MC; finish the Dome Top Shaping with CC only.

Rnd 23 (dec): *K2, ssk, k3, k2tog, k1, sm; rep from * to end of rnd—32 sts rem.

Rnd 25 (dec): *K1, ssk, k3, k2tog, sm; rep from * to end of rnd—24 sts rem.

Rnd 27 (dec): *K1, ssk, k1, k2tog, sm; rep from * to end of rnd—16 sts rem.

Rnd 29 (dec): *K2tog 2 times, rm; rep from * to end of rnd—8 sts rem.

Size Large ONLY:

Rnd 19 (dec): With CC, *sl1 wyib, ssk, sl1 wyib, k1, sl1 wyib, k2tog, sl1 wyib, sm, k9, sm; rep from * to end of rnd—64 sts rem.

Rnd 21 (dec): With MC, *k1, ssk, k1, k2tog, k1, sm, sl1 wyib, (k1, sl1 wyib) to M, sm; rep from * to end of rnd—56 sts rem.

Rnd 23 (dec): With CC, *sl1 wyib, s2kp, sl1 wyib, rm, k9, sm; rep from * to end of rnd—48 sts rem.

Rnd 25 (dec): With MC, *s2kp, sl1 wyib, (k1, sl1 wyib) to M, sm; rep from * to end of rnd—40 sts rem.

Rnd 26: With MC, purl the knit sts and slip the slipped sts purlwise wyib.

Break MC; finish the Dome Top Shaping with CC only.

Rnd 27 (dec): *K2, ssk, k3, k2tog, k1, sm; rep from * to end of rnd—32 sts rem.

Rnd 29 (dec): *K1, ssk, k3, k2tog, sm; rep from * to end of rnd—24 sts rem.

Rnd 31 (dec): *K1, ssk, k1, k2tog, sm; rep from * to end of rnd—16 sts rem.

Rnd 33 (dec): *K2tog 2 times, rm; rep from * to end of rnd—8 sts rem.

Both Sizes:

Break CC yarn, leaving an 8 in. / 20.5 cm tail. Thread tail through rem live sts and pull tight to cinch closed. Secure tail to WS.

FINISHING

Weave in all ends and wet block to dimensions. Allow to dry completely. Trim all ends.

KEY

- ▨ No stitch
- ☐ Knit on RS, purl on WS
- − Purl on RS, knit on WS
- ᴗ Crochet cast on
- ∨ Slip st purlwise: wyib on RS, wyif on WS
- ⊠ Slip st knitwise wtib
- ╱ k2tog
- ⅋ k2tog tbl
- ╲ ssk
- ⅄ sk2p
- ⊽ kfb
- ⅂ M1L
- ■ MC
- ▩ CC
- ❘ Stitch marker
- ▭ Stitch pattern repeat

LATERAL BAND

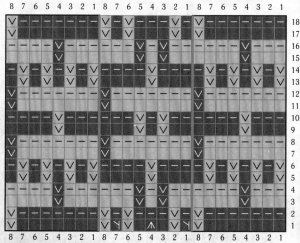

[work 8 (9) times]   [work 7 (8) times]

16

BACK NECK - SECTION 1 (left)

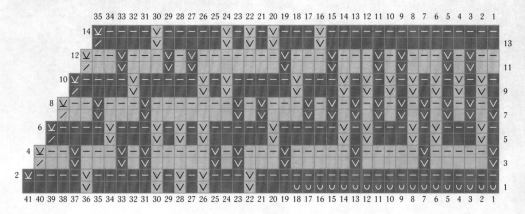

BACK NECK - SECTION 1 (right)

[work 4 (8) times]

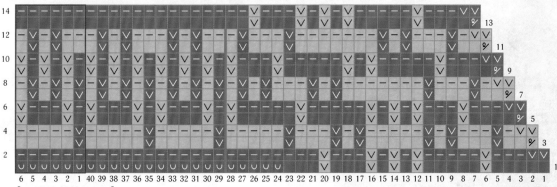

[work 6 (10) times]

LEFT CHEEK GUARD

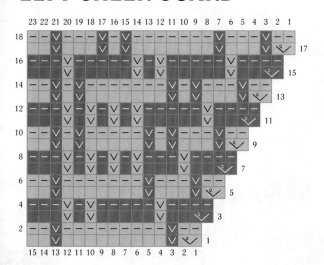

RIGHT CHEEK GUARD

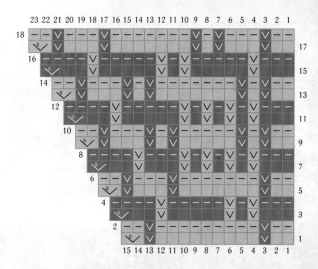

BACK NECK - SECTION 2 (left)

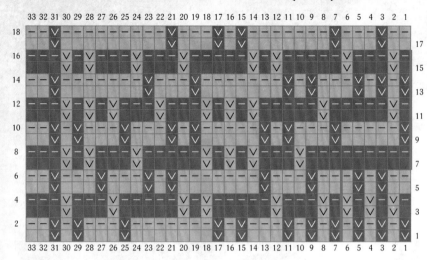

> "Let them come! There is one Dwarf yet in Moria who still draws breath!"
>
> –Gimli, *The Lord of the Rings: The Fellowship of the Ring* film

DOME TOP SHAPING - SMALL

DOME BOTTOM

[work 5 (6) times]

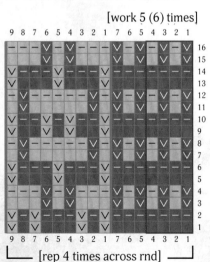

[rep 4 times across rnd]

BACK NECK - SECTION 2 (right)

[work 5 (6) times]

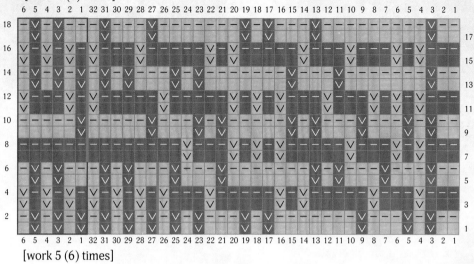

[work 5 (6) times]

DOME TOP SHAPING - LARGE

DWARF BATTLE GAUNTLETS

DESIGNED BY LILIUM ROSE

Skilled in battle, Dwarves were also masters of manufacturing weaponry and armor. Though difficult to maneuver due to their top-heaviness and long handles, axes were commonplace amongst Dwarves while in combat, as were short swords and daggers to accommodate their lack of height. Mostly used in blacksmithing, hammers could also double as weapons, as could occasionally bows. But Dwarves were renowned for their durable armor made of iron or chain mail (which they invented). They could cover their bodies with mithril, an uncommonly precious, lightweight silver metal, and their faces with forged masks. Though small, they were indeed mighty and a force to be reckoned with.

While these weathered gauntlets haven't seen many battles in their day, they're inspired by those that have. They're worked in stockinette in the round from the bottom up, and stitches are periodically bound off then cast on to create slits to give a battle-ready look. These gauntlets are finished with pyramid studs at the knuckles so you, too, can display your tenacity in battle. To arms!

SIZES

1 (2)

FINISHED MEASUREMENTS

Wrist Circumference: 6½ (8) in. / 16.5 (20.5) cm

Top of Hand Circumference: 4¾ (6½) in. / 12 (16.5) cm

Length: 8¼ in. / 21 cm

Thumb Circumference: 2 (2½) in. / 5 (6.5) cm

The gauntlets are designed to be worn with approx. 0 to 1 in. / 0 to 2.5 cm of positive ease. Shown in size 2.

YARN

DK weight yarn, shown in Brooklyn Tweed *Dapple* (2-ply; 60% US merino wool, 40% organic cotton; 165 yd. / 150 m per 1¾ oz. / 50 g hank), 1 hank in color Black Walnut

NEEDLES

US 3 / 3.25 mm, 9 in. / 23 cm long circular needle and set of double-pointed needles

US 4 / 3.5 mm, 9 in. / 23 cm long circular needle and set of double-pointed needles or size needed to obtain gauge

NOTIONS

Eight ³/₈ in. / 10 mm pyramid studs

Waste yarn or stitch holders

Tapestry needle

Stitch markers

Locking stitch markers

Scrap fabric or felt (optional)

Fabric glue or sewing needle and thread (optional)

Row counter (optional)

GAUGE

23 sts and 36 rows = 4 in. / 10 cm in
St st worked in the round on larger
needle, taken after blocking

Make sure to check your gauge.

PATTERN NOTES

These gauntlets are worked in the
round from the bottom up. The
smaller needle is used for the rolled
top and bottom cuff, and the gauge-
size needle is used for the body of
the mitts.

The gauntlets are largely the same;
the Cast On & Cuff, Body, Cuff,
and Thumb sections are worked
identically. However, the thumb
gussets are mirrored to fit each hand
properly. Be sure to make a left and
right gauntlet, differentiating the
two based on how the thumb gusset
is worked.

The thumbs are designed to be
fitted to allow for movement, while
keeping them from slipping off your
hands.

Instructions are provided for size
1 first, with size 2 in parentheses.
When only one number is provided,
it applies to both sizes.

SPECIAL TECHNIQUE

Slit Bind Off (worked over an odd
number of sts)

With the RS facing, sl1 wyif, move
yarn to back between the needles,
*sl1 wyib, pass second st on RHN
over first st on RHN (1 st BO), sl1
wyif, move yarn to back between the
needles, pass second st on RHN over
first st on RHN (1 st BO); rep from
* until 1 more st rem to be BO, sl1
wyib, pass second st on RHN over
first st on RHN (final st BO).

PATTERN INSTRUCTIONS

CAST ON & CUFF

With smaller 9 in. / 23 cm
needle, CO 38 (46) sts
using the Long Tail cast
on method. Pm for BOR
and join to work in the rnd,
being careful not to twist
the sts.

Purl all rnds until the cuff
measures 1½ in. / 4 cm
from the CO edge.

BODY

Switch to larger needles.
Knit all rnds until the
gauntlet measures 2 in. /
5 cm from the CO edge.
On the final rnd, place a
SSM after 19 (23) sts (the
halfway point of the rnd).

Make Slits

Rnd 1: K4 (5), BO 11 (13)
sts using the Slit bind
off method (see Special
Technique), sl rem st on
RHN purlwise to LHN, with
RS still facing, CO 11 (13)
sts using the Cable cast on
method, move yarn to the
front between the needles,
slip the first st on the RHN
purlwise to the LHN, move
yarn to the back between
the needles, slip the first st
on the LHN purlwise back
to the RHN, knit to BOR.

Rnds 2–7: Knit.

Rnd 8: Work as for Rnd 1.

Rnds 9–14: Knit.

Rnd 15: Work as for Rnd 1.

Rnds 16–19: Knit.

Rnd 20 (dec): K1, k2tog, knit
to 3 sts before SSM, ssk,
k1, sm, k1, k2tog, knit to
3 sts before BOR M, ssk,
k1—34 (42) sts.

Rnd 21: Knit.

Rnd 22: K3 (4), BO 11 (13) sts using the Slit bind off method, sl rem st on RHN purlwise to LHN, with RS still facing, CO 11 (13) sts using the Cable cast on method, move yarn to the front between the needles, slip the first st on the RHN purlwise to the LHN, move yarn to the back between the needles, slip the first st on the LHN purlwise back to the RHN, knit to BOR.

Rnds 23–26: Knit.

Rnd 27 (dec): Work as for Rnd 20—30 (38) sts.

Rnd 28: Knit.

Rnd 29: K3 (4), BO 9 (11) sts using the Slit bind off method, sl rem st on RHN purlwise to LHN, with RS still facing, CO 9 (11) sts using the Cable cast on method, move yarn to the front between the needles, slip the first st on the RHN purlwise to the LHN, move yarn to the back between the needles, slip the first st on the LHN purlwise back to the RHN, knit to BOR.

THUMB GUSSET— LEFT GAUNTLET

Rnd 1 (inc): Knit to 4 (5) sts before BOR M, pm-A, M1L, k2 (3), M1R, pm-B, k2—32 (40) sts.

Rnds 2 and 3: Knit.

Rnd 4 (inc): Knit to M-A, sm, M1L, knit to M-B, M1R, sm, k2—34 (42) sts.

Rnd 5: Knit.

Rnd 6: K3 (4), BO 9 (11) sts using the Slit bind off method, sl rem st on RHN purlwise to LHN, with RS still facing, CO 9 (11) sts using the Cable cast on method, move yarn to the front between the needles, slip the first st on the RHN purlwise to the LHN, move yarn to the back between the needles, slip the first st on the LHN purlwise back to the RHN, knit to BOR.

Rnd 7: Knit to M-A, rm, place 6 (7) thumb gusset sts on waste yarn or stitch holder, CO 2 (3) sts using the Backward Loop method, rm, knit to BOR—30 (38) sts rem.

THUMB GUSSET— RIGHT GAUNTLET

Rnd 1 (inc): Knit to SSM, sm, k2, pm-A, M1R, k2 (3), M1L, pm-B, knit to BOR—32 (40) sts.

Rnds 2 and 3: Knit.

Rnd 4 (inc): Knit to M-A, sm, M1R, knit to M-B, M1L, sm, knit to BOR—34 (42) sts.

Rnd 5: Knit.

Rnd 6: K3 (4), BO 9 (11) sts using the Slit bind off method, sl rem st on RHN purlwise to LHN, with RS still facing, CO 9 (11) sts using the Cable cast on method, move yarn to the front between the needles, slip the first st on the RHN purlwise to the LHN, move yarn to the back between the needles, slip the first st on the LHN purlwise back to the RHN, knit to BOR.

Rnd 7: Knit to M-A, rm, place 6 (7) thumb gusset sts on waste yarn or stitch holder, CO 2 (3) sts using the Backward Loop method, rm, knit to BOR—30 (38) sts rem.

CUFF

Knit every rnd until the gauntlet measures 1¾ in. / 4.5 cm from the CO sts on Rnd 7 of the Thumb Gusset, or until the gauntlet is 1 in. / 2.5 cm short of your total desired length.

Switch to smaller needles.

Purl every rnd for 1 in. / 2½ cm.

Bind off all sts loosely purlwise.

THUMB

Place the 6 (7) live sts from the waste yarn or stitch holder onto the smaller dpns. Join the working yarn and, starting at the gap at the end of the live sts, pick up and knit 2 sts into the gap, 2 (3) sts into the CO edge, 2 stitches into the second gap, then knit across the live 6 (7) sts—12 (14) sts.

Switch to larger dpns.

Knit 3 rnds.

Purl 3 rnds.

Bind off all sts loosely purlwise.

FINISHING

Weave in all ends to the WS. Wet block the gauntlets. When dry, trim all ends.

Try on the gauntlets. Using locking markers, place a marker into the stitch over the top of each of your 4 knuckles. (If the gauntlets are a gift, approximate the placement by evenly spacing the 4 markers across the top of the mitt, approx. ½ in. / 1 cm below the reverse St st cuff.)

Using the locking markers as guides, carefully place the pyramid studs on the RS of the fabric, with the teeth pressed through the fabric so the points show on the WS. Press the points inward to lock the stud in place. If desired, adhere felt or scrap fabric to the back of the studs using fabric glue or sewing needle and thread to keep the metal from causing friction against your knuckles.

"Bring your pretty face to my axe."

—Gimli, *The Lord of the Rings: The Two Towers* film

ELVEN ARMOR PULLOVER

DESIGNED BY ANGELA HAHN

Worn during the opening battle in *The Fellowship of the Ring*, Elven armor was designed to reflect the Elvish people—a very old race—at that point in their history. The battle in Dagorlad between Men and Elves against Sauron and the Orcs took place in the springtime of their existence. Organic-looking armor inspired by young saplings made with biological materials protected the Elves from the crude weapons of their enemies, while allowing them to move freely and swiftly during the crusade.

This cropped, semifitted pullover is inspired by the layered wrappings on the armor of the Noldorin Elves. The base sweater and sleeves are worked from the bottom up in the round, then joined for the yoke. Stitches from the base sweater are picked up and knit as overlapping stockinette stitch strips to mimic the crisscross wrappings. Although they are unlikely to turn aside the point of an arrow or the edge of a sword, they are a striking accent and add a pleasant weight to the body and cuffs.

SIZES

1 (2, 3, 4) [5, 6, 7] {8, 9, 10}

FINISHED MEASUREMENTS

Chest Circumference: 33¼ (36, 39½, 42¼) [45¼, 48, 51½] {54¼, 56½, 59¼} in. / 84.5 (91.5, 100.5, 107.5) [115, 122, 131]{138, 143.5, 150.5} cm

Garment designed to be worn with 0 to 3 in. / 0 to 7.5 cm positive ease. The garment is a size 2 modeled on a 34 in. / 86 cm chest.

YARN

DK weight yarn, shown in Spun Right Round *Squish DK* (100% superwash superfine merino; 250 yd. / 229 m per 4 oz. / 115 g hank) in color Hoof It, 6 (6, 7, 7) [8, 8, 9] {9, 10, 10} hanks

NEEDLES

US 6 / 4 mm, 16 to 40 in. / 40 to 100 cm long circular needles and set of double-pointed needles or size needed to obtain gauge

NOTIONS

Additional 40 to 60 in. / 100 to 150 cm long gauge-size circular needle for body wrappings (optional)

Waste yarn or stitch holders

Stitch markers

Removable stitch markers

Row counter

Tapestry needle

GAUGE

22 sts and 30 rows = 4 in. / 10 cm over St st worked in the round, taken after blocking

Make sure to check your gauge.

PATTERN NOTES

This pullover is worked from the bottom up in the round. The body is worked first, then stitches are placed on hold for the underarms. Then the sleeves are worked from the cuff to the underarm. The two are then joined and the yoke is shaped.

The entirety of the garment is constructed in stockinette stitch. The wrappings are added to the garment once the body, yoke, and sleeves are complete.

Written instructions are provided for pattern; a chart is provided for the yoke shaping.

Rounds that contain both increases and decreases (and thus do not change the overall stitch count) are used to shape the front and sleeves, creating an inverted V in the front, and slanted cuffs on the sleeves. These increases and decreases are also used as markers for the placement of the wrappings.

Instructions are written for size 1 first, with additional sizes in parentheses, brackets, and braces. When only one number is provided, it applies to all sizes.

References to right and left are relative to how the garment is worn on the body, not how it appears laid flat.

PATTERN STITCHES

Stockinette St in the round (worked over any number of sts)

Rnd 1: Knit all sts.

Rep Rnd 1 for patt.

Stockinette St worked flat (worked over any number of sts)

Row 1 (RS): Knit.

Row 2 (WS): Purl.

Rep Rows 1 and 2 for patt.

PATTERN INSTRUCTIONS

CAST ON & BODY

Note: Two kinds of shaping rnds are used in the Body: Inc/Dec Rnds are used to create the front inverted V of the Body and do not change the stitch count. The Side Inc Rnds increase the Body circumference from hem to chest. These shaping rnds are worked simultaneously; read through entire section before beginning.

Using a circular needle in a length appropriate for the circumference of your garment and the Long Tail cast on method, CO 41 (45, 50, 54) [58, 62, 67] {71, 74, 78} sts for Right Front, pm for right side seam, CO 82 (90, 100, 108) [116, 124, 134] {142, 148, 156} sts for Back, pm for left side seam, CO 41 (45, 50, 54) [58, 62, 67] {71, 74, 78} sts for Left Front. Pm for BOR and join to work in the rnd, being careful not to twist the sts—164 (180, 200, 216) [232, 248, 268] {284, 296, 312} sts total.

*Knit 2 rnds.

Inc/Dec Rnd: K1, M1L, work est patt to 3 sts before right SSM, ssk, k1, sm, work est patt to left SSM, sm, k1, k2tog, work est patt to last st, M1R, k1—no change in st count.

Rep from * 19 more times (60 total rnds worked).

AT THE SAME TIME, beginning on Rnd 10, work the Side Inc Rnd, below, every 10th rnd a total of 6 times as follows (60 total rnds worked):

Side Inc Rnd: **Work est patt to 5 sts before SSM, M1R, work 5 sts in est patt, sm, work 5 sts in est patt, M1L; rep from ** 1 time, work est patt to end of rnd—4 sts inc.

24 sts inc; 188 (204, 224, 240) [256, 272, 292] {308, 320, 336} sts.

Rnd 61: Knit.

Body Separation Rnd (Rnd 62): *Knit to SSM, sm, k3 (4, 5, 6) [7, 8, 9] {10, 10, 10}, place the last 6 (8, 10, 12) [14, 16, 18] {20, 20, 20} sts and SSM on stitch holder or waste yarn for the underarm, pm for raglan; rep from * 1 time, knit to end of rnd—176 (188, 204, 216) [228, 240, 256] {268, 280, 296} sts rem.

Set the body aside while working the Sleeves, leaving the live sts on the working needle; do not break working yarn.

SLEEVES (MAKE 2 THE SAME)

Note: Like the body, two kinds of shaping rnds are used in the Sleeves: Inc/Dec Rnds are used to create the angled bottom edge of the Sleeve and do not change the stitch count. The Sleeve Inc Rnds increase the Sleeve circumference from cuff to underarm. These shaping rnds are worked simultaneously; read through entire section before beginning.

Using the set of dpns and the Long Tail cast on method, CO 26 (28, 29, 30) [31, 32, 33] {34, 35, 36} sts, pm for Center of sleeve, CO 26 (28, 29, 30) [31, 32, 33] {34, 35, 36} more sts. Pm for BOR and join to work in the rnd, being careful not to twist the sts—52 (56, 58, 60) [62, 64, 66] {68, 70, 72} sts total.

*Knit 2 rnds.

Inc/Dec Rnd: K1, k2tog, knit to 1 st before Center M, M1R, k1, sm, k1, M1L, knit to last 3 sts, ssk, k1—no change in st count.

Rep from * 26 (26, 26, 27) [27, 27, 27] {27, 27, 27} more times.

Then knit 1 rnd (82 (82, 82, 85) [85, 85, 85] {85, 85, 85} rnds worked)

AT THE SAME TIME,
beginning on Rnd 12 (10, 8, 6) [6, 4, 4] {4, 4, 4}, work the Sleeve Inc Rnd, below, every 12 (10, 8, 6) [6, 4, 4] {4, 4, 4}th rnd 6 (4, 5, 4) [14, 6, 12] {15, 18, 18} times, then every 0 (12, 10, 8) [0, 6, 6] {6, 6, 6}th rnd 0 (3, 4, 7) [0, 10, 6] {4, 2, 2} times.

Sleeve Inc Rnd: Work 5 sts in est patt, M1L, work in est patt to last 5 sts (slip Center M as encountered), M1R, work in patt to end of rnd—2 sts inc.

Note: On rnds that are both Inc/Dec and Sleeve Inc Rnds, work Sleeve Inc M1Rs 6 sts before end of rnd.

12 (14, 18, 22) [28, 32, 36] {38, 40, 40} sts inc; 64 (70, 76, 82) [90, 96, 102] {106, 110, 112} sts.

Final Rnd (Rnd 83 (83, 83, 86) [86, 86, 86] {86, 86, 86}): Knit to 3 (4, 5, 6) [7, 8, 9] {10, 10, 10} sts before the end of rnd, place the next 6 (8, 10, 12) [14, 16, 18] {20, 20, 20} sts on waste yarn or stitch holder for the underarm (removing BOR M as the sts are placed on hold)—58 (62, 66, 70) [76, 80, 84] {86, 90, 92} live sleeve sts. Break yarn, leaving a 24 in. / 60 cm tail.

Place these live sts on a separate length of waste yarn or stitch holder, including the Center M, and set aside while the second sleeve is worked.

Repeat all instructions for the second sleeve but leave the 58 (62, 66, 70) [76, 80, 84] {86, 90, 92} live sleeve sts on the dpns.

YOKE

Note: Body and Sleeve Inc/Dec Rnds will continue every 3rd rnd/row of Yoke up to the neck edge. Raglan Dec Rnds and Front Neck Dec Rnds are worked simultaneously. Rnds or rows that do not include any shaping are worked even in St st. Read through entire section before beginning.

Begin the Joining Rnd, below, for all sizes by picking up the Body of the sweater. Work will begin at the BOR M with the working yarn still attached.

Sizes 1–6 ONLY:
Joining Rnd: K1, M1L, work est patt to 3 sts before raglan M, ssk, k1, sm {Right Front}. Pick up the sleeve that is still on the dpns; continuing with the working yarn across the sleeve sts: K1, k2tog, work est patt to 1 st before Center M, M1R, k1, sm, k1, M1L, work est patt to 3 sts before end of Sleeve sts, ssk, k1, pm for raglan {Right Sleeve}. Work est patt to raglan M, sm {Back}. Place the live sleeve sts of the second sleeve onto a spare needle or the dpns; continuing with the working yarn across the sleeve sts: K1, k2tog, work est patt to 1 st before Center M, M1R, k1, sm, k1, M1L, work est patt to 3 sts before end of Sleeve sts, ssk, k1, pm for raglan {Left Sleeve}. K1, k2tog, work est patt to last st before the BOR M, M1R, k1—292 (312, 336, 356) [380, 400, -] {-, -, -} sts total.

Sizes 7–10 ONLY:
Joining Rnd: K1, M1L, work est patt to 7 sts before raglan M, ssk, k2, ssk, k1, sm {Right Front}. Pick up the sleeve that is still on the dpns; continuing with the working yarn across the sleeve sts, k1, k2tog, work est patt to 1 st before Center M, M1R, k1, sm, k1, M1L, work est patt to 3 sts before end of Sleeve sts, ssk, k1, pm for raglan {Right Sleeve}. K4, k2tog, work est patt to 6 sts before raglan M, ssk,

k4 {Back}. Place the live sleeve sts of the second sleeve onto a spare needle or the dpns; continuing with the working yarn across the sleeve sts: K1, k2tog, work est patt to 1 st before Center M, M1R, k1, sm, k1, M1L, work est patt to 3 sts before end of Sleeve sts, ssk, k1, pm for raglan {Left Sleeve}. K1, k2tog, k2, k2tog, work est patt to last st before the BOR M, M1R, k1— - (-, -, -) [-, -, 420] {436, 456, 476} sts total.

All Sizes:
Find your size listed at the top of the columns of the Yoke Shaping Chart—A on page 34. Work the shaping as indicated, through Charts A and B, following the shaping rnd/row instructions below. Once the Front Neck Shaping begins on round 18 (18, 15, 15) [18, 18, 18] {18, 18, 18}, the Yoke will be worked flat; at the end of the round, turn work to the WS for the next row. From this point forward, shaping will be worked on the RS and the WS of the Yoke.

Note: Color has been added to the RS shaping rows of the Yoke Shaping Tracking Chart for ease of reading; WS row shaping may occur and will be in the grey squares.

Working in the Rnd RS Shaping

R (Raglan Dec Rnd): *Work est patt to 6 sts before raglan M, ssk, k4, sm, k4, k2tog; rep from * 3 more times, work est patt to end—8 sts dec.

RB (Body Only Raglan Dec Rnd): *Work est patt to 6 sts before raglan M, ssk, k4, sm, work est patt to next M, sm, k4, k2tog; rep from * 1 more time, work est patt to end—4 sts dec.

ID + R (Inc/Dec + Raglan Rnd): K1, M1L, work est patt to 7 sts before raglan M, ssk, k2, ssk, k1, sm {Right Front}, k1, k2tog, k2, k2tog, work est patt to 1 st before Center M, M1R, k1, sm, k1, M1L, work est patt to 7 sts before raglan M, ssk, k2, ssk, k1, sm {Right Sleeve}, k4, k2tog, work est patt to 6 sts before raglan M, ssk, k4, sm {Back}, k1, k2tog, k2, k2tog, work est patt to 1 st before Center M, M1R, k1, sm, k1, M1L, work est patt to 7 sts before raglan M, ssk, k2, ssk, k1, sm {Left Sleeve}, k1, k2tog, k2, k2tog, work est patt to 1 st before BOR M, M1R, k1 {Left Front}—8 sts dec.

ID + RB (Inc/Dec + Body Only Raglan Dec Rnd): K1, M1L, work est patt to 7 sts before raglan M, ssk, k2, ssk, k1, sm {Right Front}, k1, k2tog, work est patt to 1 st before Center M, M1R, k1, sm, k1, M1L, work est patt to 3 sts before raglan M, ssk, k1, sm {Right Sleeve}, k4, k2tog, work est patt to 6

sts before raglan M, ssk, k4, sm {Back}, k1, k2tog, work est patt to 1 st before Center M, M1R, k1, sm, k1, M1L, work est patt to 3 sts before raglan M, ssk, k1, sm {Left Sleeve}, k1, k2tog, k2, k2tog, work est patt to 1 st before BOR M, M1R, k1 {Left Front}—4 sts dec.

ID (Inc/Dec Rnd): K1, M1L, work est patt to 3 sts before raglan M, ssk, k1, sm {Right Front}, k1, k2tog, work est patt to 1 st before Center M, M1R, k1, sm, k1, M1L, work est patt to 3 sts before raglan M, ssk, k1, sm {Right Sleeve}, work est patt to raglan M, sm {Back}, k1, k2tog, work est patt to 1 st before Center M, M1R, k1, sm, k1, M1L, work est patt to 3 sts before raglan M, ssk, k1, sm {Left Sleeve}, k1, k2tog, work est patt to last st before BOR M, M1R, k1 {Left Front}—no change in st count.

Working Flat: RS and WS Row Shaping

ID + R + N (Inc/Dec + Raglan + Neck Dec Rnd, **RS**): K1, ssk, work est patt to 7 sts before raglan M, ssk, k2, ssk, k1, sm {Right Front}, k1, k2tog, k2, k2tog, work est patt to 1 st before Center M, M1R, k1, sm, k1, M1L, work est patt to 7 sts before raglan M, ssk, k2, ssk, k1, sm {Right Sleeve}, k4, k2tog, work est patt to 6 sts before raglan M, ssk, k4, sm {Back}, k1, k2tog, k2, k2tog, work est patt to 1 st before Center M, M1R, k1, sm, k1, M1L, work est

patt to 7 sts before raglan M, ssk, k2, ssk, k1, sm {Right Sleeve}, k1, k2tog, k2, k2tog, work est patt to 3 sts before BOR M, k2tog, k1 {Left Front}—10 sts dec.

N (Neck Dec Row, **RS**): K1, ssk, work est patt to 3 sts before BOR M, k2tog, k1—2 sts dec (1 st in each Front).

N (Neck Dec Row, **WS**): P1, p2tog, work in patt to 3 sts, before BOR M, ssp, p1—2 sts dec (1 st in each Front).

ID + R (Inc/Dec + Raglan Dec Row, **RS**): Work est patt to 3 sts before raglan M, ssk, k1, sm {Right Front}, k1, k2tog, k2, k2tog, work est patt to 1 st before Center M, M1R, k1, sm, k1, M1L, work est patt to 7 sts before raglan M, ssk, k2, ssk, k1, sm {Right Sleeve}, k4, k2tog, work est patt to 6 sts before raglan M, ssk, k4, sm {Back}, k1, k2tog, k2, k2tog, work est patt to 1 st before Center M, M1R, k1, sm, k1, M1L, work est patt to 7 sts before raglan M, ssk, k2, ssk, k1, sm {Left Sleeve}, k1, k2tog, work est patt to end of row {Left Front}—8 sts dec.

ID + R (Inc/Dec + Raglan Dec Row, **WS**): Work est patt to 3 sts before raglan M, p2tog, p1, sm {Left Front}, p1, ssp, p2, ssp, work est patt to 1 st before Center M, M1LP, p1, sm, p1, M1RP, work est patt to 7 sts before raglan M, p2tog, p2, p2tog, p1, sm {Left Sleeve}, p4, ssp, work est patt to 6 sts before

raglan M, p2tog, p4, sm {Back}, p1, ssp, p2, ssp, work est patt to 1 st before Center M, M1LP, p1, sm, p1, M1RP, work est patt to 7 sts before raglan M, p2tog, p2, p2tog, p1, sm {Right Sleeve}, p1, ssp, work est patt to end of row {Right Front}—8 sts dec.

R + N (Raglan + Neck Dec Row, **RS**): K1, ssk, *work est patt to 6 sts before raglan M, ssk, k4, sm, k4, k2tog; rep from * 3 more times, work est patt to 3 sts before BOR M, k2tog, k1—10 sts dec.

ID (Inc/Dec Row, **WS**): Work est patt to raglan M, sm {Left Front}, p1, ssp, work est patt to 1 st before Center M, M1LP, p1, sm, p1, M1RP, work est patt to 3 sts before raglan M, p2tog, p1, sm {Left Sleeve}, work est patt to raglan M, sm {Back}, p1, ssp, work est patt to 1 st before Center M, M1LP, p1, sm, p1, M1RP, work est patt to 3 sts before raglan M, p2tog, p1, sm {Right Sleeve}, work est patt to end of row {Right Front}— no change in st count.

ID + N (Inc/Dec + Neck Dec Row, **RS**): K1, ssk, work est patt to raglan M, sm {Right Front}, k1, k2tog, work est patt to 1 st before Center M, M1R, k1, sm, k1, M1L, work est patt to 3 sts before raglan M, ssk, k1, sm {Right Sleeve}, work est patt to raglan M, sm {Back}, k1, k2tog, work est patt to 1 st before Center M, M1R, k1, sm, k1, M1L, work est patt to 3 sts

before raglan M, ssk, k1, sm {Right Sleeve}, work est patt to 3 sts before BOR M, k2tog, k1—2 sts dec (1 st in each Front).

ID + N (Inc/Dec + Neck Dec Row, **WS**): P1, p2tog, work est patt to raglan M, sm {Left Front}, p1, ssp, work est patt to 1 st before Center M, M1LP, p1, sm, p1, M1RP, work est patt to 3 sts before raglan M, p2tog, p1, sm {Left Sleeve}, work est patt to raglan M, sm {Back}, p1, ssp, work est patt to 1 st before Center M, M1LP, p1, sm, p1, M1RP, work est patt to 3 sts before raglan M, p2tog, p1, sm {Right Sleeve}, work est patt to 3 sts before BOR M, ssp, p1—2 sts dec (1 st in each Front).

R (Raglan Dec Row, **RS**): *Work est patt to 6 sts before raglan M, ssk, k4, sm, k4, k2tog; rep from * 3 more times, work est patt to end—8 sts dec.

All Sizes—at Yoke Shaping Chart Completion:
212 (230, 250, 268) [292, 310, 330] {346, 366, 386} sts dec;
80 (82, 86, 88) [88, 90, 90] {90, 90, 90} sts rem:
1 st each for Right and Left Fronts
16 sts each for Left and Right Sleeves
46 (48, 52, 54) [54, 56, 56] {56, 56, 56} sts for the Back
FINAL WS DEC ROW (sts dec on Back only):

Size 1 Only:
Purl to M, rm, purl to M, rm, p6, p2tog, (p14, p2tog) 2 times, p6, rm, purl to end of row (rm final M as encountered).

Size 2 Only:
Purl to M, rm, purl to M, rm, p3, p2tog, (p8, p2tog) 4 times, p3, rm, purl to end of row (rm final M as encountered).

Size 3 Only:
Purl to M, rm, purl to M, rm, p4, p2tog, (p5, p2tog) 6 times, p4, rm, purl to end of row (rm final M as encountered).

Sizes 4 and 5 Only:
Purl to M, rm, purl to M, rm, (p5, p2tog) 7 times, p5, rm, purl to end of row (rm final M as encountered).

Sizes 6–10 Only:
Purl to M, rm, purl to M, rm, p3, p2tog, (p4, p2tog) 8 times, p3, rm, purl to end of row (rm final M as encountered).

3 (5, 7, 7) [7, 9, 9] {9, 9, 9} sts dec; 77 (77, 79, 81) [81, 81, 81] {81, 81, 81} sts rem.

With RS facing, bind off all sts knitwise.

FINISHING

Place live Body and Sleeve underarm sts on 2 needles held parallel. Use long yarn tail at underarm to graft sts closed using Kitchener stitch. Weave in ends and block to finished measurements.

BODY WRAPPINGS

Place Markers—All Sizes:

On Body Rnd 6 (the second Inc/Dec rnd from the bottom of the sweater), clip removable M into Inc/Dec Rnd dec sts (worked as ssk or k2tog). Rep this on every 3rd Inc/Dec Rnd 6 more times on Body Rnds 15, 24, 33, 43, 51, and 60.

Note: Marked dec sts should fall 1 st forward of the side seam (between the Fronts and Back; do not mark Body inc sts, which are 5 sts are from sides). Last sts marked should fall just under underarms.

Place Markers—Sizes 1 (2, -, -) [5, 6, 7] {8, 9, 10} ONLY:

On Body Rnd 6 (the second Inc/Dec rnd from the bottom of the sweater), clip removable M into Inc/Dec Rnd inc sts (worked as M1L or M1R). Rep this on every 4th Inc/Dec Rnd 6 more times on Body Rnds 18, 30, 42, and 55, and Yoke Rnds / Rows 6 and 17 (or Rnds 68 and 79 if counting contiguously up the front of the garment).

Place Markers—Sizes 3 and 4 ONLY:

On Body Rnd 6 (the second Inc/Dec rnd from the bottom of the sweater), clip removable M into Inc/Dec Rnd inc sts (worked as M1L or M1R). Rep this on the 3rd next Inc/Dec Rnd 1 time, then every 4th Inc/Dec Rnd 5 more times on Body Rnds 15, 27, 39, and 52, and Yoke Rnds / Rows 3 and 14 (or Rnds 65 and 76 if counting contiguously up the front of the garment).

Note: Marked inc sts will be 1 st on each side of the center front. Last sts marked should fall just below the bottom of the V-neck shaping.

Picking Up Sts for Wrappings:

Lay sweater flat with the front of the sweater facing up. Optional: Use a 40 to 60 in. / 100 to 150 cm long circular needle (basing the length on selected garment size) to make it easier to check line of sts picked up. Pointy needles and/or using a needle a size smaller than the gauge-size needle may make it easier to pick up sts. If you opt for the smaller needle, be sure to use the gauge-size needle when working wrappings.

Advance needle by pushing tip under right leg of each st and out through center of the st, sliding picked up sts along needle. DO NOT KNIT STS: All sts will be picked up on the circular needle before beginning to knit.

When crossing rnds while picking up sts diagonally across Front (for Wrappings 2–6), use number of rnds crossed vs number of sts in each side of Front to gauge when to switch rnds (i.e., if crossing 7 rnds, and Left Front has 57 sts, then switch rnds approx. every 8 sts).

Note: The picked up sts will be on the working needle in reverse orientation. On the first knit row, knit all sts through the back loop to avoid twisted sts.

The garment is rotated 180 degrees after picking up the stitches to knit the wrappings. As a result, the sts will appear to begin and end half a st off from the center front and sides. This does not matter.

Increases are used in wrappings to shape them to base garment, but total st counts are not required and are not provided.

Leave approx. 10 in. / 25½ cm tails when joining the working yarn to begin knitting. These tails will be used to tack down ends of wrappings to the face of the garment.

Wrapping 1:

With RS facing, using marked sts in Body Rnd 6 as a guide, using circular needle, and beginning with first st of the rnd (at Center Front), pick up right leg of each st in rnd to 1 st after marked dec st at right side seam, pm for SSM, pick up right leg of each st in rnd to 1 st before marked dec st at left side, pm for SSM, pick up right leg of each st in rnd to end of rnd. ***Rotate work 180 degrees so the neckline edge of the garment is closest to you.***

Row 1 (RS): Beginning with last st picked up, join working yarn leaving a 10 in. / 25½ cm tail and knit all sts tbl. Do not join to work in the rnd.

Row 2 (WS): Purl.

Row 3 (inc): K1, M1L, knit to 1 st before right SSM, M1R, k1, sm, knit to left SSM, sm, k1, M1L, knit to last st, M1R, k1—4 sts inc.

Row 4: Purl.

Row 5 (inc): Knit to 1 st before right SSM, M1R, k1, sm, knit to left SSM, sm, k1, M1L, knit to end of row—2 sts inc.

Rows 6–9: Rep [Rows 2–5] 1 time—6 sts inc.

Rows 10–12: Rep [Rows 2–4] 1 time—4 sts inc.

With RS facing, BO all sts knitwise.

Sizes 3 and 4 ONLY:

Work Wrapping 2 as for Wrapping 1, using marked sts in Body Rnd 15 as guide.

Wrappings 3–6: Work as for Wrappings 1 and 2, EXCEPT that each line of sts picked up will move across multiple rnds on Front, because wrappings are spaced farther apart at center Front than at sides (wrappings will remain parallel across Back): Third wrapping will move across 4 rnds; fourth will move across 7 rnds; fifth will move across 10 rnds; and sixth will move across 13 rnds.

Sizes 1 (2, -, -) [5, 6, 7] {8, 9, 10} ONLY:

Wrappings 2–6: Work as for Wrapping 1, EXCEPT that each line of sts picked up will move across multiple rnds on Front, because wrappings are spaced farther apart at center Front than at sides: Second wrapping will move across 4 rnds; third will move across 7 rnds; fourth will move across 10 rnds; fifth will move across 13 rnds; and sixth will move across 16 rnds.

All Sizes:

Wrapping 7, Part 1:

Beginning at neckline edge at the juncture of Back and Left Sleeve, and using row of sts just below the BO edge, pick up 1 st for every BO st along Left Sleeve, pm for raglan; pick up 1 st for every two rows along Left Front neck edge using column of sts next to selvage st and ending at M placed in M1L just below base of

V-neck; cont diagonally across Right Front to right center underarm (will cross 19 (19, 16, 16) [19, 19, 19] {19, 19, 19} rnds), pm for right side seam; pick up sts horizontally across back, ending at Left center underarm. *Rotate work 180 degrees so the neckline edge of the garment is closest to you.*

Row 1 (RS, inc): Beginning with the last st picked up at the Left underarm, join working yarn leaving a 10 in. / 25.5 cm tail and knit all sts tbl, CO 1 st using the Knitted cast on method. Do not join to work in the rnd—1 st inc.

Row 2 (WS, inc): Purl to end, CO 1 st using the Knitted cast on method—1 st inc.

Row 3 (inc): Knit to right SSM, sm, k1, M1L, knit to 1 st before raglan M, M1R, k1, sm, k1, M1L, knit to last 2 sts, M1R, k2—4 sts inc.

Row 4: Purl.

Rows 5–12: Rep [Rows 3 and 4] 4 more times—16 sts inc.

With RS facing, BO all sts knitwise.

Part 2:

Beginning at the Left center underarm, pick up sts diagonally across Left Front to base of V-neck, picking up sts across Part 1 of the wrap; pick up 1 st for every two rows along Right Front neck edge using column of sts next to selvage st; pm for raglan; pick up 1 st for every BO st along neck edge of Right Sleeve, pm for raglan; pick up one st for every BO st

along Back neck. *Rotate work 180 degrees so the neckline edge of the garment is closest to you.*

Row 1 (RS, inc): Beginning with the last st picked up at the back neck, join working yarn leaving a 10 in. / 25.5 cm tail and knit all sts tbl, CO 1 st using the Knitted cast on method. Do not join to work in the rnd—1 st inc.

Row 2 (WS, inc): Purl to end, then CO 1 st using the Knitted cast on method—1 st inc.

Row 3 (inc): K5, M1L, knit to 4 sts before raglan M, M1R, k4, sm, k1, M1L, knit to 1 st before raglan M, M1R, k1, sm, k1, M1L, knit to last 2 sts, M1L, k2—6 sts inc.

Row 4: Purl.

Rows 5–12: Rep [Rows 3 and 4] 4 more times—16 sts inc.

With RS facing, BO all sts knitwise.

TACKING DOWN WRAPPINGS:

Beginning with Wrapping 1, use yarn tail from BO and tapestry needle to tack end of wrapping down along line of picked up sts. Overlap beginning end of wrapping over end just tacked down, and use yarn tail from CO to tack end down along next line of picked up sts.

Rep for Wrappings 2–6.

Wrapping 7:

Use tapestry needle and yarn tails from CO and

BO to seam ends of Part 1 and Part 2 to form one continuous wrapping (extra sts CO at ends will be used for seam allowances).

Note: If Wrapping 7 tends to flip up at shoulders/ back neck, use short lengths of yarn and tapestry needle to tack WS near BO edge of wrapping down at raglan "seams," center of Back neck, and center of Right Front neck edge.

SLEEVE WRAPPINGS:

All wrappings are parallel to cuff and to each other, and begin and end at Center column on top of sleeve, not at the BOR on the underside of the sleeve.

Use inc and dec sts in Inc/ Dec Rnds as guides; these inc and dec sts are 1 st away from the BOR and the Center column on the top of the sleeve. Do not use Sleeve Shaping Rnd inc, which are farther away from the BOR. When picking up sts for wrap, pm on each side of the BOR, adjacent to the inc sts (2 markers placed).

Wrapping 1:

Use inc and dec sts in Sleeve Rnd 6 (second Inc/Dec rnd from CO) as guides.

Wrapping 2:

Use inc and dec sts in Sleeve Rnd 15 (fifth Inc/Dec rnd from CO) as guides.

Schematic

Dimensions provided for base garment, before wraps are added.

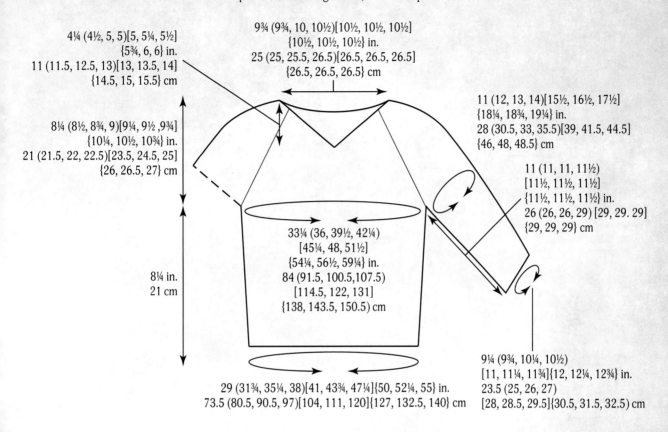

4¼ (4½, 5, 5)[5, 5¼, 5½]
{5¾, 6, 6} in.
11 (11.5, 12.5, 13)[13, 13.5, 14]
{14.5, 15, 15.5} cm

9¾ (9¾, 10, 10½)[10½, 10½, 10½]
{10½, 10½, 10½} in.
25 (25, 25.5, 26.5)[26.5, 26.5, 26.5]
{26.5, 26.5, 26.5} cm

11 (12, 13, 14)[15½, 16½, 17½]
{18¼, 18¾, 19¼} in.
28 (30.5, 33, 35.5)[39, 41.5, 44.5]
{46, 48, 48.5} cm

8¼ (8½, 8¾, 9)[9¼, 9½ ,9¾]
{10¼, 10½, 10¾} in.
21 (21.5, 22, 22.5)[23.5, 24.5, 25]
{26, 26.5, 27} cm

11 (11, 11, 11½)
[11½, 11½, 11½]
{11½, 11½, 11½} in.
26 (26, 26, 29) [29, 29. 29]
{29, 29, 29} cm

33¼ (36, 39½, 42¼)
[45¼, 48, 51½]
{54¼, 56½, 59¼} in.
84 (91.5, 100.5,107.5)
[114.5, 122, 131]
{138, 143.5, 150.5) cm

8¼ in.
21 cm

9¼ (9¾, 10¼, 10½)
[11, 11¼, 11¾]{12, 12¼, 12¾} in.
23.5 (25, 26, 27)
[28, 28.5, 29.5]{30.5, 31.5, 32.5) cm

29 (31¾, 35¼, 38)[41, 43¾, 47¼]{50, 52¼, 55} in.
73.5 (80.5, 90.5, 97)[104, 111, 120]{127, 132.5, 140} cm

Wrapping 3:

Use inc and dec sts in Sleeve Rnd 24 (eighth Inc/Dec rnd from CO) as guides.

After picking up sts for wrapping, *rotate work 180 degrees so the neckline edge of the garment is closest to you.*

Work each wrapping the same:

Row 1 (RS): Beginning with last st picked up, join working yarn leaving a 10 in. / 25.5 cm tail and knit all sts tbl. Do not join to work in the rnd.

Row 2 (WS): Purl.

Row 3 (inc): K1, M1L, knit to 1 st before M, M1R, k1, sm, k1, M1L, knit to last st, M1R, k1—4 sts inc.

Row 4: Purl.

Row 5 (inc): Knit to 1 st before M, M1R, k1, sm, k1, M1L, knit to end of row—2 sts inc.

Rows 6–9: Rep [Rows 2–5] 1 time—6 sts inc.

Rows 10–12: Rep [Rows 2–4] 1 time—4 sts inc.

With RS facing, BO all sts knitwise.

Tack down Sleeve wrappings as for Body, EXCEPT reverse direction of overlap on one sleeve, so that it is a mirror image of the other sleeve.

Weave in ends and steam block wrappings.

KEY

☐	RS est patt (St st)
■	WS est patt (St st)
R	RS Raglan decrease (8 st dec)
RB	RS Raglan Body Only decrease (4 st dec)
ID+R	RS Inc/Dec + Raglan decrease (8 sts dec)
ID+RB	RS Inc/Dec + Raglan Body Only decrease (4 sts dec)
ID+R	WS Inc/Dec + Raglan decrease (8 sts dec)
ID	RS Inc/Dec
ID	WS Inc/Dec
ID+R+N	RS Inc/Dec, Raglan and Neck Shaping decrease (10 sts dec)
N	RS Neck decrease (2 sts dec)
N	WS Neck decrease (2 sts dec)
R+N	RS Raglan and Neck decrease (10 sts dec)
ID+N	WS Inc/Dec and Neck decrease (2 sts dec)
———	Start of Neck Shaping (working flat)
END	Return to written instructions

YOKE SHAPING CHART - A

Yoke Row/ Rnd No.	Size 1	Size 2	Size 3	Size 4	Size 5	Size 6	Size 7	Size 8	Size 9	Size 10
1	R	R	R	R	R	R	R	R	R	R
2							RB	RB	RB	RB
3	ID+R	ID+R	ID+R	ID+R	ID+R	ID+R	ID+R	ID+R	ID+R	ID+R
4								RB	RB	RB
5		R	R	R	R	R	R	R	R	R
6	ID+R	ID	ID	ID	ID	ID	ID	ID+RB	ID+RB	ID+RB
7		R	R	R	R	R	R	R	R	R
8									RB	RB
9	ID+R	ID+R	ID+R	ID+R	ID+R	ID+R	ID+R	ID+R	ID+R	ID+R
10										RB
11			R	R	R	R	R	R	R	R
12	ID+R	ID+R	ID	ID	ID	ID	ID	ID	ID	ID+RB
13			R	R	R	R	R	R	R	R
14										RB
15	ID+R	ID+R	ID+R+N	ID+R+N	ID+R	ID+R	ID+R	ID+R	ID+R	ID+R
16										
17			N	N						
18	ID+R+N	ID+R+N	ID+R	ID+R	ID+R+N	ID+R+N	ID+R+N	ID+R+N	ID+R+N	ID+R+N
19			N	N						
20	N	N			N	N	N	N	N	N
21	ID+R	ID+R	ID+R+N	ID+R+N	ID+R	ID+R	ID+R	ID+R	ID+R	ID+N
22	N	N			N	N	N	N	N	N
23			N	N						
24	ID+R+N	ID+R+N	ID+R	ID+R	ID+R+N	ID+R+N	ID+R+N	ID+R+N	ID+R+N	ID+R+N
25			N	N						
26	N	N			N	N	N	N	R+N	R+N
27	ID+R	ID+R	ID+R+N	ID+R+N	ID+R	ID+R	ID+R	ID+R	ID	ID
28	N	N			N	N	N	N	R+N	R+N
29										
30	ID+R+N	ID+R+N	ID+R	ID+R	ID+R+N	ID+R+N	ID+R+N	ID+R+N	ID+R+N	ID+R+N
31			N	N						
32	N	N			N	N	R+N	R+N	R+N	R+N
33	ID+R	ID+R	ID+R+N	ID+R+N	ID+R	ID+R	ID	ID	ID	ID
34	N	N			N	N	R+N	R+N	R+N	R+N
35			N	N						
36	ID+R+N	ID+R+N	ID+R	ID+R	ID+R+N	ID+R+N	ID+R+N	ID+R+N	ID+R+N	ID+R+N
37			N	N						
38	N	N			N	R+N	R+N	R+N	R+N	R+N
39	ID+R	ID+R	ID+R+N	ID+R+N	ID+R	ID	ID	ID	ID	ID
40	N	N			N	R+N	R+N	R+N	R+N	R+N
41			N	N						

YOKE SHAPING CHART - B

Yoke Row/Rnd No.	Size 1	Size 2	Size 3	Size 4	Size 5	Size 6	Size 7	Size 8	Size 9	Size 10
42	ID+R+N	ID+R+N	ID+R	ID+R	ID+R+N	ID+R+N	ID+R+N	ID+R+N	ID+R+N	ID+R+N
43			N	N						
44	N	N			R+N	R+N	R+N	R+N	R+N	R+N
45	ID+R	ID+R	ID+R+N	ID+R+N	ID	ID	ID	ID	ID	ID
46	N	N			R+N	R+N	R+N	R+N	R+N	R+N
47			N	N						
48	ID+R+N	ID+R+N	ID+R	ID+R	ID+R+N	ID+R+N	ID+R+N	ID+R+N	ID+R+N	ID+R+N
49			N	N						
50	N	N			R+N	R+N	R+N	R+N	R+N	R+N
51	ID+R	ID+R	ID+R+N	ID+R+N	ID	ID	ID	ID	ID	ID
52	N	N			R+N	R+N	R+N	R+N	R+N	R+N
53			N	R+N						
54	ID+R+N	ID+R+N	ID+R	ID	ID+R+N	ID+R+N	ID+R+N	ID+R+N	ID+R+N	ID+R+N
55			N	R+N						
56	N	N			R+N	R+N	R+N	R+N	R+N	R
57	ID+R	ID+R	ID+R+N	ID+R+N	ID	ID	ID	ID	ID	ID+N
58	N	N			R+N	R+N	R+N	R+N	R+N	R
59			R+N	R+N						
60	ID+R+N	ID+R+N	ID	ID	ID+R+N	ID+R+N	ID+R+N	ID+R+N	ID+R	ID+R+N
61	END		R+N	R+N					N	
62		R+N			R+N	R+N	R+N	R+N	R	R
63		END	ID+R+N	ID+R+N	ID	ID	ID	ID	ID	ID+N
64			END		R+N	R+N	R+N	R	R+N	R
65				R+N				N		
66				END	ID+R+N	ID+R+N	ID+R+N	ID+R	ID+R	ID+R+N
67									N	
68					R+N	R+N	R	R+N	R	R
69					END	ID	ID+N	ID	ID	ID+N
70						R+N	R	R+N	R	
71						END	N			
72							ID+R+N	ID+R	ID+R	ID+R+N
73							END	N		
74								R+N	R	
75								END	ID	ID+N
76									R+N	R
77									END	
78										ID+R+N
79										END

"Tangado haid!
Leithio i philinn!"

Translation:
Hold positions!
Fire the arrows!

—Elrond, *The Lord of the Rings:
The Fellowship of the Ring* film

ELVEN ROYALTY CLOAK

DESIGNED BY BETHANY HICK

Exquisite Rivendell is home to the Half-Elves west of the Misty Mountains. After the War of Sauron and Elves, Elrond created it as a stronghold to protect the Elves from the siege. Nestled in a valley with flowing waterfalls, trees, the Hall of Fire, and inhabited by many members of Elven royalty, it became a refuge of education and peace, eventually serving as the meeting place of the Council of Elrond where the Fellowship is formed.

As timeless as Middle-earth, this lace cloak fit for Elven royalty is a must knit for any *Lord of the Rings* fan! Beginning at the bottom edge, a lace border is worked flat, then moves into a larger lace motif. After decreases are cleverly hidden within the stockinette, an eyelet row is worked before moving into the hood. Instructions are also given for an oversized, more mysterious hood. Don't want a hood? No problem! Simply omit and bind off.

SIZES

1 (2, 3, 4, 5) [6, 7, 8, 9]

FINISHED MEASUREMENTS

Circumference Around Upper Chest and Arms: 57¾ (61¾, 65¾, 69¾, 73¾) [77¾, 81¾, 85¾, 89¾] in. / 146.5 (157, 167, 177, 187.5) [197.5, 207.5, 218, 228] cm

Designed to be worn with 21¾ to 29 ¾ in. / 55 to 75.5 cm of positive ease measured at the full chest circumference.

The sample garment is the Oversize Hood Option in a size 2 modeled on a 36 in. / 91 cm chest with 22 ¾ in. / 58 cm positive ease.

YARN

Fingering weight yarn, shown in The Plucky Knitter *Primo Fingering* (75% superwash merino, 20% cashmere, 5% nylon; 440 yd. / 402 m per 4 oz. / 115 g hank) in color Smoke and Mirrors

No Hood Option: 2 (2, 2, 2, 2) [2, 2, 3, 3] hanks

Fitted Hood Option: 2 (2, 2, 2, 3) [3, 3, 3, 3] hanks

Oversized Hood Option: 2 (2, 2, 3, 3) [3, 3, 3, 3] hanks

NEEDLES

US 9 / 5.5 mm, 32 to 40 in. / 80 to 100 cm long circular needle or size needed to obtain gauge

NOTIONS

Additional gauge-size circular needle or dpn (for Hooded options only)

Stitch markers (optional)

Row counter (optional)

Tapestry needle

1½ in. / 4 cm wide ribbon in a complementary color (approx. 1 yd. / 1 m)

GAUGE

17 sts and 21 rows = 4 in. / 10 cm in St st worked flat, taken after blocking

Make sure to check your gauge.

PATTERN NOTES

The cloak is worked flat from the bottom up, beginning with charted lacework, and transitioning to written instructions for the yoke and hood options.

To work from the charts, read all RS (odd-numbered) rows from right to left. The WS rows are not charted except for the final row of the chart to ensure that the lacework pattern is ended with a WS row; read this WS row from left to right.

To work the uncharted WS rows from the chart, work as per Row 2 of the Cloak St st pattern stitches.

The count of stitches in the charted lacework section fluctuates throughout the chart; it is recommended to place markers between each repeat to track your stitches.

If using hand-dyed yarn, consider alternating skeins as this project is worked.

Instructions are provided for size 1 first, with additional sizes in parentheses and brackets. When only one number is provided, it applies to all sizes.

PATTERN STITCHES

Stockinette St (worked over any number of sts)

Row 1 (RS): Knit.

Row 2 (WS): Purl.

Rep Rows 1 and 2 for patt.

Cloak St st (worked over any number of sts)

Row 1 (RS): Yo, k2tog, knit to end.

Row 2 (WS): Yo, ssk, purl to last 2 sts, k2.

Rep Rows 1 and 2 for patt.

PATTERN INSTRUCTIONS

CAST ON & CHARTED LACEWORK

CO 315 (337, 359, 381, 403) [425, 447, 469, 491] sts using the Long Tail cast on method. Do not join to work in the rnd.

Begin working from Chart A. Work [Rows 1–56] 1 time. The patt rep is worked 14 (15, 16, 17, 18) [19, 20, 21, 22] times across each row. At chart completion: 147 (157, 167, 177, 187) [197, 207, 217, 227] sts total.

YOKE

Work Rows 1 and 2 of Cloak St st 1 (1, 1, 2, 2) [2, 2, 3, 3] time(s).

Dec Row 1 (RS): Yo, k2tog, k1, *k3, k2tog; rep from * to last 4 sts, k4—119 (127, 135, 143, 151) [159, 167, 175, 183] sts.

Beginning with a WS row, work 3 (3, 3, 3, 5) [5, 5, 5, 7] rows of Cloak St st.

Dec Row 2 (RS): Yo, k2tog, k1, *k2tog, k2; rep from * to last 4 sts, k4—91 (97, 103, 109, 115) [121, 127, 133, 139] sts.

Beginning with a WS row, work 1 (3, 3, 3, 3) [5, 5, 5, 5] row(s) of Cloak St st.

Dec Row 3 (RS): Yo, k2tog, k1, *k2, k2tog, k2; rep from * to last 4 sts, k4—77 (82, 87, 92, 97) [102, 107, 112, 117] sts.

Beginning with a WS row, work 1 (1, 1, 3, 3) [3, 5, 5, 5] row(s) of Cloak St st.

Dec Row 4 (RS): Yo, k2tog, k6 (3, 1, 3, 1) [5, 3, 1, 3], *k1 (3, 3, 3, 3) [3, 3, 2, 2], k2tog, k2 (3, 3, 4, 4) [3, 3, 3, 2]; rep from * to last 9 (5, 4, 6, 4) [7, 6, 4, 4] sts, knit to end—65 (73, 77, 83, 87) [91, 95, 97, 99] sts.

Work Row 2 of Cloak St st 1 time.

HOOD

The first 8 rows are worked for all hood options and sizes; then are broken out into individual instructions.

Row 1 (RS): Yo, k2tog, knit to end.

Row 2 (WS): Yo, ssk, knit to end.

Row 3: Yo, k2tog, k4 (1, 4, 4, 2) [1, 4, 1, 2], k2tog, *(yo) 2 times, s2kp; rep from * to last 6 (5, 6, 6, 6) [5, 6, 5, 6] sts, (yo) 2 times, ssk, knit to end.

Row 4: Yo, ssk, k3 (2, 3, 3, 3) [2, 3, 2, 3], (k1, p1) into double yo, *k1, (k1, p1) into double yo; rep from * to last 7 (4, 7, 7, 5) [4, 7, 4, 5] sts, knit to end.

Work Rows 1 and 2 of Cloak St st 2 times (4 rows total).

No Hood Option

With RS facing, BO loosely purlwise. Proceed to Finishing.

Fitted Hood Option

Work Rows 1 and 2 of Cloak St st 26 times (52 rows total).

Divide the sts in half over the two ends of the circular needle (the needle closer to you should have 1 less stitch than the one further from you); fold the needle in half and hold the two ends of the needle parallel. Turn the hood inside out so the WS is facing. Using the spare gauge-size needle, BO sts using the Three-Needle bind off method until 3 sts rem: 1 st on the closer needle, 2 sts on the further needle. Insert the third needle knitwise into the single stitch on the closer needle and into both sts on the back needle, and knit all 3 sts together. Pass the previous stitch over and off the needle. Break yarn; pull tail through final stitch to secure. Turn hood back RS out. Proceed to Finishing.

Oversized Hood Option

Inc Row (RS): Yo, k2tog, k2 (2, 2, 2, 1) [2, 2, 2, 1], *M1L, k3; rep from * to last 4 (3, 4, 4, 3) [3, 4, 3, 3] sts, M1L, knit to end—84 (95, 100, 108, 114) [119, 124, 127, 130] sts.

Work the WS row of Cloak St st 1 time. Then work Rows 1 and 2 of Cloak St st 30 times (61 rows total).

For an even number of sts: Divide the sts evenly over the two ends of the circular needle; fold the needle in half and hold the two ends of the needle parallel. Turn the hood inside out so the WS is facing. Using the spare gauge-size needle, BO all sts using the Three-Needle

bind off method. Break yarn; pull tail through final stitch to secure. Turn hood back RS out. Proceed to Finishing.

For an odd number of sts: Divide the sts in half over the two ends of the circular needle (the needle closer to you should have 1 less stitch than the one further from you); fold the needle in half and hold the two ends of the needle parallel. Turn the hood inside out so the WS is facing. Using the spare gauge-size needle, BO sts using the Three-Needle bind off method until 3 sts rem: 1 st on the closer needle, 2 sts on the further needle. Insert the third

needle knitwise into the single stitch on the closer needle and into both sts on the back needle, and knit all 3 sts together. Pass the previous stitch over and off the needle. Break yarn; pull tail through final stitch to secure. Turn hood back RS out. Proceed to Finishing.

FINISHING

Weave in all loose ends to the WS with tapestry needle. Wet block to dimensions in the schematic. Once dry, trim all ends.

Weave the ribbon through the eyelets created at the base of the hood. Trim to desired length.

"'Rivendell' said Frodo. 'Very good: I will go east, and I will make for Rivendell . . .' He spoke lightly, but his heart was moved suddenly with a desire to see the house of Elrond Halfelven, and breathe the air of that deep valley where many of the Fair Folk still dwelt in peace."

—The Lord of the Rings: The Fellowship of the Ring
by J.R.R. Tolkien

Schematic

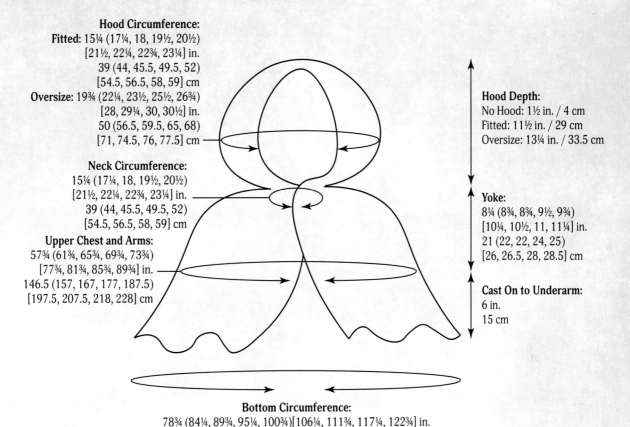

Hood Circumference:
Fitted: 15¼ (17¼, 18, 19½, 20½)
[21½, 22¼, 22¾, 23¼] in.
39 (44, 45.5, 49.5, 52)
[54.5, 56.5, 58, 59] cm
Oversize: 19¾ (22¼, 23½, 25½, 26¾)
[28, 29¼, 30, 30½] in.
50 (56.5, 59.5, 65, 68)
[71, 74.5, 76, 77.5] cm

Neck Circumference:
15¼ (17¼, 18, 19½, 20½)
[21½, 22¼, 22¾, 23¼] in.
39 (44, 45.5, 49.5, 52)
[54.5, 56.5, 58, 59] cm

Upper Chest and Arms:
57¾ (61¾, 65¾, 69¾, 73¾)
[77¾, 81¾, 85¾, 89¾] in.
146.5 (157, 167, 177, 187.5)
[197.5, 207.5, 218, 228] cm

Hood Depth:
No Hood: 1½ in. / 4 cm
Fitted: 11½ in. / 29 cm
Oversize: 13¼ in. / 33.5 cm

Yoke:
8¼ (8¾, 8¾, 9½, 9¾)
[10¼, 10½, 11, 11¼] in.
21 (22, 22, 24, 25)
[26, 26.5, 28, 28.5] cm

Cast On to Underarm:
6 in.
15 cm

Bottom Circumference:
78¾ (84¼, 89¾, 95¼, 100¾)[106¼, 111¾, 117¼, 122¾] in.
200 (214, 228, 242, 256)[270, 284, 298, 312] cm

CHART A

KEY

- ▉ No stitch
- ☐ k on RS, p on WS
- ⊟ p on RS, k on WS
- ╱ k2tog on RS, ssk on WS
- ╲ ssk on RS, k2tog on WS
- ⊼ s2kp
- ⊙ yo
- ▉ ⟋ 3-to-2
- ⟋⊙⟍ 3-to-3
- ⟍⊼⊙⟋ 5-to-3
- ⟍⊙⟍⊙⟍ 5-to-5
- ⟍⊙⟍⊙⟍⊙⟍⊙⟍ 3-to-9
- ☐ Pattern repeat

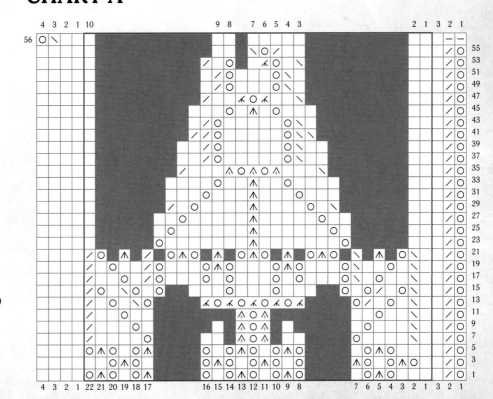

SHIELDMAIDEN VEST

DESIGNED BY CASSANDRA CRUIKSHANK

Raised by King Théoden after her father Éomund was killed by Orcs and her mother died from grief, Éowyn lived in Meduseld. The primary caregiver for her uncle who was enthralled by neighboring Saruman and his puppet Wormtongue, she is a fierce leader of Rohan and loyal to her family, doing everything she can to bring her uncle back to health and power. After Gandalf heals Théoden, Éowyn's attempts to join the battle against evil are continually thwarted by her family, and she finally disguises herself as a man alongside the Hobbit Merry and escapes. Skilled with a blade, an accomplished rider, and often dismissed because of her gender, she is essential to the destruction of Sauron.

Dress like the warrior princess you are! Inspired by the armor Éowyn wears, this vest is worked in the round from the bottom up until the sleeve shaping. The front and back are then worked flat before being joined into the round again for the neckline. This cap-sleeved vest and costume replica from *The Lord of the Rings: The Two Towers* film features a faux-quilted pattern throughout created with knits and purls, with stranded colorwork details running along the bottom edge, middle, neckline, and sleeve caps. The sleeve caps are worked separately with German short rows, then joined into the arm openings with single crochet.

SIZES

1 (2, 3, 4, 5) [6, 7, 8, 9] {10, 11, 12, 13}

FINISHED MEASUREMENTS

Chest Circumference: 29 (32¾, 36¼, 40, 43½) [47¼, 51, 54½, 58] {61¾, 65½, 69, 72¾} in. / 73.5 (83, 92, 101.5, 110.5)[120, 129.5, 138.5, 147.5]{157, 166.5, 175.5, 185} cm

Garment designed to be worn with 2 to 4 in. / 5 to 10 cm positive ease.

YARN

Fingering weight yarn, shown in Urban Girl Yarns *Virginia* (90% superwash merino, 10% nylon; 480 yd. / 439 m per 4½ oz. / 125 g hank)

Colorways:

- **Main Color (MC):** Kodiak, 1 (1, 1, 2, 2) [2, 3, 3, 4] {4, 4, 5, 5} hank(s)
- **Contrast Color (CC):** Valor, 1 (1, 1, 1, 1) [1, 1, 2, 2] {2, 2, 2, 2} hank(s)

NEEDLES

US 2 / 2.75 mm, 16 in. / 40 cm long circular needle

US 4 / 3.5 mm, 24 to 40 in. / 60 to 100 cm long circular needle or size needed to obtain gauge

NOTIONS

Spare gauge-size needle

Stitch marker

Locking stitch markers

Waste yarn

Tapestry needle

E-4 / 3.5 mm crochet hook (or size equivalent to the gauge-size needle)

GAUGE

22 sts and 40 rnds = 4 in. / 10 cm in reverse St st worked in the round on the larger needle, taken after blocking

Make sure to check your gauge.

PATTERN NOTES

This vest is worked from the bottom up in the round for the body; the front and back halves of the yoke are separated at the underarm and worked flat to the shoulder.

The stranded colorwork patterns are provided in chart form only. Short rows are incorporated into the sleeve colorwork pattern, which is worked flat.

When working the stranded colorwork patterns, catch floats longer than five stitches. Carry CC yarn below MC for color dominance, except for when catching floats.

When catching floats in the colorwork pattern, stagger the catch location to avoid puckering of the fabric and/or the contrast color showing through where it is not intended.

Instructions are provided for size 1 first, with additional sizes in parentheses, brackets, and braces. When only one number is provided, it applies to all sizes.

PATTERN STITCHES

Reverse St st (worked over any number of sts)

Rnd 1: Purl.

Rep Rnd 1 for patt.

PATTERN INSTRUCTIONS

CAST ON

With MC and the larger needle, CO 160 (180, 200, 220, 240)[260, 280, 300, 320]{340, 360, 380, 400} sts using the Long Tail cast on method. Pm for BOR and join to work in the rnd., being careful. Not to twist the sts. *The BOR M will be located at the right side seam.*

Purl 1 round.

BOTTOM COLORWORK BAND

Begin Chart A, reading all rows from right to left as for working in the rnd, joining CC as required. Work [Rows 1–9] 3 times, then [Rows 1 and 2] 1 more time (29 total rows worked; chart is worked 16 (18, 20, 22, 24)[26, 28, 30, 32]{34, 36, 38, 40} times across each rnd). When complete, break CC.

BODY

Textural Pattern
Begin Chart B, reading all rows from right to left as for working in the rnd. Rep Rows 1–10 until the garment measures 8½ (8½, 8½, 9, 9)[9, 9½, 9½, 9½]{10½, 10½, 10½, 10½} in. / 21.5 (21.5, 21.5, 23, 23)[23, 24, 24, 24]{26.5, 26.5, 26.5, 26.5} cm from the CO edge, ending with any row (chart is worked 16 (18, 20, 22, 24)[26, 28, 30,

32]{34, 36, 38, 40} times across each rnd).

Colorwork Band
Begin Chart A, reading all rows from right to left as for working in the rnd, joining CC as required. Work [Rows 1–9] 1 time, then [Rows 1 and 2] 1 more time (11 rnds total; chart is worked 16 (18, 20, 22, 24)[26, 28, 30, 32]{34, 36, 38, 40} times across each rnd). When complete, break CC.

Textural Pattern
Begin Chart B, reading all rows from right to left as for working in the rnd. Rep Rows 1–10 until the garment measures 12½ (12½, 12½, 13½, 13½)[13½, 14½, 14½, 14½]{15½, 15½, 15½, 15½} in. / 32 (32, 32, 34.5, 34.5)[34.5, 37, 37, 37]{39.5, 39.5, 39.5, 39.5} cm from the CO edge, ending with an odd-numbered row (chart is worked 16 (18, 20, 22, 24)[26, 28, 30, 32]{34, 36, 38, 40} times across each rnd). *Make a note of which row you ended on to continue the pattern up the yoke.*

DIVIDE FOR YOKE / ARMHOLES

Setup Rnd: Resuming on the next row of Chart B (an even-numbered row), work 75 (85, 95, 105, 115) [125, 134, 144, 153]{163, 173, 182, 192} sts in est patt, BO 10 (10, 10, 10, 10)[10, 12, 12, 14]{14, 14, 16, 16} sts knitwise, cont in est patt across the next 70 (80, 90, 100, 110)[120, 128, 138, 146]{156, 166, 174, 184} sts, BO 10 (10, 10, 10, 10)[10, 12, 12, 14]{14, 14, 16, 16} sts, rm BOR M as encountered—140 (160, 180, 200, 220)[240, 256, 276, 292]{312, 332, 348, 368} sts rem.

The first 70 (80, 90, 100, 110)[120, 128, 138, 146]{156, 166, 174, 184} sts make up the back yoke; the remaining 70 (80, 90, 100, 110)[120, 128, 138, 146]{156, 166, 174, 184} sts make up the front yoke. Place the front yoke sts on hold using waste yarn.

BACK YOKE

The textural pattern will now follow Chart C, which is the same stitch pattern as Chart B, but worked flat. Begin with the next odd-numbered row to cont in est patt (odd-numbered rows are RS rows).

Row 1 (RS): BO 3 (5,5, 5, 7)[7, 7, 9, 9]{11, 11, 11, 11} sts knitwise, work est patt to end of row.

Row 2 (WS): BO 3 (5,5, 5, 7)[7, 7, 9, 9]{11, 11, 11, 11} sts purlwise, work est patt to end of row.

64 (70, 80, 90, 96)[106, 114, 120, 128]{134, 144, 152, 162} sts rem.

Sizes 1– 9 ONLY:

Row 3 (dec): P1, p2tog, work est patt to last 3 sts, ssp, p1—2 sts dec.

Row 4: Work est patt to end of row.

Rep [Rows 3 and 4] 2 (5, 8, 13, 16)[19, 21, 23, 25]{-, -, -, -} more times.

Sizes 10-13 ONLY:

Row 3 (dec): P1, p2tog, work est patt to last 3 sts, ssp, p1—2 sts dec.

Row 4 (dec): K1, ssk, work est patt to last 2 sts, k2tog, k1—2 sts dec.

Rep [Rows 3 and 4] - (-, -, -, -)[-, -, -, -]{1, 2, 3, 6} more times.

Next Row (RS, dec): P1, p2tog, work est patt to last 3 sts, ssp, p1—2 sts dec.

Next Row (WS): Work est patt to end of row.

Rep last 2 rows - (-, -, -, -)[-, -, -, -]{23, 25, 25, 23} more times.

All Sizes:

6 (12, 18, 28, 34)[40, 44, 48, 52]{56, 64, 68, 76} sts dec; 58 (58, 62, 62, 62)[66, 70, 72, 76]{78, 80, 84, 86} sts rem.

If needed, cont in est patt even (no more decreases) until the yoke measures 4 (4, 4½, 5, 5)[5½, 5½, 5½, 6]{6, 6½, 7, 7) in. / 10 (10, 11.5, 12.5, 12.5)[14, 14, 14, 15]{15, 16.5, 18, 18} from the divide for yoke, ending with a WS row.

BACK NECK SHAPING

Bind Off Row (RS): Resuming on the next row of Chart C, work 16 (16, 18, 18, 18)[20, 20, 20, 22]{22, 22, 24, 24} sts in est patt, place these just worked sts on hold using waste yarn (these will make up the back right shoulder). BO 26 (26, 26, 26, 26)[26, 30, 32, 32]{34, 36, 36, 38} sts knitwise, cont in est patt to end of row.

BACK LEFT SHOULDER

Setup Row (WS): Work est patt to end of row.

Row 1 (RS): BO 3 sts knitwise, work est patt to end of row—3 sts dec.

Row 2 (WS, dec): Work est patt to last 3 sts, k2tog, k1—1 st dec.

Row 3 (dec): P1, p2tog, work est patt to end of row—1 st dec.

Row 4 (dec): Work est patt to last 3 sts, k2tog, k1—1 st dec.

Rep [Rows 3 and 4] 0 (0, 1, 1, 1)[2, 2, 2, 3]{3, 3, 4, 4} more times.

6 (6, 8, 8, 8)[10, 10, 10, 12]{12, 12, 14, 14} sts dec; 10 sts rem.

Cont est patt even (no more decreases) until the back measures 6 (6, 6½, 7, 7)[7, 7½, 7½, 8]{8, 8½, 8½, 9) in. / 15 (15, 16.5, 18, 18)[18, 19, 19, 20.5]{20.5, 21.5, 21.5, 23} cm from the divide for yoke, ending with a WS row. Break yarn; place sts on hold using waste yarn.

BACK RIGHT SHOULDER

Place 16 (16, 18, 18, 18)[20, 20, 20, 22]{22, 22, 24, 24} sts of the back right shoulder onto larger needle. Rejoin MC with the WS facing.

Setup Row (WS): BO 3 sts purlwise, work est patt to end of row—3 sts dec.

Row 1 (RS, dec): Work est patt to last 3 sts, p2tog, p1—1 st dec.

Row 2 (WS, dec): K1, k2tog, work est patt to end of row—1 st dec.

Rep [Rows 1 and 2] 0 (0, 1, 1, 1)[2, 2, 2, 3]{3, 3, 4, 4} more times.

Next Row (RS, dec): Work est patt to last 3 sts, p2tog, p1—1 st dec.

Next Row (WS): Work est patt to end of row.

6 (6, 8, 8, 8)[10, 10, 10, 12]{12, 12, 14, 14} sts dec; 10 sts rem.

Cont est patt even (no more decreases) until the back measures 6 (6, 6½, 7, 7)[7, 7½, 7½, 8]{8, 8½, 8½, 9) in. / 15 (15, 16.5, 18, 18)[18, 19, 19, 20.5]{20.5, 21.5, 21.5, 23} cm from the divide for yoke, ending with a WS row. Break yarn; place sts on hold using waste yarn.

FRONT YOKE

Place 70 (80, 90, 100, 110)[120, 128, 138, 146]{156, 166, 174, 184} sts of the front yoke onto the larger needle. Rejoin MC with the RS facing. Begin working from Chart C to maintain est patt.

Row 1 (RS): BO 3 (5,5, 5, 7)[7, 7, 9, 9]{11, 11, 11, 11} sts knitwise, work est patt to end of row.

Row 2 (WS): BO 3 (5,5, 5, 7)[7, 7, 9, 9]{11, 11, 11, 11} sts purlwise, work est patt to end of row.

64 (70, 80, 90, 96)[106, 114, 120, 128]{134, 144, 152, 162} sts rem.

Sizes 1–9 ONLY:

Row 3 (dec): P1, p2tog, work est patt to last 3 sts, ssp, p1—2 sts dec.

Row 4: Work est patt to end of row.

Rep [Rows 3 and 4] 2 (3, 6, 8, 8)[8, 11, 11, 13]{-, -, -, -} more times.

Sizes 10–13 ONLY:

Row 3 (dec): P1, p2tog, work est patt to last 3 sts, ssp, p1—2 sts dec.

Row 4 (dec): K1, ssk, work est patt to last 2 sts, k2tog, k1—2 sts dec.

Rep [Rows 3 and 4] - (-, -, -, -)[-, -, -, -]{1, 2, 3, 6} more times.

Next Row (RS, dec): P1, p2tog, work est patt to last 3 sts, ssp, p1—2 sts dec.

Next Row (WS): Work est patt to end of row.

Rep last 2 rows - (-, -, -, -)[-, -, -, -]{11, 13, 13, 11} more times.

All Sizes:

6 (8, 14, 18, 18)[18, 24, 24, 28]{32, 40, 42, 52} sts dec; 58 (62, 66, 72, 78)[88, 90, 96, 100]{102, 104, 110, 110} sts rem.

FRONT NECK SHAPING

Size 1 ONLY:

Row 1 (RS): Work est patt to end of row.

Row 2 (WS): Work est patt to end of row.

Row 3: Work 27 sts in est patt, place these just worked sts on hold using waste yarn (these will make up the front left shoulder). BO 4 sts knitwise, cont in est patt to end of row—27 sts rem for front right shoulder.

Row 4: Work est patt to end of row.

Sizes 2–13 ONLY:

Row 1 (RS, dec): P1, p2tog, work - (26, 28, 31, 34)[39, 40, 43, 45]{46, 47, 50, 50} sts in est patt, place these just-worked sts on hold using waste yarn (these will make up the front left shoulder). BO 4 sts knitwise, cont in est patt to last 3 sts, ssp, p1—- (28, 30, 33, 36)[41, 42, 45, 47]{48, 49, 52, 52} sts rem for front right shoulder.

Row 2: Work est patt to end of row.

FRONT RIGHT SHOULDER

Size 1 ONLY:

Row 1 (RS, dec): P1, p2tog, work est patt to end of row—1 st dec.

Row 2 (WS): Work est patt to end of row.

Rows 3–10: Rep [Rows 1 & 2] 4 more times—22 sts rem.

Row 11 (dec): P1, p2tog, work est patt to end of row—1 st dec.

Row 12 (dec): Work est patt to last 2 sts, k2tog, k1—1 st dec.

Rows 13–22: Rep [Rows 11 & 12] 5 more times - 10 sts rem.

Sizes 2 (3) ONLY:

Row 1 (RS, dec): P1, p2tog, work est patt to last 3 sts, ssp, p1—26 (28) sts rem.

Row 2 (WS): Work est patt to end of row.

Row 3 (dec): P1, p2tog, work est patt to end of row—1 st dec.

Row 4: Work est patt to end of row.

Rows 5–10: Rep [Rows 3 & 4] 3 more times—22 (24) sts rem.

Row 11 (dec): P1, p2tog, work est patt to end of row—1 st dec.

Row 12 (dec): Work est patt to last 2 sts, k2tog, k1—1 st dec.

Rows 13–22 (13-24): Rep [Rows 11 & 12] 5 (6) more time(s)—10 sts rem.

Size 4 ONLY:

Row 1 (RS, dec): P1, p2tog, work est patt to last 3 sts, ssp, p1—2 sts dec.

Row 2 (WS): Work est patt to end of row.

Rows 3–8: Rep [Rows 1 & 2] 3 more times—25 sts rem.

Row 9 (dec): P1, p2tog, work est patt to end of row—24 sts rem.

Row 10: Work est patt to end of row.

Row 11 (dec): P1, p2tog, work est patt to end of row—1 st dec.

Row 12 (dec): Work est patt to last 2 sts, k2tog, k1—1 st dec

Rows 13–24: Rep [Rows 11 & 12] 6 more times—10 sts rem.

Size 5 ONLY:

Row 1 (RS, dec): P1, p2tog, work est patt to last 3 sts, ssp, p1—2 sts dec.

Row 2 (WS): Work est patt to end of row.

Rows 3–10: Rep [Rows 1 & 2] 4 more times—26 sts rem.

Row 11 (dec): P1, p2tog, work est patt to last 3 sts, ssp, p1—2 sts dec.

Row 12 (dec): Work est patt to last 2 sts, k2tog, k1—1 st dec.

Rows 13–14: Rep [Rows 11 & 12] 1 more time—20 sts rem.

Row 15 (dec): P1, p2tog, work est patt to end of row—1 st dec.

Row 16 (dec): Work est patt to last 2 sts, k2tog, k1—1 st dec.

Rows 17–24: Rep [Rows 15 & 16] 4 more times—10 sts rem.

Size 6 ONLY:

Row 1 (RS, dec): P1, p2tog, work est patt to last 3 sts, ssp, p1—2 sts dec.

Row 2 (WS): Work est patt to end of row.

Rows 3–10: Rep [Rows 1 & 2] 4 more times—31 sts rem.

Row 11 (dec): P1, p2tog, work est patt to last 3 sts, ssp, p1—2 sts dec.

Row 12 (dec): Work est patt to last 2 sts, k2tog, k1—1 st dec.

Rows 13–20: Rep [Rows 11 & 12] 4 more times—16 sts rem.

Row 21 (dec): P1, p2tog, work est patt to end of row—1 st dec.

Row 22 (dec): Work est patt to last 2 sts, k2tog, k1—1 st dec.

Rows 23–26: Rep [Rows 21 & 22] 2 more times—10 sts rem.

Size 7 ONLY:

Row 1 (RS, dec): P1, p2tog, work est patt to last 3 sts, ssp, p1—2 sts dec.

Row 2 (WS): Work est patt to end of row.

Rows 3–10: Rep [Rows 1 & 2] 4 more times—32 sts rem.

Row 11 (dec): P1, p2tog, work est patt to last 3 sts, ssp, p1—2 sts dec.

Row 12 (dec): Work est patt to last 2 sts, k2tog, k1—1 st dec.

Rows 13–18: Rep [Rows 11 & 12] 3 more times—20 sts rem.

Row 19 (dec): P1, p2tog, work est patt to end of row—1 st dec.

Row 20 (dec): Work est patt to last 2 sts, k2tog, k1—1 st dec.

Rows 21–28: Rep [Rows 19 & 20] 4 more times—10 sts rem.

Sizes 8 (9, 11) ONLY:

Row 1 (RS, dec): P1, p2tog, work est patt to last 3 sts, ssp, p1—2 sts dec.

Row 2 (WS): Work est patt to end of row.

Rows 3–10: Rep [Rows 1 & 2] 4 more times—35 (37, 39) sts rem.

Row 11 (dec): P1, p2tog, work est patt to last 3 sts, ssp, p1—2 sts dec.

Row 12 (dec): Work est patt to last 2 sts, k2tog, k1—1 st dec.

Rows 13–22: Rep [Rows 11 & 12] 5 more times—17 (19, 21) sts rem.

Row 23 (dec): P1, p2tog, work est patt to end of row—1 st dec.

Row 24 (dec): Work est patt to last 2 sts, k2tog, k1—1 st dec.

Rows 25–28 (25-30, 25-32): Rep [Rows 23 & 24] 2 (3, 4) more times—11 sts rem.

Next Row (RS, dec): P1, p2tog, work est patt to end of row—10 sts rem.

Next Row (WS): Work est patt to end of row.

Sizes 10 (13) ONLY:

Row 1 (RS, dec): P1, p2tog, work est patt to last 3 sts, ssp, p1—2 sts dec.

Row 2 (WS): Work est patt to end of row.

Rows 3–10: Rep [Rows 1 & 2] 4 more times—38 (42) sts rem.

Row 11 (dec): P1, p2tog, work est patt to last 3 sts, ssp, p1—2 sts dec.

Row 12 (dec): Work est patt to last 2 sts, k2tog, k1—1 st dec.

Rows 13–22: Rep [Rows 11 & 12] 5 more times—20 (24) sts rem.

Row 23 (dec): P1, p2tog, work est patt to end of row—1 st dec.

Row 24 (dec): Work est patt to last 2 sts, k2tog, k1—1 st dec.

Rows 25–32 (25-36): Rep [Rows 23 & 24] 4 (6) more times—10 sts rem.

Size 12 ONLY:

Row 1 (RS, dec): P1, p2tog, work est patt to last 3 sts, ssp, p1—2 sts dec.

Row 2 (WS): Work est patt to end of row.

Rows 3–10: Rep [Rows 1 & 2] 4 more times—42 sts rem.

Row 11 (dec): P1, p2tog, work est patt to last 3 sts, ssp, p1—2 sts dec.

Row 12 (dec): Work est patt to last 2 sts, k2tog, k1—1 st dec.

Rows 13-24: Rep [Rows 11 & 12] 6 more times—21 sts rem.

Row 25 (dec): P1, p2tog, work est patt to end of row—1 st dec.

Row 26 (dec): Work est patt to last 2 sts, k2tog, k1—1 st dec.

Rows 27-30: Rep [Rows 25 & 26] 4 more times—11 sts rem.

Next Row (RS, dec): P1, p2tog, work est patt to end of row—10 sts rem.

Next Row (WS): Work est patt to end of row.

All Sizes:

Beginning with a RS row, cont est patt even (no more decreases) until the front measures 6 (6, 6½, 7, 7)[7, 7½, 7½, 8]{8, 8½, 8½, 9} in. / 15 (15, 16.5, 18, 18)[18, 19, 19, 20.5]{20.5, 21.5, 21.5, 23} cm from the divide for yoke, ending with a WS row.

Place the live 10 sts of the back right shoulder onto a spare gauge-size needle and hold parallel with the front right shoulder sts. Turn the garment inside out and join the front and back right shoulder sts together using the Three Needle bind off method. Break yarn. Turn the garment RS out.

FRONT LEFT SHOULDER

Place 27 (28, 30, 33, 36) [41, 42, 45, 47]{48, 49, 52, 52} sts of the front left shoulder onto the larger needle. Rejoin MC with the WS facing.

Setup Row (WS): Work est patt to end of row.

Size 1 ONLY:

Row 1 (RS, dec): Work est patt to last 3 sts, ssp, p1—1 st dec.

Row 2 (WS): Work est patt to end of row.

Rows 3-10: Rep [Rows 1 & 2] 4 more times—22 sts rem.

Row 11 (dec): Work est patt to last 3 sts, ssp, p1– 1 st dec.

Row 12 (dec): K1, ssk, work est patt to end of row—1 st dec.

Rows 13–22: Rep [Rows 11 & 12] 5 more times - 10 sts rem.

Sizes 2 (3) ONLY:

Row 1 (RS, dec): P1, p2tog, work est patt to last 3 sts, ssp, p1—26 (28) sts rem.

Row 2 (WS): Work est patt to end of row.

Row 3 (dec): Work est patt to last 3 sts, ssp, p1—1 st dec.

Row 4: Work est patt to end of row.

Rows 5–10: Rep [Rows 3 & 4] 3 more times—22 (24) sts rem.

Row 11 (dec): Work est patt to last 3 sts, ssp, p1—1 st dec.

Row 12 (dec): K1, ssk, work est patt to end of row—1 st dec.

Rows 13–22 (13-24): Rep [Rows 11 & 12] 5 (6) more time(s)—10 sts rem.

Size 4 ONLY:

Row 1 (RS, dec): P1, p2tog, work est patt to last 3 sts, ssp, p1—2 sts dec.

Row 2 (WS): Work est patt to end of row.

Rows 3-8: Rep [Rows 1 & 2] 3 more times—25 sts rem.

Row 9 (dec): Work est patt to last 3 sts, ssp, p1—24 sts rem.

Row 10: Work est patt to end of row.

Row 11 (dec): Work est patt to last 3 sts, ssp, p1—1 st dec.

Row 12 (dec): K1, ssk, work est patt to end of row—1 st dec.

Rows 13–24: Rep [Rows 11 & 12] 6 more times—10 sts rem.

Size 5 ONLY:

Row 1 (RS, dec): P1, p2tog, work est patt to last 3 sts, ssp, p1—2 sts dec.

Row 2 (WS): Work est patt to end of row.

Rows 3–10: Rep [Rows 1 & 2] 4 more times—26 sts rem.

Row 11 (dec): P1, p2tog, work est patt to last 3 sts, ssp, p1—2 sts dec.

Row 12 (dec): K1, ssk, work est patt to end of row—1 st dec.

Rows 13–14: Rep [Rows 11 & 12] 1 more time—20 sts rem.

Row 15 (dec): Work est patt to last 3 sts, ssp, p1—1 st dec.

Row 16 (dec): K1, ssk, work est patt to end of row—1 st dec.

Rows 17–24 (dec): Rep [Rows 15 & 16] 4 more times—10 sts rem.

Size 6 ONLY:

Row 1 (RS, dec): P1, p2tog, work est patt to last 3 sts, ssp, p1—2 sts dec.

Row 2 (WS): Work est patt to end of row.

Rows 3–10: Rep [Rows 1 & 2] 4 more times—31 sts rem.

Row 11 (dec): P1, p2tog, work est patt to last 3 sts, ssp, p1—2 sts dec.

Row 12 (dec): K1, ssk, work est patt to end of row—1 st dec.

Rows 13–20: Rep [Rows 11 & 12] 4 more times—16 sts rem.

Row 21 (dec): Work est patt to last 3 sts, ssp, p1—1 st dec.

Row 22 (dec): K1, ssk, work est patt to end of row—1 st dec.

Rows 23–26 (dec): Rep [Rows 21 & 22] 2 more times—10 sts rem.

Size 7 ONLY:

Row 1 (RS, dec): P1, p2tog, work est patt to last 3 sts, ssp, p1—2 sts dec.

Row 2 (WS): Work est patt to end of row.

Rows 3–10: Rep [Rows 1 & 2] 4 more times—32 sts rem.

Row 11 (dec): P1, p2tog, work est patt to last 3 sts, ssp, p1—2 sts dec.

Row 12 (dec): K1, ssk, work est patt to end of row—1 st dec.

Rows 13–18: Rep [Rows 11 & 12] 3 more times—20 sts rem.

Row 19 (dec): Work est patt to last 3 sts, ssp, p1—1 st dec.

Row 20 (dec): K1, ssk, work est patt to end of row—1 st dec.

Rows 21–28 (dec): Rep [Rows 21 & 22] 2 more times—10 sts rem.

Sizes 8 (9, 11) ONLY:

Row 1 (RS, dec): P1, p2tog, work est patt to last 3 sts, ssp, p1—2 sts dec.

Row 2 (WS): Work est patt to end of row.

Rows 3–10: Rep [Rows 1 & 2] 4 more times—35 (37, 39) sts rem.

Row 11 (dec): P1, p2tog, work est patt to last 3 sts, ssp, p1—2 sts dec.

Row 12 (dec): K1, ssk, work est patt to end of row—1 st dec.

Rows 13–22: Rep [Rows 11 & 12] 5 more times—17 (19, 21) sts rem.

Row 23 (dec): Work est patt to last 3 sts, ssp, p1—1 st dec.

Row 24 (dec): K1, ssk, work est patt to end of row—1 st dec.

Rows 25–28 (25-30, 25-32): Rep [Rows 23 & 24] 2 (3, 4) more times—11 sts rem.

Next Row (RS, dec): Work est patt to last 3 sts, ssp, p1— 10 sts rem.

Next Row (WS): Work est patt to end of row.

Sizes 10 (13) ONLY:

Row 1 (RS, dec): P1, p2tog, work est patt to last 3 sts, ssp, p1—2 sts dec.

Row 2 (WS): Work est patt to end of row.

Rows 3–10: Rep [Rows 1 & 2] 4 more times—38 (42) sts rem.

Row 11 (dec): P1, p2tog, work est patt to last 3 sts, ssp, p1—2 sts dec.

Row 12 (dec): K1, ssk, work est patt to end of row—1 st dec.

Rows 13–22: Rep [Rows 11 & 12] 5 more times—20 (24) sts rem.

Row 23 (dec): Work est patt to last 3 sts, ssp, p1— 1 st dec.

Row 24 (dec): K1, ssk, work est patt to end of row—1 st dec.

Rows 25-32 (25-36): Rep [Rows 23 & 24] 4 (6) more times—10 sts rem.

Size 12 ONLY:

Row 1 (RS, dec): P1, p2tog, work est patt to last 3 sts, ssp, p1—2 sts dec.

Row 2 (WS): Work est patt to end of row.

Rows 3-10: Rep [Rows 1 & 2] 4 more times—42 sts rem.

Row 11 (dec): P1, p2tog, work est patt to last 3 sts, ssp, p1—2 sts dec.

Row 12 (dec): K1, ssk, work est patt to end of row—1 st dec.

Rows 13-24: Rep [Rows 11 & 12] 6 more times—21 sts rem.

"No living man am I! You look upon a woman! Éowyn I am, Éomund's daughter. Begone if you be not deathless!"

–Éowyn, *The Lord of the Rings: The Return of the King* by J.R.R. Tolkien

Schematic

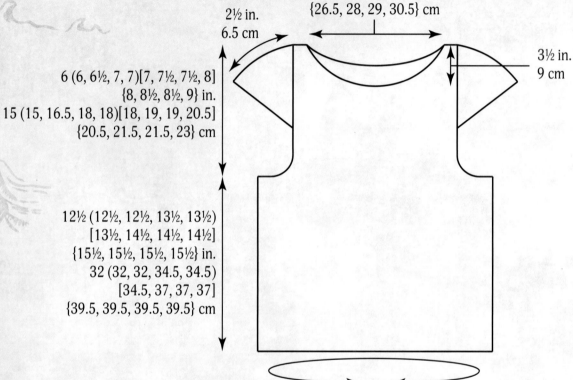

7 (7, 7½, 7½, 7½)[8¼, 9, 9½, 10]
{10½, 11, 11½, 12 } in.
18 (18, 19, 19, 19)[21, 23, 24, 25.5]
{26.5, 28, 29, 30.5} cm

2½ in.
6.5 cm

3½ in.
9 cm

6 (6, 6½, 7, 7)[7, 7½, 7½, 8]
{8, 8½, 8½, 9} in.
15 (15, 16.5, 18, 18)[18, 19, 19, 20.5]
{20.5, 21.5, 21.5, 23} cm

12½ (12½, 12½, 13½, 13½)
[13½, 14½, 14½, 14½]
{15½, 15½, 15½, 15½} in.
32 (32, 32, 34.5, 34.5)
[34.5, 37, 37, 37]
{39.5, 39.5, 39.5, 39.5} cm

29 (32¾, 36¼, 40, 43½)[47¼, 51, 54½, 58]{61¾, 65½, 69, 72¾} in.
73.5 (83, 92, 101.5, 110.5)[120, 129.5, 138.5, 147.5]{157, 166.5, 175.5, 185} cm

KEY

- ▨ No stitch
- ■ MC
- ▨ CC
- □ Knit on RS, purl on WS
- − Purl on RS, knit on WS
- ⊂ Turn work, left edge
- ⊃ Turn work, right edge
- � Make DS
- ⋀ kDS on RS, pDS on WS
- ▭ Pattern repeat

CHART A

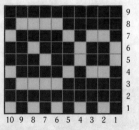

CHART B

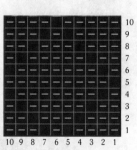

50

Row 25 (dec): Work est patt to last 3 sts, ssp, p1– 1 st dec.

Row 26 (dec): K1, ssk, work est patt to end of row—1 st dec.

Rows 27-30: Rep [Rows 25 & 26] 4 more times—11 sts rem.

Next Row (dec): Work est patt to last 3 sts, ssp, p1– 10 sts rem.

Next Row (WS): Work est patt to end of row.

All Sizes:

Beginning with a RS row, cont est patt even (no more decreases) until the front measures 6 (6, 6½, 7, 7)[7, 7½, 7½, 8]{8, 8½, 8½, 9} in. / 15 (15, 16.5, 18, 18)[18, 19, 19, 20.5]{20.5, 21.5, 21.5, 23} cm from the divide for yoke, ending with a WS row.

Place the live 10 sts of the back left shoulder onto a spare gauge-size needle and hold parallel with the front left shoulder sts.

Turn the garment inside out and join the front and back left shoulder sts together using the Three Needle bind off method. Break yarn. Turn the garment RS out.

SLEEVES (MAKE 2 THE SAME)

Using MC and the larger needle, CO 40 (40, 50, 50, 60)[60, 70, 70, 70]{80, 80, 80, 90} sts using the Long Tail cast on method. Do not join to work in the rnd.

Knit 2 rows.

Begin Chart D, reading all RS (odd-numbered) rows from right to left and all WS (even numbered) rows from left to right, joining CC as required.

Work [Rows 1-24] 1 time (pattern repeat is worked

1 (1, 2, 2, 3)[3, 4, 4, 4]{5, 5, 5, 6} times). When complete, break CC.

With RS facing, BO all sts knitwise.

NECK EDGING

Using MC and the smaller needle, beginning at either shoulder seam, pick up and knit sts evenly around the neckline in multiples of 10. Pm for BOR and join to work in the rnd.

Begin Chart A, reading all rows from right to left as for working in the rnd, joining CC as required.

Work [Rows 1-9] 1 time, then [Rows 1 and 2] 1 more time (11 rnds total). When complete, break CC.

BO all sts loosely knitwise.

FINISHING

Center a sleeve over shoulder seam, right sides together, with the bound off edge aligned with the armhole edge (the cast on edge becomes the outer edge of the sleeve). Use locking markers to keep the sleeve in position.

Using MC and the crochet hook, beginning at the bottom center of the armhole, join MC yarn and, working from right to left, 1 sc into each knit st around the armhole edge, catching the sleeve edge as you go to secure the sleeve to the upper portion of the armhole. Break yarn leaving an 8 in. / 20 cm tail, finishing last sc by drawing yarn through rem loop.

Repeat for second sleeve.

Weave in ends and wet block to finished measurements. When dry, trim ends. Block well.

CHART C

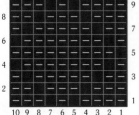

CHART D

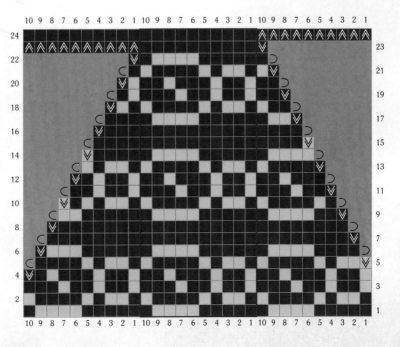

FELLOWSHIP SCARF

DESIGNED BY TANIS GRAY

To take on the near-impossible task of bringing the One Ring to Mordor to destroy it, and in turn stopping Sauron from ravaging Middle-earth, the Fellowship was formed at the Council of Elrond in Rivendell. To match the number of Nazgûl hunting the Ring, it was decided there should be nine members in the Fellowship—Gandalf, a Wizard; Legolas, an Elf; Gimli, a Dwarf; Boromir and Aragorn, both Men; and Merry, Pippin, Samwise, and Frodo the ring bearer, four Hobbits. An odd brotherhood, each member was chosen to represent their race, despite animosity and distrust between some of the party.

Channel your inner Hobbit and prepare to pack for your next journey across Middle-earth! This replica of Pippin's scarf as seen in the films is a simple 8-stitch by 8-stitch tessellating houndstooth pattern worked in a stranded colorwork tube knit in the round from the bottom up so there is no visible wrong side. The live stitches at the ends are closed with alternating fringe. No matter whether you're Hobbit-sized or Gandalf-sized, it's easy to shorten or add length.

SIZES
One size

FINISHED MEASUREMENTS
Width: 7 in. / 18 cm

Length (not including fringe): 60 in. / 152.5 cm

YARN
Worsted weight yarn, shown in Blue Moon Fiber Arts *Targhee Worsted* (100% Targhee wool; 616 yd. / 563 m per 8½ oz. / 240 g hank)

Colorways:

- **Color 1 (C1):** Antiquated System, 1 hank
- **Color 2 (C2):** Winter Solstice, 1 hank

NEEDLES
US 7 / 4.5 mm, 16 in. / 40 cm long circular needle or size needed to obtain gauge

NOTIONS
Stitch marker

Tapestry needle

US G-6 / 4 mm crochet hook

GAUGE
25 sts and 25 rnds = 4 in. / 10 cm in stranded colorwork pattern in the round, taken after blocking

Make sure to check your gauge.

PATTERN NOTES
The scarf is worked in the round from the bottom up as a tube.

Although gauge is not critical for this project, a difference in gauge may result in different finished dimensions and yardage requirements.

When attaching the fringe, be sure to hold both layers together to flatten the tube into a scarf and close up the open ends.

PATTERN INSTRUCTIONS

CAST ON

Using C2, CO 88 sts using the Long Tail cast on method. Pm for BOR and join to work in the rnd, being careful not to twist the sts.

BODY OF SCARF

Begin Chart A, reading all rows from right to left as for working in the rnd, joining C1 as needed. Work [Rows 1–8] 47 times total (chart is repeated 11 times across each rnd), or until work measures approx. 60 in. / 152.5 cm from the CO edge, ending with Row 8. When complete, break C1. BO all sts loosely knitwise with C2.

FINISHING

Weave in all loose ends to the WS.

Wet block the scarf to allow the sts to relax. Complete all blocking before attaching the fringe.

FRINGE

Cut eighty-four 14 in. / 35.5 cm lengths of C1 and C2 each.

*Holding 6 strands of C1 together, fold in half. Using the crochet hook, pull the loop of the folded strands through the edge of the scarf (making sure the two edges are held together to close the scarf end). Pass the 12 tails (2 from each folded strand) through the loop and cinch down to complete 1 section of fringe.

Repeat the above with 6 strands of C2.

Continue to alternate C1 and C2 fringe sections across one end of the scarf so that you end with a total of 14 fringe sections: 7 C1 and 7 C2. A total of 42 strands each of C1 and C2 will have been used.

Repeat the above instructions from * at the other end of the scarf with the remaining 42 strands each of C1 and C2.

Trim all fringe to about 6 in. / 15 cm.

KEY

☐ Knit
■ C1
▨ C2
☐ Pattern repeat

CHART A

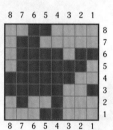

"Home is behind, the world ahead. . . . And there are many paths to tread. Through shadow, to the edge of night, until the stars are all alight. . . . Mist and shadow, cloud and shade, all shall fade . . . all shall fade."

—Pippin, *The Lord of the Rings: The Return of the King* film

CHAPTER TWO

MITTS & HATS

HORSE BANNER FINGERLESS MITTS

DESIGNED BY ANGELA HAHN

Holding horses in the highest esteem and valuing them above all else, the Rohirrim are known for their horsemanship and cavalry. Living on the vast plains of Rohan between the Misty Mountains and White Mountains with their villages nestled into hills, the Horse Lords are adept horse breeders. Mearas, their swiftest and noblest breed, are the white horses that adorn Rohan's green and white banners, and are also represented in their architecture, helmets, and armor. Rohan is also home to Éowyn, a female shieldmaiden and niece of King Théoden, who is crucial in the defeat of Sauron in *The Lord of the Rings: The Return of the King* during the Battle of the Pelennor Fields.

You, too, can represent Rohan while riding into battle with these fingerless mitts, inspired by the graphic and bold banners of Rohan. Worked in the round from the bottom up, these mitts begin with 2x2 ribbing. Mearas motifs are stitched on the back of the hand using stranded colorwork, with armored plate motifs stitched into the palm side. A thumb gusset is worked at the same time as the body of the fingerless mitt, with the final colorwork duplicate stitched onto the thumb to avoid stranding across a small circumference. Ride on!

SIZES

1 (2)

FINISHED MEASUREMENTS

Hand Circumference: 7½ (8½) in. / 19 (21.5) cm

Length: 8 (8½) in. / 20.5 (21.5) cm

Designed to be worn with 0 to 1 in. / 0 to 2.5 cm negative ease.

YARN

Fingering weight yarn, shown in Blue Sky Fibers *Woolstok Light* (100% fine Highland wool; 218 yd. / 200 m per 1¾ oz. / 50 g hank)

Colorways:

- **Main Color (MC):** #2306 Wild Thyme, 1 hank
- **Contrast Color (CC):** #2312 Drift Wood, 1 hank

NEEDLES

US 1 / 2.25 mm set of double-pointed needles

US 3 / 3.25 mm set of double-pointed needles or size needed to obtain gauge

NOTIONS

Stitch markers

Row counter (optional)

Tapestry needle

GAUGE

31 sts and 36 rnds = 4 in. / 10 cm over stranded colorwork in the round on the larger needle, taken after blocking

Make sure to check your gauge.

PATTERN NOTES

These mitts are worked in the round from the cuff up, using the smaller needle for the ribbing and the gauge-size needle for the body of the mitts. The smaller needle should be 2 sizes smaller than the larger needle when gauge is met.

The stranded colorwork patterns are provided in chart form only and are size specific; be sure to use the correct chart for your size for each hand.

When working the stranded colorwork patterns, catch floats longer than five stitches. Carry CC yarn above MC for color dominance, except for when catching floats.

Duplicate stitch is used to continue the colorwork pattern across the thumbs, to avoid having to catch floats over a small circumference.

Instructions are provided for size 1 first, with size 2 in parentheses. When only one number is provided, it applies to both sizes.

"Arise now, arise, Riders of Théoden!
Dire deeds awake: dark is it eastward.
Let horse be bridled, horn be sounded!
Forth Eorlingas!"

—The Lord of the Rings: The Two Towers
by J.R.R. Tolkien

PATTERN INSTRUCTIONS

CAST ON & BOTTOM CUFF

Using the smaller needles and CC, CO 52 (56) sts using the Long Tail cast on method. Pm for BOR and join to work in the rnd, being careful not to twist the sts.

Rib Rnd: (K2, p2) to end of rnd.

Rep Rib Rnd 4 (5) more times.

Switch to larger needles.

Join in MC and knit 4 (6) rnds.

Inc Rnd:

Size 1 ONLY: K18, M1R, (k17, M1R) 2 times—55 sts.

Size 2 ONLY: K12, M1R, (k11, M1R) 4 times—61 sts.

BODY–LEFT MITT

Begin Left Mitt chart for your size, reading all rows from right to left as for working in the rnd. Work Rows 1–26 once.

Work 51 (55) sts in patt as per Row 27 of chart, pm (for beginning of gusset), work next 3 sts as per Row 27, pm (for end of gusset), work to end of row in patt as per Row 27.

Work Rows 28–47 once, sm as encountered—69 (77) sts at completion.

Work to first M in patt as per Row 48 of chart, sm, place the next 15 (17) sts on waste yarn or stitch holder, turn work so WS is facing,

CO 5 sts using MC and the Knitted cast on method, turn work so RS is facing, sm, work to end of row in patt as per Row 48—59 (65) sts rem.

Work Rows 49–56 once, rm (gusset M) on rnd 56 as encountered (leave BOR M in place)—55 (61) sts rem.

Do not break yarns; carry CC loosely up the inside until needed for the top cuff.

Dec Rnd (using MC):

Size 1 ONLY: K17, k2tog, (k16, k2tog) 2 times—52 sts.

Size 2 ONLY: K11, k2tog, (k10, k2tog) 4 times—56 sts.

Using MC, knit 3 (5) rnds.

Break MC yarn.

TOP CUFF

Switch to smaller needles.

Knit 1 rnd.

Rib Rnd: (K2, p2) to end of rnd.

Rep Rib Rnd 3 (4) more times.

Bind off all sts in patt.

THUMB

Place the live 15 (17) sts of the thumb gusset onto 2 larger dpns. Join MC at the right edge with the RS facing and knit across all live sts. Using a third dpn, pick up and knit 1 st into the gap, pick up and knit 5 sts across the cast on edge, pick up and knit 1 more st into the gap—22 (24) sts total. Pm for BOR and join to work in the rnd.

Setup Rnd (dec): K15 (17), k2tog, k3, ssk—20 (22) sts rem.

Knit 5 (7) rnds.

Break MC yarn.

Switch to smaller needles; join CC yarn.

Dec Rnd:

Size 1 ONLY: Knit.

Size 2 ONLY: (K11, M1R) 2 times—24 sts total.

All Sizes:

Rib Rnd: (K2, p2) to end of rnd.

Rep Rib Rnd 3 (4) more times.

Bind off all sts in patt.

RIGHT MITT

Work the Cast On & Bottom Cuff as for the first mitt.

BODY–RIGHT MITT

Begin Right Mitt chart for your size, reading all rows from right to left as for working in the rnd. Work Rows 1–26 once.

Work 31 (35) sts in patt as per Row 27 of chart, pm (for beginning of gusset), work next 3 sts as per Row 27, pm (for end of gusset), work to end of row in patt as per Row 27.

Work Rows 28–47 once, sm as encountered—69 (77) sts at completion.

Work to first M in patt as per Row 48 of chart, sm, place the next 15 (17) sts on waste yarn or stitch holder, turn work so WS is facing, CO 5 sts using MC and the Knitted cast on method, turn work so RS is facing, sm, work to end of row in patt as per Row 48—59 (65) sts rem.

Work Rows 49–56 once, rm (gusset M) on rnd 56 as encountered (leave BOR M in place)—55 (61) sts rem.

Do not break yarns; carry CC loosely up the inside until needed for the top cuff.

Dec Rnd (using MC):

Size 1 ONLY: K17, k2tog, (k16, k2tog) 2 times—52 sts.

Size 2 ONLY: K11, k2tog, (k10, k2tog) 4 times—56 sts.

Using MC, knit 3 (5) rnds.

Break MC yarn.

Work the Top Cuff and Thumb as for the first mitt.

FINISHING

Weave in ends and wet block to measurements.

Once dry, thread a 24 in. / 60 cm length of CC yarn onto the tapestry needle. Beginning just above the CC sts at top of gusset, work duplicate stitch over sts indicated on Thumb charts. Weave in ends to WS.

LEFT MITT CHART - SIZE 1

KEY

■	No stitch	╱	k2tog
■	MC	╲	ssk
▨	CC	ᴜ	Knitted cast on
☐	Knit	☒	Duplicate stitch
℺	Knit tbl	—	Place sts below on waste yarn
↘	M1L	—	Stitch marker
↗	M1R		BOR

LEFT THUMB - SIZE 1

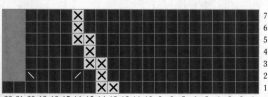

LEFT MITT CHART - SIZE 2

LEFT THUMB - SIZE 2

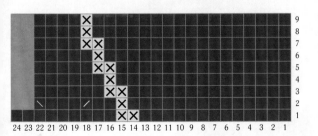

RIGHT MITT CHART - SIZE 1

RIGHT THUMB - SIZE 1

RIGHT MITT CHART - SIZE 2

RIGHT THUMB - SIZE 2

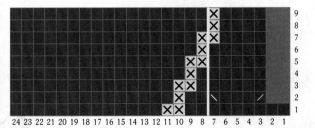

KEY

■	No stitch	╱	k2tog
■	MC	╲	ssk
▨	CC	∪	Knitted cast on
□	Knit	✕	Duplicate stitch
Ω	Knit tbl	—	Place sts below on waste yarn
⅄	M1L	—	Stitch marker
⅄	M1R		BOR

NOBLE MAIDEN HAT

DESIGNED BY TANIS GRAY

After choosing to abandon her immortality for true love against the wishes of her father Elrond, Arwen patiently waits for the Ring to be destroyed, and for Aragorn to claim his birthright as king of Gondor. Granddaughter of Galadriel, Princess Arwen is a Half-Elf who reunites the kingdoms of Men and Elf through her marriage. Said to be even lovelier than her grandmother, she gives her necklace, the Evenstar, which represents her immortality, commitment, and love, to Aragorn. While the necklace breaks in his dreams, Aragorn carefully guards the necklace until he is reunited with his princess.

Adorned with stranded colorwork Evenstars, this Arwen-inspired hat is knit seamlessly in the round from the bottom up. Begun with corrugated ribbing, the motifs come together at the crown creating a star as bright and radiant as the Elven princess herself. Knit one for you, or for your true love.

SIZES

Small (Large)

FINISHED MEASUREMENTS

Circumference: 20 (22) in. / 51 (56) cm

Height: 8 (9) in. / 20.5 (23) cm

Recommended fit is 0 to 2 in. / 0 to 5 cm negative ease. The hat fits most adult heads.

YARN

DK weight yarn, shown in Yarn Café Creations *Americano DK* (4-ply; 100% superwash merino wool; 231 yd. / 211 m per 3½ oz. / 100 g hank)

Colorways:

- **Main Color (MC):** Gentleman, 1 hank
- **Contrast Color (CC):** Dried Rose Petals, 1 hank

NEEDLES

US 3 / 3.25 mm, 16 in. / 40 cm long circular needle

US 4 / 3.5 mm, 16 in. / 40 cm long circular needle and set of 5 double-pointed needles or size needed to obtain gauge

NOTIONS

Stitch markers (5; 1 unique for BOR)

Row counter (optional)

Tapestry needle

GAUGE

Size Small: 26 sts and 32 rnds = 4 in. / 10 cm in stranded colorwork pattern in the round on the larger needle, taken after blocking

Size Large: 23½ sts and 29 rnds = 4 in. / 10 cm in stranded colorwork pattern in the round on the larger needle, taken after blocking

Make sure to check your gauge.

PATTERN NOTES

To honor the original design of the hat and ensure a wider range of available fit, rather than compromise on the stitch pattern, the hat has been graded using different gauges for the two sizes. To achieve the gauge for your finished size of hat, adjust your needle size as needed.

This hat is worked in the round from the brim up. Corrugated ribbing makes up the brim of the hat and is worked on the smaller needle (1 US size smaller than gauge). Stranded colorwork on the larger, gauge-size needles makes up the remainder of the body and crown.

Written instructions are provided for the construction of the hat; charts are provided for the colorwork body and crown of the hat.

Instructions are provided for size small first with size large in parentheses. When only one number is provided, it applies to both sizes.

When working the corrugated rib, be sure to move the CC yarn to the back between the needles after completing the purl stitch so all floats are on the WS of the hat.

When the circumference of the hat becomes too small during the crown shaping, switch to dpns for comfort.

It may be helpful to place a marker between each chart repeat in the body of the hat. Use a unique marker for the BOR.

If you tend to be a tight colorwork knitter, swatch 1 or 2 needle sizes up to test for gauge.

PATTERN INSTRUCTIONS

CAST ON & BRIM

Using the smaller needles and CC, CO 130 sts using the Long Tail cast on method. Pm for BOR and join to work in the rnd, being careful not to twist the sts.

Join MC.

Rib Rnd: *P1 with CC, k1 with MC; rep from * to end of rnd.

Rep Rib Rnd 9 more times (10 rnds total).

Do not break MC; knit 1 rnd in CC.

BODY OF HAT

Switch to larger circular needles.

Begin Chart A, reading all rows from right to left as for working in the rnd. Work [Rows 1–53] 1 time (chart is worked 5 times across each rnd).

Decreases begin on Rnd 42; change to dpns for comfort when the circumference becomes too small for the circular needle.

When the chart is complete, 10 sts rem. Break both yarns leaving a 6 in. / 15 cm tail.

Thread the tapestry needle with both tails and pull tails through rem live sts and cinch closed. Secure tails to WS.

FINISHING

Weave in all loose ends to the WS.

Wet block the hat to allow the sts to relax.

KEY

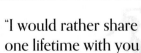

- No stitch
- Knit
- MC
- CC
- k2tog
- ssk
- cdd
- Pattern repeat

"I would rather share one lifetime with you than face all the ages of this world alone."

–Arwen to Aragorn in *The Lord of the Rings: The Fellowship of the Ring* film

CHART A

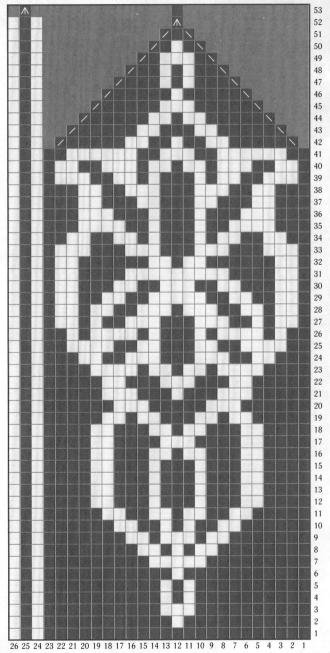

ELF WARRIOR FINGERLESS MITTS & HAT

DESIGNED BY JENNY NOTO

The Lord of Rivendell and father to Arwen, Elrond is a Half-Elf and ruler of the Eldar Elves. A member of the White Council and longtime friend of Gandalf, he fought alongside Men at the Battle of Dagorlad. Though victorious in battle, he witnessed firsthand Isildur's failure to destroy the One Ring in the fires of Mount Doom, and the effects that had on Middle-earth in the aftermath. Though many years passed, he remained focused on the defeat of Sauron, calling together the races and forming the Fellowship of the Ring, tasking them with the responsibility of finally destroying it once and for all.

Inspired by the sharp angles and scroll designs of Elrond's Elven armor, this matching hat and fingerless mitts set embodies the strength and beauty of the Elves. Knit in the round from the cuff to the fingertips with a twisted rib pattern all the way around until the palm, the fingerless mitts maintain incredible stretch. The palms are knit in stockinette to provide a smoother and more snug fit. The reversible hat is worked in the round from the brim up through the crown decreases. No cable needles are required—the traveling lines are faux cables made with strategically placed increases and decreases.

FOR THE HAT

SIZES
One size

FINISHED MEASUREMENTS
Circumference (unstretched): 14 in. / 35.5 cm

Height: 9 in. / 23 cm

Fits most adult heads. This hat is designed to be worn with up to 9 in. / 23 cm of negative ease. Although the unstretched size appears quite small, the ribbed nature of the hat allows it to comfortably stretch to fit a head up to 23 in. / 58.5 cm in circumference.

YARN
DK weight yarn, shown in Oink Pigments *Mystic* (3-ply; 100% superwash merino; 230 yd. / 210 m per 3½ oz. / 100 g hank), 1 hank in color That Is Mahogany!

NEEDLES
US 4 / 3.5 mm, 16 in. / 40 cm circular needle and set of double-pointed needles

US 6 / 4 mm, 16 in. / 40 cm long circular needle or size needed to obtain gauge

NOTIONS
Stitch marker(s)

Row counter (optional)

Tapestry needle

GAUGE
24 sts and 32 rows = 4 in. / 10 cm in St st worked in the round on larger needle, taken after steam blocking

Make sure to check your gauge.

PATTERN STITCHES

Twisted Rib in the round (worked over a multiple of 2 sts)

Rnd 1: *P1, k1 tbl; rep from * to end of rnd.

Rep Rnd 1 for patt.

PATTERN NOTES

This hat is worked in the round from the brim up, beginning with the smaller needle for the brim, changing to the larger needle for the body of the hat. The smaller needle is used again for the crown shaping of the hat.

It is recommended to swatch in St st for ease of swatching and measuring the swatch. The hat is worked in a twisted rib pattern. If you prefer to work your swatch in the twisted rib pattern, your target gauge is 34 sts and 26 rows = 4 in. / 10 cm over Twisted Rib worked in the round on larger needles, taken after steam blocking, unstretched.

While stitch markers are not written into the pattern (other than the BOR marker), using stitch markers between each pattern repeat is extremely helpful.

Written instructions are provided for the entirety of the pattern. Optional charts are provided. Read carefully through all written instructions before working from the charts to ensure no instructions get missed. Read all chart rows from right to left as for working in the round.

When the circumference of the hat becomes too small for the circular needle during the crown shaping, change to dpns to finish the hat.

PATTERN INSTRUCTIONS

CAST ON & BRIM

Using the smaller circular needle, CO 120 sts using the Long Tail cast on method. Pm for BOR and join to work in the rnd, being careful not to twist the sts.

Option 1—Brimless (modeled):

Setup Rnd: *P1, k1 tbl; rep from * to end of rnd.

Cont with smaller needle, work Rnds 1–12 of the Body of Hat section 1 time, following the written instructions or the Body chart (patt rep is worked 5 times across the rnd).

Option 2—Traditional Ribbed Brim:

Rnds 1–11: *P1, k1 tbl; rep from * to end of rnd.

BODY OF HAT

Switch to larger circular needles.

Follow written instructions below or work from Body chart.

Rnd 1: *(P1, k1 tbl) 3 times, twisted k2tog, (p1, k1 tbl) 2 times, ryo, p1, yo, (k1 tbl, p1) 2 times, twisted ssk, k1 tbl, (p1, k1 tbl) 2 times; rep from * to end of rnd.

Rnd 2: *(P1, k1 tbl) 3 times, k1 tbl, (p1, k1 tbl) 2 times, k1, p1, k2 tbl, (p1, k1 tbl) 2 times, (k1 tbl, p1) 2 times, k1 tbl; rep from * to end of rnd.

Rnd 3: *(P1, k1 tbl) 2 times, p1, twisted k2tog, (p1, k1 tbl) 2 times, ryo, k1 tbl, p1,

k1 tbl, yo, (k1 tbl, p1) 2 times, twisted ssk, (p1, k1 tbl) 2 times; rep from * to end of rnd.

Rnd 4: *(P1, k1 tbl) 7 times, p1 tbl, k1 tbl, (p1, k1 tbl) 4 times; rep from * to end of rnd.

Rnd 5: *(P1, k1 tbl) 2 times, twisted k2tog, (p1, k1 tbl) 2 times, ryo, p1, (k1 tbl, p1) 2 times, yo, (k1 tbl, p1) 2 times, twisted ssk, k1 tbl, p1, k1 tbl; rep from * to end of rnd.

Rnd 6: *(P1, k1 tbl) 2 times, k1 tbl, (p1, k1 tbl) 2 times, k1, p1, (k1 tbl, p1) 2 times, k2 tbl, (p1, k1 tbl) 2 times, k1 tbl, p1, k1 tbl; rep from * to end of rnd.

Rnd 7: *P1, k1 tbl, p1, twisted k2tog, (p1, k1 tbl) 2 times, ryo, (k1 tbl, p1) 3 times, k1 tbl, yo, (k1 tbl, p1) 2 times, twisted ssk, p1, k1 tbl; rep from * to end of rnd.

Rnd 8: *(P1, k1 tbl) 8 times, p1 tbl, k1 tbl, (p1, k1 tbl) 3 times; rep from * to end of rnd.

Rnd 9: *P1, k1 tbl, twisted k2tog, (p1, k1 tbl) 2 times, ryo, (p1, k1 tbl) 4 times, p1, yo, (k1 tbl, p1) 2 times, twisted ssk, k1 tbl; rep from * to end of rnd.

Rnd 10: *P1, k2 tbl, (p1, k1 tbl) 2 times, k1, (p1, k1 tbl) 5 times, (k1 tbl, p1) 2 times, k2 tbl; rep from * to end of rnd.

Rnd 11: *P1, twisted k2tog, (p1, k1 tbl) 2 times, ryo, (k1 tbl, p1) 5 times, k1 tbl, yo, (k1 tbl, p1) 2 times, twisted ssk; rep from * to end of rnd.

Rnd 12: *(P1, k1 tbl) 9 times, p1 tbl, k1 tbl, (p1, k1 tbl) 2 times; rep from * to end of rnd.

Rep [Rnds 1–12] 3 more times (48 total Body rnds).

CROWN SHAPING

Switch to smaller needles.
Follow written instructions below or work from Crown Shaping chart.

Rnd 1 (dec): *(P1, k1 tbl) 3 times, twisted k2tog, (p1, k1 tbl) 4 times, p1, twisted ssk, k1 tbl, (p1, k1 tbl) 2 times; rep from * to end of rnd—110 sts rem.

Rnd 2: *(P1, k1 tbl) 3 times, k1 tbl, (p1, k1 tbl) 5 times, k1 tbl, (p1, k1 tbl) 2 times; rep from * to end of rnd.

Rnd 3 (dec): *(P1, k1 tbl) 2 times, p1, twisted k2tog, (p1, k1 tbl) 4 times, p1, twisted ssk, (p1, k1 tbl) 2 times; rep from * to end of rnd—100 sts rem.

Rnd 4: *P1, k1 tbl; rep from * to end of rnd.

Rnd 5 (dec): *(P1, k1 tbl) 2 times, twisted k2tog, p1, k1 tbl, twisted k2tog, p1, twisted ssk, k1 tbl, p1, twisted ssk, k1 tbl, p1, k1 tbl; rep from * to end of rnd—80 sts rem.

Rnd 6: *P1, k1 tbl, p1, k2 tbl, p1, k1 tbl, k1, p1, k1 tbl, p1, k2 tbl, p1, k1 tbl; rep from * to end of rnd.

Rnd 7 (dec): *P1, k1 tbl, (p1, twisted k2tog) 2 times, p1, (twisted ssk, p1) 2 times, k1 tbl; rep from * to end of rnd—60 sts rem.

Rnd 8: *P1, k1 tbl; rep from * to end of rnd.

Rnd 9 (dec): *P1, k1 tbl, (twisted k2tog) 2 times, p1, (twisted ssk) 2 times, k1 tbl; rep from * to end of rnd—40 sts rem.

Rnd 10: *P1, k3 tbl; rep from * to end of rnd.

Rnd 11 (dec): *P1, twisted cdd; rep from * to end of rnd—20 sts rem.

Break yarn leaving an 8 in. / 20.5 cm tail. Thread tail through rem live sts and pull tight to cinch closed. Secure tail to WS.

FINISHING

Weave in all ends. Steam block gently to smooth out stitches and shape if needed.

KEY

- ■ No stitch
- □ knit
- − purl
- Ⓠ knit tbl
- Ⓠ purl tbl
- ○ yo
- ⊙ ryo
- ╱ twisted k2tog
- ╲ twisted ssk
- ⋀ twisted cdd
- ▭ Pattern repeat

BODY CHART

CROWN SHAPING CHART

73

FOR THE MITTS

SIZES

1 (2, 3, 4)

FINISHED MEASUREMENTS

Circumference (unstretched): 5½ (6, 6½, 7) in. / 14 (15, 16.5, 18) cm

Length: 9½ (10¼, 11, 12) in. / 24 (26, 28, 30.5) cm

The fingerless mitts are designed to be worn with up to 2 in. / 5 cm of negative ease. Although the unstretched size appears quite small, the ribbed nature of the mitt allows it to comfortably stretch to fit a hand up to 2 in. / 5 cm larger than the finished circumference.

YARN

DK weight yarn, shown in Oink Pigments *Mystic* (3-ply; 100% 17-micron superwash merino; 230 yd. / 210 m per 3½ oz. / 100 g hank), 1 (1, 1, 2) hank(s) That Is Mahogany!

NEEDLES

US 3 / 3.25 mm, 32 in. / 80 cm long circular needle or size needed to obtain gauge

NOTIONS

Stitch marker (optional)

Row counter (optional)

Waste yarn or stitch holder

Tapestry needle

GAUGE

Size 1: 26 sts and 36 rows = 4 in. / 10 cm in St st worked in the round, taken after steam blocking

Size 2: 24 sts and 33 rows = 4 in. / 10 cm in St st worked in the round, taken after steam blocking

Size 3: 22 sts and 31 rows = 4 in. / 10 cm in St st worked in the round, taken after steam blocking

Size 4: 20.5 sts and 28 rows = 4 in. / 10 cm in St st worked in the round, taken after steam blocking

Make sure to check your gauge.

PATTERN STITCHES

Twisted Rib in the round (worked over a multiple of 2 sts)

Rnd 1: *P1, k1 tbl; rep from * to end of rnd.

Rep Rnd 1 for patt.

PATTERN NOTES

To honor the original design of the fingerless mitts and ensure a wider range of available fit, rather than compromise on the stitch pattern, these fingerless mitts have been graded using different gauges for each size. To achieve the gauge for your finished size of mitts, adjust your needle size as needed.

These fingerless mitts are worked in the round from the cuff up, using the Magic Loop method. If desired, you may use dpns rather than the Magic Loop method.

It is recommended to swatch in St st for ease of swatching and measuring the swatch. The fingerless mitts are worked in a twisted rib pattern. If you prefer to work your swatch in the twisted rib pattern, your target gauge is 35 (32, 29.5, 27.5) sts and 32 (29, 27, 25) rows = 4 in. / 10 cm over Twisted Rib worked in the round on larger needles, taken after steam blocking, unstretched.

Written instructions are provided for the entirety of the pattern. Optional charts are provided. Read carefully through all written instructions before working from the chart to ensure no instructions get missed. Read all chart rows from right to left as for working in the round.

The mitts are made as mirror images to one another. The cast on, cuffs, ribbing, and thumbs are identical; the thumb gussets are mirrors of each other. Be sure to work from the correct instructions for each mitt to ensure the thumb position is correct.

PATTERN INSTRUCTIONS

CAST ON

CO 48 sts using the Twisted German cast on method. Pm for BOR (if desired) and join to work in the rnd, being careful not to twist the sts.

Setup Rnd: *P1, k1 tbl; rep from * to end of rnd.

CUFF–BOTH MITTS

Follow written instructions below or work from Cuff chart.

Rnd 1: *(P1, k1 tbl) 3 times, twisted k2tog, (p1, k1 tbl) 2 times, ryo, p1, yo, (k1 tbl, p1) 2 times, twisted ssk, k1 tbl, (p1, k1 tbl) 2 times; rep from * once more.

Rnd 2: *(P1, k1 tbl) 3 times, k1 tbl, (p1, k1 tbl) 2 times, k1, p1, k2 tbl, (p1, k1 tbl) 2 times, (k1 tbl, p1) 2 times, k1 tbl; rep from * once more.

Rnd 3: *(P1, k1 tbl) 2 times, p1, twisted k2tog, (p1, k1 tbl) 2 times, ryo, k1 tbl, p1, k1 tbl, yo, (k1 tbl, p1) 2 times, twisted ssk, (p1, k1 tbl) 2 times; rep from * once more.

Rnd 4: *(P1, k1 tbl) 7 times, p1 tbl, k1 tbl, (p1, k1 tbl) 4 times; rep from * once more.

Rnd 5: *(P1, k1 tbl) 2 times, twisted k2tog, (p1, k1 tbl) 2 times, ryo, p1, (k1 tbl, p1) 2 times, yo, (k1 tbl, p1) 2 times, twisted ssk, k1 tbl, p1, k1 tbl; rep from * once more.

Rnd 6: *(P1, k1 tbl) 2 times, k1 tbl, (p1, k1 tbl) 2 times, k1, p1, (k1 tbl, p1) 2 times, k2 tbl, (p1, k1 tbl) 2 times, k1 tbl, p1, k1 tbl; rep from * once more.

Rnd 7: *P1, k1 tbl, p1, twisted k2tog, (p1, k1 tbl) 2 times, ryo, (k1 tbl, p1) 3 times, k1 tbl, yo, (k1 tbl, p1) 2 times, twisted ssk, p1, k1 tbl; rep from * once more.

Rnd 8: *(P1, k1 tbl) 8 times, p1 tbl, k1 tbl, (p1, k1 tbl) 3 times; rep from * once more.

Rnd 9: *P1, k1 tbl, twisted k2tog, (p1, k1 tbl) 2 times, ryo, (p1, k1 tbl) 4 times, p1, yo, (k1 tbl, p1) 2 times, twisted ssk, k1 tbl; rep from * once more.

Rnd 10: *P1, k2 tbl, (p1, k1 tbl) 2 times, k1, (p1, k1 tbl) 5 times, (k1 tbl, p1) 2 times, k2 tbl; rep from * once more.

Rnd 11: *P1, twisted k2tog, (p1, k1 tbl) 2 times, ryo, (k1 tbl, p1) 5 times, k1 tbl, yo, (k1 tbl, p1) 2 times, twisted ssk; rep from * once more.

Rnd 12: *(P1, k1 tbl) 9 times, p1 tbl, k1 tbl, (p1, k1 tbl) 2 times; rep from * once more.

Rep [Rnds 1–12] 3 more times (48 total Cuff rnds).

GUSSET SETUP–BOTH MITTS

Follow written instructions below or work Rows 1–4 of the Left or Right Gusset chart.

Rnd 1: (P1, k1 tbl) 3 times, twisted k2tog, (p1, k1 tbl) 2 times, ryo, p1, yo, (k1 tbl, p1) 2 times, twisted ssk, (k1 tbl, p1) 3 times, k23.

Rnd 2: (P1, k1 tbl) 3 times, k1 tbl, (p1, k1 tbl) 2 times, k1, p1, k2 tbl, (p1, k1 tbl) 2 times, (k1 tbl, p1) 3 times, k23.

Rnd 3: (P1, k1 tbl) 2 times, p1, twisted k2tog, (p1, k1 tbl) 2 times, ryo, k1 tbl, p1, k1 tbl, yo, (k1 tbl, p1) 2 times, twisted ssk, (p1, k1 tbl) 2 times, p1, k23.

Rnd 4: (P1, k1 tbl) 7 times, p1 tbl, (k1 tbl, p1) 5 times, k23.

THUMB GUSSET– LEFT MITT

Follow written instructions below or work Rows 5–20 of the Left Gusset chart.

Rnd 5 (inc): (P1, k1 tbl) 2 times, twisted k2tog, (p1, k1 tbl) 2 times, ryo, p1, (k1 tbl, p1) 2 times, yo, (k1 tbl, p1) 2 times, twisted ssk, (k1 tbl, p1) 2 times, k19, M1R, k1, M1L, k3—50 sts.

Rnd 6: (P1, k1 tbl) 2 times, k1 tbl, (p1, k1 tbl) 2 times, k1, p1, (k1 tbl, p1) 2 times, k2 tbl, (p1, k1 tbl) 2 times, (k1 tbl, p1) 2 times, k25.

Rnd 7 (inc): P1, k1 tbl, p1, twisted k2tog, (p1, k1 tbl) 2 times, ryo, (k1 tbl, p1) 3 times, k1 tbl, yo, (k1 tbl, p1) 2 times, twisted ssk, p1, k1 tbl, p1, k19, M1R, k3, M1L, k3—52 sts.

Rnd 8: (P1, k1 tbl) 8 times, p1 tbl, (k1 tbl, p1) 4 times, k27.

Rnd 9 (inc): P1, k1 tbl, twisted k2tog, (p1, k1 tbl) 2 times, ryo, (p1, k1 tbl) 4 times, p1, yo, (k1 tbl, p1) 2 times, twisted ssk, k1 tbl, p1, k19, M1R, k5, M1L, k3—54 sts.

Rnd 10: P1, k2 tbl, (p1, k1 tbl) 2 times, k1, (p1, k1 tbl) 5 times, (k1 tbl, p1) 2 times, k2 tbl, p1, k29.

Rnd 11 (inc): P1, twisted k2tog, (p1, k1 tbl) 2 times, ryo, (k1 tbl, p1) 5 times, k1 tbl, yo, (k1 tbl, p1) 2 times, twisted ssk, p1, k19, M1R, k7, M1L, k3—56 sts.

Rnd 12: (P1, k1 tbl) 9 times, p1 tbl, (k1 tbl, p1) 3 times, k31.

Rnd 13 (inc): (P1, k1 tbl) 3 times, twisted k2tog, (p1, k1 tbl) 2 times, ryo, p1, yo, (k1 tbl, p1) 2 times, twisted ssk, (k1 tbl, p1) 3 times, k19, M1R, k9, M1L, k3—58 sts.

Rnd 14: (P1, k1 tbl) 3 times, k1 tbl, (p1, k1 tbl) 2 times, k1, p1, k2 tbl, (p1, k1 tbl) 2 times, (k1 tbl, p1) 3 times, k33.

Rnd 15 (inc): (P1, k1 tbl) 2 times, p1, twisted k2tog, (p1, k1 tbl) 2 times, ryo, k1 tbl, p1, k1 tbl, yo, (k1 tbl, p1) 2 times, twisted ssk, (p1, k1 tbl) 2 times, p1, k19, M1R, k11, M1L, k3—60 sts.

Rnd 16: (P1, k1 tbl) 7 times, p1 tbl, (k1 tbl, p1) 5 times, p1, k35.

Rnd 17 (inc): (P1, k1 tbl) 2 times, twisted k2tog, (p1, k1 tbl) 2 times, ryo, p1, (k1 tbl, p1) 2 times, yo, (k1 tbl, p1) 2 times, twisted ssk, (k1 tbl, p1) 2 times, k19, M1R, k13, M1L, k3—62 sts.

Rnd 18: (P1, k1 tbl) 2 times, k1 tbl, (p1, k1 tbl) 2 times, k1, p1, (k1 tbl, p1) 2 times, k2 tbl, (p1, k1 tbl) 2 times, (k1 tbl, p1) 2 times, k37.

Rnd 19 (dec): P1, k1 tbl, p1, twisted k2tog, (p1, k1 tbl) 2 times, ryo, (k1 tbl, p1) 3 times, k1 tbl, yo, (k1 tbl, p1) 2 times, twisted ssk, p1, k1 tbl, p1, k19, place the next 15 thumb sts onto waste yarn, turn, CO 3 sts using the Knitted cast on method, turn, k3—50 sts.

Rnd 20 (dec): (P1, k1 tbl) 8 times, p1 tbl, (k1 tbl, p1) 4 times, k18, k2tog, k1, ssk, k2—48 sts.

THUMB GUSSET–RIGHT MITT

Follow written instructions below or work Rows 5–20 of the Right Gusset chart.

Rnd 5 (inc): (P1, k1 tbl) 2 times, twisted k2tog, (p1, k1 tbl) 2 times, ryo, p1, (k1 tbl, p1) 2 times, yo, (k1 tbl, p1) 2 times, twisted ssk, (k1 tbl, p1) 2 times, k3, M1R, k1, M1L, k19—50 sts.

Rnd 6: (P1, k1 tbl) 2 times, k1 tbl, (p1, k1 tbl) 2 times, k1, p1, (k1 tbl, p1) 2 times, k2 tbl, (p1, k1 tbl) 2 times, (k1 tbl, p1) 2 times, k25.

Rnd 7 (inc): P1, k1 tbl, p1, twisted k2tog, (p1, k1 tbl) 2 times, ryo, (k1 tbl, p1) 3 times, k1 tbl, yo, (k1 tbl, p1) 2 times, twisted ssk, p1, k1 tbl, p1, k3, M1R, k3, M1L, k19—52 sts.

Rnd 8: (P1, k1 tbl) 8 times, p1 tbl, (k1 tbl, p1) 4 times, k27.

Rnd 9 (inc): P1, k1 tbl, twisted k2tog, (p1, k1 tbl) 2 times, ryo, (p1, k1 tbl) 4 times, p1, yo, (k1 tbl, p1) 2 times, twisted ssk, k1 tbl, p1, k3, M1R, k5, M1L, k19—54 sts.

Rnd 10: P1, k2 tbl, (p1, k1 tbl) 2 times, k1, (p1, k1 tbl) 5 times, (k1 tbl, p1) 2 times, k2 tbl, p1, k29.

Rnd 11 (inc): P1, twisted k2tog, (p1, k1 tbl) 2 times, ryo, (k1 tbl, p1) 5 times, k1 tbl, yo, (k1 tbl, p1) 2 times, twisted ssk, p1, k3, M1R, k7, M1L, k19—56 sts.

Rnd 12: (P1, k1 tbl) 9 times, p1 tbl, (k1 tbl, p1) 3 times, k31.

Rnd 13 (inc): (P1, k1 tbl) 3 times, twisted k2tog, (p1, k1 tbl) 2 times, ryo, p1, yo, (k1 tbl, p1) 2 times, twisted ssk, (k1 tbl, p1) 3 times, k3, M1R, k9, M1L, k19—58 sts.

Rnd 14: (P1, k1 tbl) 3 times, k1 tbl, (p1, k1 tbl) 2 times, k1, p1, k2 tbl, (p1, k1 tbl) 2 times, (k1 tbl, p1) 3 times, k33.

Rnd 15 (inc): (P1, k1 tbl) 2 times, p1, twisted k2tog, (p1, k1 tbl) 2 times, ryo, k1 tbl, p1, k1 tbl, yo, (k1 tbl, p1) 2 times, twisted ssk, (p1, k1 tbl) 2 times, p1, k3, M1R, k11, M1L, k19—60 sts.

Rnd 16: (P1, k1 tbl) 7 times, p1 tbl, (k1 tbl, p1) 5 times, k35.

Rnd 17 (inc): (P1, k1 tbl) 2 times, twisted k2tog, (p1, k1 tbl) 2 times, ryo, p1, (k1 tbl, p1) 2 times, yo, (k1 tbl, p1) 2 times, twisted ssk, (k1 tbl, p1) 2 times, k3, M1R, k13, M1L, k19—62 sts.

Rnd 18: (P1, k1 tbl) 2 times, k1 tbl, (p1, k1 tbl) 2 times, k1, p1, (k1 tbl, p1) 2 times, k2 tbl, (p1, k1 tbl) 2 times, (k1 tbl, p1) 2 times, k37.

Rnd 19 (dec): P1, k1 tbl, p1, twisted k2tog, (p1, k1 tbl) 2 times, ryo, (k1 tbl, p1) 3 times, k1 tbl, yo, (k1 tbl, p1) 2 times, twisted ssk, p1, k1 tbl, p1, k3, place the next 15 thumb sts onto waste yarn, turn, CO 3 sts using the Knitted cast on method, turn, k19—50 sts.

Rnd 20 (dec): (P1, k1 tbl) 8 times, p1 tbl, (k1 tbl, p1) 4 times, k2, k2tog, k1, ssk, k18—48 sts.

PALM–BOTH MITTS

Follow written instructions below or work from Palm chart.

Rnd 1: P1, k1 tbl, twisted k2tog, (p1, k1 tbl) 2 times, ryo, (p1, k1 tbl) 4 times, p1, yo, (k1 tbl, p1) 2 times, twisted ssk, k1 tbl, p1, k23.

Rnd 2: P1, k2 tbl, (p1, k1 tbl) 2 times, k1, (p1, k1 tbl) 5 times, (k1 tbl, p1) 2 times, k2 tbl, p1, k23.

Rnd 3: P1, twisted k2tog, (p1, k1 tbl) 2 times, ryo, (k1 tbl, p1) 5 times, k1 tbl, yo, (k1 tbl, p1) 2 times, twisted ssk, p1, k23.

Rnd 4: (P1, k1 tbl) 9 times, p1 tbl, (k1 tbl, p1) 3 times, k23.

Rnd 5: (P1, k1 tbl) 3 times, twisted k2tog, (p1, k1 tbl) 2 times, ryo, p1, yo, (k1 tbl, p1) 2 times, twisted ssk, (k1 tbl, p1) 3 times, k23.

Rnd 6: (P1, k1 tbl) 3 times, k1 tbl, (p1, k1 tbl) 2 times, k1, p1, k2 tbl, (p1, k1 tbl) 2 times, (k1 tbl, p1) 3 times, k23.

Rnd 7: (P1, k1 tbl) 2 times, p1, twisted k2tog, (p1, k1 tbl) 2 times, ryo, k1 tbl, p1, k1 tbl, yo, (k1 tbl, p1) 2 times, twisted ssk, (p1, k1 tbl) 2 times, p1, k23.

Rnd 8: (P1, k1 tbl) 7 times, p1 tbl, (k1 tbl, p1) 5 times, k23.

Rnd 9: (P1, k1 tbl) 2 times, twisted k2tog, (p1, k1 tbl) 2 times, ryo, p1, (k1 tbl, p1) 2 times, yo, (k1 tbl, p1) 2 times, twisted ssk, (k1 tbl, p1) 2 times, k23.

Rnd 10: (P1, k1 tbl) 2 times, k1 tbl, (p1, k1 tbl) 2 times, k1, p1, (k1 tbl, p1) 2 times, k2 tbl, (p1, k1 tbl) 2 times, (k1 tbl, p1) 2 times, k23.

Rnd 11: P1, k1 tbl, p1, twisted k2tog, (p1, k1 tbl) 2 times, ryo, (k1 tbl, p1) 3 times, k1 tbl, yo, (k1 tbl, p1) 2 times, twisted ssk, p1, k1 tbl, p1, k23.

Rnd 12: (P1, k1 tbl) 8 times, p1 tbl, (k1 tbl, p1) 4 times, k23.

Rep [Rnds 1–12] until the mitt is approx. ½ in. / 1 cm short of the desired total length, ending with Rnd 4, 8, or 12.

RIBBING–BOTH MITTS

Rnds 1–4: *P1, k1 tbl; rep from * to end of rnd.

BO in patt. Break yarn. Proceed to Thumb section.

THUMB—BOTH MITTS

Place the live 15 thumb sts onto the needle. Rejoin yarn to the right edge of the CO sts and pick up and knit 4 sts across the CO edge. Pm for BOR (if desired) and join to work in the rnd—19 sts.

Rnd 1: Knit.

Rnd 2 (dec): [K4, k2tog] 3 times, k1—16 sts.

Rnds 3 and 4: Knit.

Rnds 5—8: *K1 tbl, p1; rep from * to end of rnd.

BO in patt. Break yarn.

FINISHING

Weave in all ends. Steam block gently to smooth out stitches and shape if needed. Trim ends.

> "Isildur kept the Ring. It should have ended that day, but evil was allowed to endure. There's no strength left in the world of Men. They're scattered, divided, leaderless."
>
> –Elrond, *The Lord of the Rings: The Fellowship of the Ring* film

KEY

- No stitch
- knit
- purl
- knit tbl
- purl tbl
- yo
- ryo
- k2tog
- twisted k2tog
- ssk
- twisted ssk
- M1L
- M1R
- Knitted cast on
- Place sts below on waste yarn
- Pattern repeat

CUFF CHART

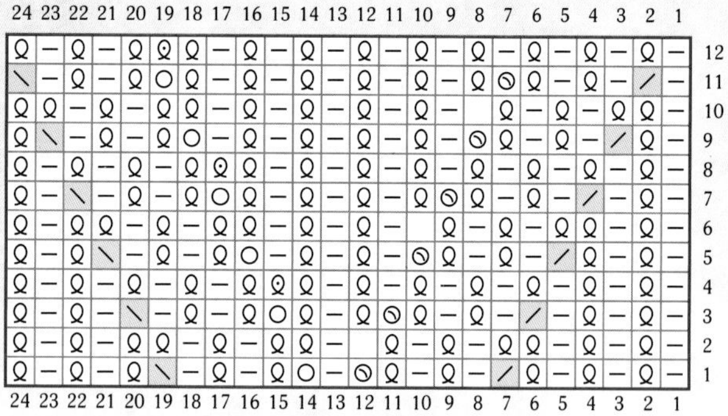

PALM CHART

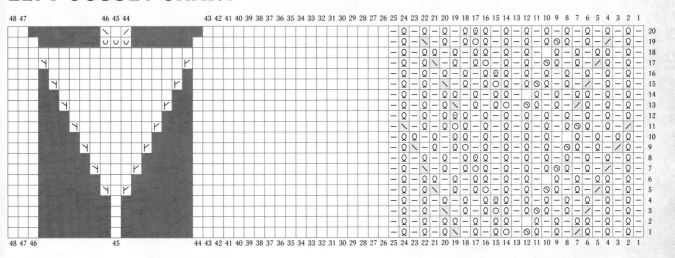

LEFT GUSSET CHART

RIGHT GUSSET CHART

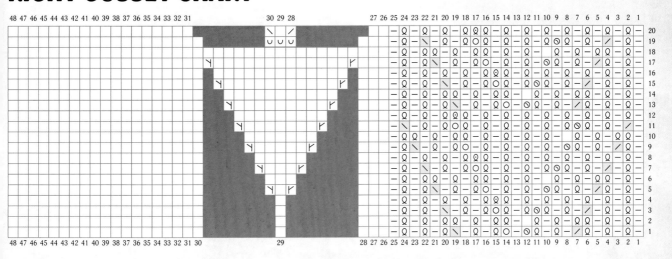

LADY OF THE WOODS HEADBAND

DESIGNED BY TANIS GRAY

The Lady of Lothlórien and bearer of the water ring Nenya, one of the three rings of power given to the Elves, Galadriel is renowned for her wisdom, beauty, power, and ability to see into the hearts of others. Over 8,000 years old, she protects her lands and people with the power of her ring alongside her husband, Celeborn. She is tested and briefly enthralled by its power when the Fellowship brings the One Ring into her woods and it is offered freely to her by Frodo. Accepting that the time of the Elves is ending, she passes the test and instead helps the group continue their journey.

Rule your corner of Middle-earth and keep those pointed ears warm with a headband fit for a queen. Begun with a provisional (or temporary) cast on, the headband is worked in the round with a stranded colorwork crown motif tipped with flowers inspired by Galadriel's circlet. A purled turning ridge is created to act like a hinge, then the back side of the band is worked in stockinette. The cast on is removed, and the live stitches are grafted together.

SIZES

1 (2, 3, 4, 5)

FINISHED MEASUREMENTS

Circumference: 18 (19, 20, 21, 22) in. / 46 (48.5, 51, 53.5, 56) cm

Height: 2½ in. / 6.5 cm

Designed to fit with 2 to 4 in. / 5 to 10 cm negative ease.

YARN

Fingering weight yarn, shown in Urth Yarns *16 Fingering* (100% extrafine merino; 220 yd. / 201 m per 1¾ oz. / 50 g hank)

Colorways:

- **Main Color (MC):** #N70 Dark Grey, 1 hank
- **Contrast Color (CC):** #N100 Silver, 1 hank

NEEDLES

US 1 / 2.25 mm, 16 in. / 40 cm long circular knitting needle or size needed to obtain gauge

NOTIONS

Spare 16 in. / 40 cm long gauge-size circular knitting needle

Stitch markers (3; 1 unique for BOR)

Row counter

Smooth fingering weight waste yarn

US B-1 / 2.25 mm crochet hook

GAUGE

34 sts and 49 rnds = 4 in. / 10 cm in stranded colorwork in the round, taken after blocking

Make sure to check your gauge.

PATTERN NOTES

This headband is worked in the round. A Crochet Provisional cast on method is used to start the headband. The two long edges (the cast on and the live sts at the top edge) are grafted together with Kitchener stitch to create a closed tube for a seamless-looking headband.

Written instructions are provided for the construction of the headband; a colorwork chart is provided to direct color changes while the headband is created. The colorwork chart is the same number of stitches for all sizes; the difference in circumference is made up by knitting a larger section at the back of the headband in stockinette stitch in the MC.

Instructions are provided for size 1 first, with additional sizes in parentheses. When only one number is provided, it applies to all sizes.

PATTERN INSTRUCTIONS

PROVISIONAL CAST ON

Using smooth waste yarn and crochet hook, CO 153 (161, 171, 179, 187) sts using the Crochet Provisional cast on - Chain Method. Use MC to pick up the sts into the back of the chain. Pm for BOR and join to work in the rnd, being careful not to twist the sts.

Setup Rnd: P9 (13, 18, 22, 26), pm, p135, pm, purl to end of rnd.

These markers will center the colorwork motif over the top of the headband.

KEY

☐ Knit
▩ MC
☐ CC

HEADBAND

Begin working from Chart A, reading all rows from right to left as for working in the rnd, joining CC as required. Work Rows 1–31 once between the markers as follows:

Knit to M with MC, sm, work Chart A across 135 sts to next M, sm, knit to end of rnd with MC.

When the chart is complete, break CC and remove M (except BOR M).

Purl 1 rnd.

Knit 29 rnds. When complete, do not bind off. Break the MC yarn leaving a tail approx. 3 times the length of the live sts. Leave the live sts on the working needle.

CHART A

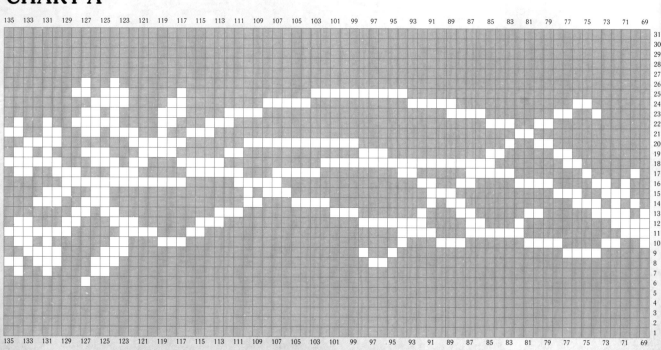

FINISHING

Return to the cast on edge and carefully unravel the provisional cast on, placing the live sts onto a spare gauge-size needle.

Fold the headband in half, WS together (RS facing out), with the live sts parallel on two needles.

Thread a tapestry needle with the long tail of MC and graft the live sts together using Kitchener stitch to form a seamless headband.

Carefully weave the tail into the hollow created by the two sides of the headband. Wet block to dimensions.

"... No sign of age was upon them, unless it were in the depths of their eyes; for these were keen as lances in the starlight, and yet profound, the wells of deep memory."

—The Lord of the Rings: The Fellowship of the Ring by J.R.R. Tolkien

CHART A

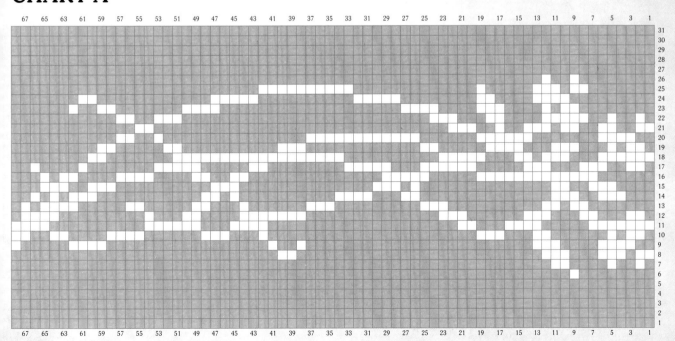

WATCHFUL EYE MITTENS

DESIGNED BY THERESE SHARP

Once a good Wizard and trusted confidant of Gandalf's, Saruman the White was the head of the Istari Order. Although he originally opposed Sauron and his possession of the One Ring, Saruman's knowledge of dark magic and hunger for power led to his eventual alliance with evil. Fueled by the desire to obtain the One Ring for himself, or at least become Sauron's right hand, he gives control of Isengard to Mordor, and the Watchful Eye of Sauron. Aided by Orcs, he destroys the natural beauty of Nan Curunír digging for Uruk-hai.

Rule over Isengard in these stranded colorwork mittens illustrating Barad-dûr, or the Dark Tower, holding the Eye of Sauron aloft on the hand side. Beginning with a 1x1 twisted ribbed cuff, the palm side has vertical striping with an afterthought thumb positioned with waste yarn. Once the body of the mitten is complete, stitches are picked up and knit for the thumb.

SIZES

Small (Medium, Large, Extra Large)

FINISHED MEASUREMENTS

Hand Circumference: 8¼ (8¾, 9½, 10½) in. / 21 (22, 24, 26.5) cm

Total Length: 10 (10½, 11¼, 12) in. / 25.5 (26.5, 28.5, 30.5) cm

Designed to fit with 0 to ¾ in. / 0 to 2 cm positive ease.

YARN

Fingering weight yarn, shown in Robin's Promise Yarn Co. *Songbird* (4-ply; 75% superwash merino, 25% nylon; 463 yd. / 423 m per 3½ oz. / 100 g hank)

Colorways:

- **Main Color (MC):** Japanese Flycatcher Feather, 1 hank
- **Contrast Color 1 (CC1):** Kestral Feather, 1 hank
- **Contrast Color 2 (CC2):** Guianan Cock-of-the-Rock, 1 hank

NEEDLES

US 1.5 / 2.5 mm, 32 in. / 80 cm long circular needle or set of 5 double-pointed needles

US 4 / 3.5 mm, 32 in. / 80 cm long circular needle or set of 5 double-pointed needles or size needed to obtain gauge

NOTIONS

Stitch markers (2; 1 unique for BOR)

Waste yarn

Tapestry needle

GAUGE

Small: 42 sts and 40 rows = 4 in. / 10 cm in stranded knitting pattern worked in the rnd, taken after blocking

Medium: 39 sts and 37 rows = 4 in. / 10 cm in stranded knitting pattern worked in the rnd, taken after blocking

Large: 36 sts and 34 rows = 4 in. / 10 cm in stranded knitting pattern worked in the rnd, taken after blocking

Extra Large: 33 sts and 31 rows = 4 in. / 10 cm in stranded knitting pattern worked in the rnd, taken after blocking

Make sure to check your gauge.

PATTERN NOTES

To honor the original design of the mittens and ensure a wider range of available fit, rather than compromise on the stitch pattern, these mittens have been graded using different gauges for each size. To achieve the gauge for your finished size of mittens, adjust your needle size as needed.

These mittens are worked in the round from the bottom up. Stranded knitting creates the colorwork motif. When working the stranded colorwork, catch floats longer than five stitches.

The twisted ribbed cuff is worked on the smaller needle, and the body of the mitt is worked using the larger needle. The afterthought thumb is worked on the smaller needle.

Written instructions are provided for the construction of the mittens; a colorwork chart is provided for the body of the mittens.

These mitts are nearly identical to each other; the position of the thumb differentiates the two. Take care to follow the thumb placement for the opposing mittens to ensure both wear as intended.

Waste yarn will be used to hold the stitches for the afterthought thumb while the body of the mitten is completed. A smooth waste yarn in fingering weight is recommended to make transferring the stitches back to the working needle easier.

Instructions are provided for size small first, with larger sizes in parentheses. When only one set of numbers is provided, it applies to all sizes.

PATTERN STITCHES

Twisted Rib (worked over a multiple of 2 sts)

All Rnds: *K1tbl, p1; rep from * to end of rnd.

PATTERN INSTRUCTIONS

CAST ON & CUFF

Using the smaller needle and CC1, CO 82 sts using the Long Tail cast on method. Pm for BOR and join to work in the rnd, being careful not to twist the sts. Work in Twisted Rib until the cuff measures approx. 2 in. / 5 cm from the CO edge.

Next Rnd (inc): *K18, kfb; rep from * 3 more times; knit to end of rnd—86 sts.

BODY

Change to larger needle. Begin Mitten chart, reading all rows from right to left as for working in the round and joining MC as required. Work Rows 1–22 once (Row 23, where there are marks for thumb placement, will be worked in tandem with written instructions that differ for each mitten).

THUMB PLACEMENT AND BODY CONT'D

For Left Mitten:

Work across all sts in patt (per Row 23) to the last 15 sts. Slip the last 15 sts of the rnd onto waste yarn. Using MC and CC1, cast on 15 new stitches in the colorwork pattern shown in the orange / left thumb placement box of the chart using the Backward Loop method.

For Right Mitten:

Work across the first 44 sts in patt (per Row 23). Slip the next 15 sts to waste yarn. Using MC and CC1, cast on 15 new stitches in the colorwork pattern shown in the green / right thumb placement box of the chart using the Backward Loop method. Cont to the end of rnd in patt (per Row 23).

Both Mittens:

Work Rows 24–79 of the chart, joining CC2 as required; 6 sts rem at chart completion. Break all yarn except MC. If not already the case, transfer the rem 6 sts to 2 needles (3 sts per needle).

Break MC leaving an 8 in. / 20.5 cm tail. Graft the live sts on the 2 needles held parallel using Kitchener stitch.

AFTERTHOUGHT THUMB

Place the live 15 sts from the thumb placement onto the smaller needle.

Join MC to the left edge of the live sts when the palm of the mitten is facing you.

Pick up and knit 1 st into the gap between the live sts and the cast on sts, pm (SSM), pick up and knit 15 sts along the cast on edge of the back of the thumb, pick up and knit 1 more stitch to close the gap at the right edge of the thumbhole. Pm for BOR and join to work in the rnd—32 sts total.

Setup Rnd (dec): *K14, k2tog, sm; rep from * once more—30 sts rem.

Work in St st (knit every rnd) for 25 rnds, or until the thumb is approx. ¾ in. / 2 cm short of the desired total length.

Thumb Decrease Rnd (dec): *Ssk, knit to 2 sts before M, k2tog, sm; rep from * once more—4 sts dec.

Rep Thumb Decrease Rnd 5 more times.

24 sts dec; 6 sts rem.

Break MC, leaving an 8 in. / 20.5 cm tail. If not already the case, transfer the rem 6 sts to 2 needles (3 sts per needle). Graft the live sts on the 2 needles held parallel using Kitchener stitch.

FINISHING

Weave in all ends and wet block to measurements. Allow to dry completely. Trim all ends.

KEY

- ■ No stitch
- □ Knit
- ■ MC
- ▨ CC1
- ▨ CC2
- ◪ k2tog
- ◪ ssk
- ▢ Right thumb
- ▢ Left thumb

> "Who now has the strength
> to stand against the armies
> of Isengard . . . and Mordor?"
>
> —Saruman, *The Lord of the Rings:*
> *The Two Towers* film

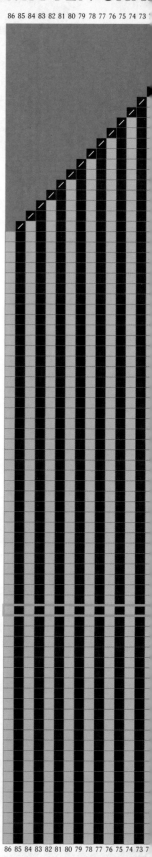

CHAPTER THREE

COWLS, SHAWLS & PULLOVERS

ROOTS & BRANCHES COWL

DESIGNED BY CARISSA BROWNING

Created to protect the forests of Middle-earth, Ents were originally sentient treelike creatures until the Elves taught them how to speak. Incredibly strong and patient, they can walk through the forests and converse with the trees, protecting them from Orcs and other threats. When Saruman begins to clear-cut the forests to aid Sauron, destroying every living thing in his path, the Ents have an Entmoot—a rare gathering of Ents—and decide to fight back by breaching the dams surrounding Isengard.

Alternating light and dark brioche gives this Entmoot-inspired cowl the illusion of depth and a bark-like texture. An Italian cast on and tubular bind off allow the stitches to flow smoothly over the edges of the fabric, while sporadic knotholes lend extra personality. Worked in the round from the bottom up, it can easily be customized by adding more repeats or lengthening/shortening the tree trunks.

SIZES

One size

FINISHED MEASUREMENTS

Circumference: 26 in. / 66 cm

Height: 12 in. / 30.5 cm

YARN

Bulky weight yarn, shown in Queen City Yarn *Plaza Midwood Bulky* (3-ply; 100% superwash merino; 106 yd. / 97 m per 3½ oz. / 100 g hank)

Colorways:

- **Light Color (LC):** Edge of the Galaxy, 1 hank
- **Dark Color (DC):** Avocado Toast, 1 hank

NEEDLES

US 10 / 6 mm, 16 in. / 40 cm long circular needle or size needed to obtain gauge

NOTIONS

4 stitch markers (1 unique for BOR)

Removable stitch marker (1)

Row counter (optional)

Tapestry needle

GAUGE

12 sts and 13 rounds = 4 in. / 10 cm over 2-color brioche rib worked in the round, taken after blocking

Make sure to check your gauge.

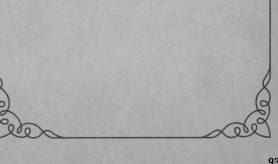

PATTERN NOTES

This cowl is worked in the round from the bottom up using one needle size throughout.

Written instructions are provided for the entirety of the pattern. Optional charts are provided. Read carefully through all written instructions before working from the charts to ensure no instructions get missed.

Knotholes are worked into the fabric of the "trunks" of the trees. Each knothole temporarily adds 2 sts to the total stitch count of the cowl. These stitches are decreased out at the top of the knothole.

The original design includes 4 knotholes, and the pattern provides instructions for their specific placement. You may choose to place additional knotholes as desired in either stitch 2 or stitch 20 of any pattern repeat. Adding significantly more knotholes may alter the circumference of the cowl and require additional yardage.

Ensure all knotholes have been completed and the overall stitch count is 80 stitches before moving on to the Branches section at the top of the cowl.

PATTERN STITCHES

2-Color Brioche Rib in the round (worked over a multiple of 2 sts)

Rnd 1 LC: *Sl1yo, k1; rep from * to end of rnd.

Rnd 1 DC: *Brp1, sl1yo; rep from * to end of rnd.

Rnd 2 LC: *Sl1yo, brk1; rep from * to end of rnd.

Rnd 2 DC: *Brp1, sl1yo; rep from * to end of rnd.

Rep Rnd 2 LC & DC for patt.

Knothole (worked into 1 st in est brioche pattern)

Follow written instructions below or work from the Knothole chart.

Rnd 1 LC: Brkyobrk—2 sts inc; 3 sts total for base of knothole.

Rnd 1 DC: Sl1yo, p1, sl1yo.

Rnd 2 LC: Brk1, sl1yo, brk1.

Rnd 2 DC: Sl1yo, brp1, sl1yo.

Rnds 3 and 4 LC & DC: Rep [Rnd 2 LC & DC] 2 times.

Rnd 5 LC: BrLsl dec—2 sts dec; 1 st rem for top of knothole.

PATTERN INSTRUCTIONS

CAST ON & SETUP

CO 80 sts using the Two-Color Italian cast on method, beginning with LC and a purl st.

Be sure to work the setup rows included in the cast on method before proceeding.

Pm for BOR and join to work in the rnd, being careful not to twist the sts.

ROOTS

Follow written instructions below or work from the Roots chart. The pattern repeat is worked 4 times across each rnd; work Rnds 1–9 LC and DC one time.

Rnd 1 LC: *(Sl1yo, k1) 10 times, pm; rep from * 3 more times (the final M will be the BOR M).

Rnd 1 DC: *(Brp1, sl1yo) 5 times, brk1, sl1yo, (brp1, sl1yo) 4 times, sm; rep from * 3 more times.

Rnd 2 LC: *Sl1yo, brk1; rep from * to end of rnd (sm as encountered).

Rnd 2 DC: *(Brp1, sl1yo) 5 times, brk1, sl1yo, (brp1, sl1yo) 4 times, sm; rep from * 3 more times.

Rnd 3 LC & DC: Rep [Rnd 2 LC & DC] 1 time.

Rnd 4 LC (dec): *[Sl1yo, brLsl dec, (sl1yo, brk1) 3 times] 2 times, sm; rep from * 3 more times—64 sts.

Rnd 4 DC (inc): *(Brp1, sl1yo) 4 times, br4st inc, sl1yo, (brp1, sl1yo) 3 times, sm; rep from * 3 more times—80 sts.

Rnd 5 LC: *(Sl1yo, brk1) 4 times, (sl1yo, p1) 2 times, (sl1yo, brk1) 4 times, sm; rep from * 3 more times.

Rnd 5 DC: *(Brp1, sl1yo) 4 times, (brk1, sl1yo) 3 times, (brp1, sl1yo) 3 times, sm; rep from * 3 more times.

Rnd 6 LC (dec): *(Sl1yo, brk1) 2 times, sl1yo, brRsl dec, (sl1yo, brp1) 2 times, (sl1yo, brk1) 2 times, sl1yo, brRsl dec, sm; rep from * 3 more times—64 sts.

Rnd 6 DC (inc): *(Brp1, sl1yo) 3 times, brkyobrk, sl1yo, brk1, sl1yo, brkyobrk, (sl1yo, brp1) 2 times, sl1yo, sm; rep from * 3 more times—80 sts.

Rnd 7 LC: *(Sl1yo, brk1) 3 times, sl1yo, p1, (sl1yo, brp1) 2 times, sl1yo, p1, (sl1yo, brk1) 3 times, sm; rep from * 3 more times.

Rnd 7 DC: *(Brp1, sl1yo) 3 times, (brk1, sl1yo) 5 times, (brp1, sl1yo) 2 times, sm; rep from * 3 more times.

Rnd 8 LC (dec): *Sl1yo, brLsl dec, sl1yo, brk1, (sl1yo, brp1) 4 times, sl1yo, brLsl dec, sl1yo, brk1, sm; rep from * 3 more times—64 sts.

Rnd 8 DC (inc): *(Brp1, sl1yo) 2 times, brkyobrk, (sl1yo, brk1) 3 times, sl1yo, brkyobrk, sl1yo, brp1, sl1yo, sm; rep from * 3 more times—80 sts.

Rnd 9 LC: *(Sl1yo, brk1) 2 times, sl1yo, p1, (sl1yo, brp1) 4 times, sl1yo, p1, (sl1yo, brk1) 2 times, sm; rep from * 3 more times.

Rnd 9 DC: *(Brp1, sl1yo) 2 times, (brk1, sl1yo) 7 times, brp1, sl1yo, sm; rep from * 3 more times.

TRUNKS & KNOTHOLES

Read carefully through this section before beginning as multiple steps occur at the same time.

Rnd 1 LC: *(Sl1yo, brk1) 2 times, (sl1yo, brp1) 6 times, (sl1yo, brk1) 2 times, sm; rep from * 3 more times.

Rnd 1 DC: *(Brp1, sl1yo) 2 times, (brk1, sl1yo) 7 times, brp1, sl1yo, sm; rep from * 3 more times.

Rnds 2–20 LC & DC: Rep [Rnd 1 LC & DC] 19 more times.

AT THE SAME TIME:

On Rnd 3 LC, in the second st of the rnd, work a Knothole—2 sts inc; 82 sts total. The Knothole will conclude on Rnd 7 LC—2 sts dec; 80 sts total.

On Rnd 7 LC, in the 42nd st of the rnd, work a Knothole—2 sts inc; 82 sts total. The Knothole will conclude on Rnd 11 LC—2 sts dec; 80 sts total.

On Rnd 11 LC, in the 22nd st of the rnd, work a Knothole—2 sts inc; 82 sts total. The Knothole will conclude on Rnd 15 LC—2 sts dec; 80 sts total.

On Rnd 15 LC, in the 62nd st of the rnd, work a Knothole—2 sts inc; 82 sts total. The Knothole will conclude on Rnd 19 LC—2 sts dec; 80 sts total.

BRANCHES

Follow written instructions below or work from the Branches chart. The pattern repeat is worked 4 times across each rnd; work Rnds 1–8 LC and DC one time.

Rnd 1 LC (inc): *Sl1yo, brk1, sl1yo, brkyobrk, (sl1yo, brp1) 6 times, sl1yo, brk1, sl1yo, brkyobrk, sm; rep from * 3 more times—96 sts.

Rnd 1 DC (dec): *(Brp1, sl1yo) 2 times, p1, sl1yo, brLsl dec, sl1yo, (brk1, sl1yo) 3 times, brRsl dec, sl1yo, brp1, sl1yo, p1, sl1yo, sm; rep from * 3 more times—80 sts.

Rnd 2 LC: *(Sl1yo, brk1) 3 times, (sl1yo, brp1) 4 times, (sl1yo, brk1) 3 times, sm; rep from * 3 more times.

Rnd 2 DC: *(Brp1, sl1yo) 3 times, (brk1, sl1yo) 5 times, (brp1, sl1yo) 2 times, sm; rep from * 3 more times.

Rnd 3 LC (inc): *Sl1yo, brkyobrk, (sl1yo, brk1) 2 times, (sl1yo, brp1) 4 times, sl1yo, brkyobrk, (sl1yo, brk1) 2 times, sm; rep from * 3 more times—96 sts.

Rnd 3 DC (dec): *Brp1, sl1yo, p1, sl1yo, (brp1, sl1yo) 2 times, brLsl dec, sl1yo, brk1, sl1yo, brRsl dec, sl1yo, p1, sl1yo, (brp1, sl1yo) 2 times, sm; rep from * 3 more times—80 sts.

Rnd 4 LC: *(Sl1yo, brk1) 4 times, (sl1yo, brp1) 2 times, (sl1yo, brk1) 4 times, sm; rep from * 3 more times.

Rnd 4 DC: *(Brp1, sl1yo) 4 times, (brk1, sl1yo) 3 times, (brp1, sl1yo) 3 times, sm; rep from * 3 more times.

Rnd 5 LC (inc): *(Sl1yo, brk1) 3 times, sl1yo, brkyobrk, (sl1yo, brp1) 2 times, (sl1yo, brk1) 3 times, sl1yo, brkyobrk, sm; rep from * 3 more times—96 sts.

Rnd 5 DC (dec): *(Brp1, sl1yo) 4 times, p1, sl1yo, br4st dec, sl1yo, (brp1, sl1yo) 3 times, p1, sl1yo, sm; rep from * 3 more times—80 sts.

Rnd 6 LC: *Sl1yo, brk1; rep from * to end of rnd (sm as encountered).

Rnd 6 DC: *(Brp1, sl1yo) 5 times, brk1, sl1yo, (brp1, sl1yo) 4 times, sm; rep from * 3 more times.

Rnds 7 and 8 LC & DC: Rep [Rnd 6 LC & DC] 2 times.

Final Rnd LC: *Sl1 wyif, brk1; rep from * to end of rnd (rm as encountered).

Break LC.

Break DC leaving a tail roughly 100 in. / 254 cm long (or approx. 4 times the length of the edge to be bound off).

Thread the tapestry needle with the long tail of DC yarn. Beginning with the Slipped Stitch Round, BO all sts using the Sewn Tubular bind off method, noting that the first st BO will be a purl st.

FINISHING

Weave in ends. Gently wet block the cowl to dimensions and allow to dry completely. Trim all ends.

> "Curse him, root and branch! Many of those trees were my friends, creatures I had known from nut and acorn; many had voices of their own that are lost forever now. And there is a waste of stump and bramble where once there were singing groves. I have been idle. I have let things slip. It must stop!"
>
> –Treebeard, *The Lord of the Rings: The Two Towers* by J.R.R. Tolkien

KEY

- No stitch
- LC
- DC
- knit
- purl
- sl1yo
- brk
- brp
- brLsl dec
- brRsl dec
- br4st dec
- brkyobrk
- br4st inc
- Pattern repeat

ROOTS CHART

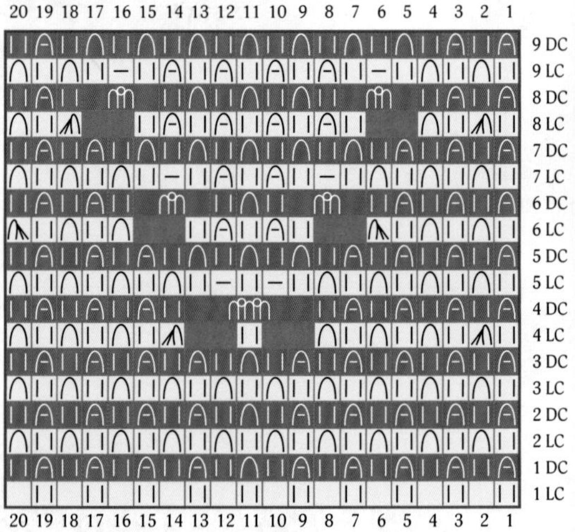

KNOTHOLE CHART

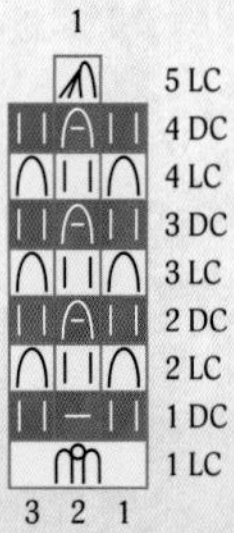

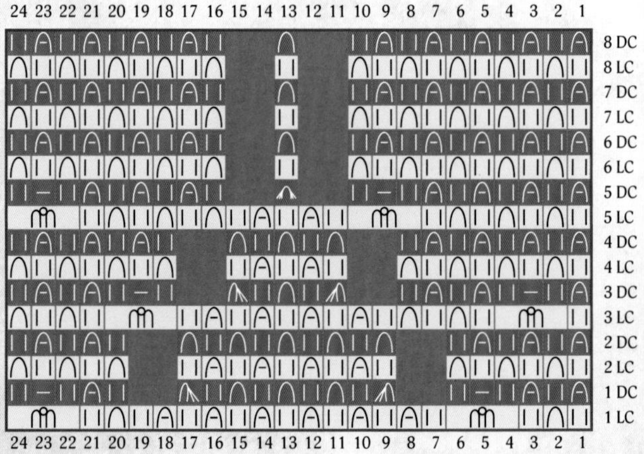

YOU SHAWL NOT PASS

DESIGNED BY CARISSA BROWNING

Exiled deep underground in the Mines of Moria, a Balrog ("demon of night") was awakened by the Dwarves many years ago. At a turning point in *The Fellowship of the Ring* where it is believed that the first member of the Fellowship falls, the group flees from a winged Balrog named Durin's Bane over the bridge of Khazad-dûm. Made of fire and shadow with blazing wings, it has a large human shape with a ram's head and horns and carries a sword and whip made of flame. It is here where Gandalf bellows the iconic line, "You shall not pass!"

"Fly, you fools!" This multicolored shawl is inspired by the Balrog's fiery wings and the Fellowship's encounter with it. Begun by casting on for the long straight edge along the top, the shawl is created by joining two semicircles of expanding chevrons with a wedge of garter in the center. Formed by rapid increases in each end section, paired with slower decreases leaning toward the center, the body tapers to a point while the lacy wings unfurl in their full, flame-tipped glory. The pointed edges are pulled out while blocking, pointy and sinister like the wings of a Balrog.

SIZES

One size

FINISHED MEASUREMENTS

Wingspan (along top edge): 87 in. / 221 cm

Center Depth: 17 in. / 43 cm

Wing Radius (from cast on to flame tip): 25 in. / 63.5 cm

YARN

Fingering weight yarn, shown in Knitcircus Yarns *Breathtaking BFL Fingering* (4-ply; 100% superwash Blue-Faced Leicester wool; 410 yd. / 375 m per 3½ oz. / 100 g cake)

Colorways:

- **Main Color (MC):** Quoth the Raven, 2 cakes
- **Contrast Color (CC):** Leaf Pile Leap Panoramic Gradient, 1 cake

NEEDLES

US 4 / 3.5 mm, 32 to 40 in. / 80 to 100 cm long circular needle or size needed to obtain gauge

NOTIONS

2 stitch markers

16 locking stitch markers (optional)

Row counter (optional)

T-pins / blocking pins

Tapestry needle

GAUGE

18 sts and 38 rows = 4 in. / 10 cm over garter stitch worked flat, taken after blocking

Make sure to check your gauge.

PATTERN NOTES

This shawl is worked flat from the top center edge, downward and outward. Use the length of needle that feels most comfortable to you.

Written instructions are provided for the entirety of the shawl.

The first and last st of each WS row is slipped to maintain a smooth selvage edge.

If desired, a locking stitch marker can be placed through the fabric to denote the center of each chevron where the double decrease will be. Move stitch markers up every 4 to 8 rows.

PATTERN INSTRUCTIONS

CAST ON & SETUP

Using MC, CO 162 sts using the Long Tail cast on method. Do not join to work in the rnd.

Row 1 (RS, inc): K1, {k1, yo, k1, yo, k1} into next st, knit to last 2 sts, {k1, yo, k1, yo, k1} into next st, k1—170 sts.

Row 2 (WS): Sl1 wyif, p5, knit to last 6 sts, p5, sl1 wyif.

Row 3 (inc): K1, (k1, yo) 4 times, pm, ssk, knit to last 7 sts, k2tog, pm, (yo, k1) 4 times, k1—176 sts.

Row 4 (WS, and all WS rows unless otherwise noted): Sl1 wyif, purl to M, sm, p1, knit to 1 st before M, p1, sm, purl to last st, sl1 wyif.

Row 5 (inc): K1, (k1, yo) to M, sm, ssk, knit to 2 sts before M, k2tog, sm, (yo, k1) to last st, k1—190 sts; 17 sts in each wing, 156 center sts.

Row 7 (dec): K1, (k1, yo, sk2p, yo) to M, sm, ssk, knit to 2 sts before M, k2tog, sm, (yo, sk2p, yo, k1) to last st, k1—188 sts; 17 sts in each wing, 154 center sts.

Row 9 (dec): Work as for Row 7—186 sts; 17 sts in each wing, 152 center sts.

Row 11 (dec): Work as for Row 7—184 sts; 17 sts in each wing, 150 center sts.

Row 13 (inc): Work as for Row 5—214 sts; 33 sts in each wing, 148 center sts.

Row 15 (dec): Work as for Row 7—212 sts; 33 sts in each wing, 146 center sts.

Row 17 (dec): Work as for Row 7—210 sts; 33 sts in each wing, 144 center sts.

Row 19 (dec): Work as for Row 7—208 sts; 33 sts in each wing, 142 center sts.

Row 21 (inc): K1, (k1, yo, k3, yo) to M, sm, ssk, knit to 2 sts before M, k2tog, sm, (yo, k3, yo, k1) to last st, k1—238 sts; 49 sts in each wing, 140 center sts.

Row 22: Sl1 wyif, purl to M, sm, p1, knit to 1 st before M, p1, sm, purl to last st, sl1 wyif.

CHEVRONS

Row 1 (RS, dec): K1, (k1, yo, k1, sk2p, k1, yo) to M, sm, ssk, knit to 2 sts before M, k2tog, sm, (yo, k1, sk2p, k1, yo, k1) to last st, k1—236 sts; 49 sts in each wing, 138 center sts.

Row 2 (WS, and all WS rows unless otherwise noted): Sl1 wyif, purl to M, sm, p1, knit to 1 st before M, p1, sm, purl to last st, sl1 wyif.

Row 3 (dec): Work as for Row 1—234 sts; 49 sts in each wing, 136 center sts.

Row 5 (dec): Work as for Row 1—232 sts; 49 sts in each wing, 134 center sts.

Row 7 (inc): K1, (k1, yo, k5, yo) to M, sm, ssk, knit to 2 sts before M, k2tog, sm, (yo, k5, yo, k1) to last st, k1—262 sts; 65 sts in each wing, 132 center sts.

Row 9 (dec): K1, (k1, yo, k2, sk2p, k2, yo) to M, sm, ssk, knit to 2 sts before M, k2tog, sm, (yo, k2, sk2p, k2, yo, k1) to last st, k1—260 sts; 65 sts in each wing, 130 center sts.

Row 11 (dec): Work as for Row 9—258 sts; 65 sts in each wing, 128 center sts.

Row 13 (dec): Work as for Row 9—256 sts; 65 sts in each wing, 126 center sts.

Row 15 (inc): K1, (k1, yo, k7, yo) to M, sm, ssk, knit to 2 sts before M, k2tog, sm, (yo, k7, yo, k1) to last st, k1—286 sts; 81 sts in each wing, 124 center sts.

Row 17 (dec): K1, (k1, yo, k3, sk2p, k3, yo) to M, sm, ssk, knit to 2 sts before M, k2tog, sm, (yo, k3, sk2p, k3, yo, k1) to last st, k1—284 sts; 81 sts in each wing, 122 center sts.

Row 19 (dec): Work as for Row 17—282 sts; 81 sts in each wing, 120 center sts.

Row 21 (dec): Work as for Row 17—280 sts; 81 sts in each wing, 118 center sts.

Row 23 (inc): K1, (k1, yo, k9, yo) to M, sm, ssk, knit to 2 sts before M, k2tog, sm, (yo, k9, yo, k1) to last st, k1—310 sts; 97 sts in each wing, 116 center sts.

Row 24: Sl1 wyif, purl to M, sm, p1, knit to 1 st before M, p1, sm, purl to last st, sl1 wyif.

CONTINUE CHEVRONS

Read carefully through this section before beginning as multiple steps occur at the same time.

Rep [Rows 17–24 of the Chevron section] 9 more times, then [Rows 19–22 of the Chevron section] 1 more time (78 total rows)—520 sts; 241 sts in each wing, 38 center sts.

For each 8-row rep, the center sts will decrease by 8 stitches (2 sts on each RS row), and the wings will increase by 16 stitches (16 sts on Row 23).

AT THE SAME TIME, as you cont the reps, inc the sts in the wings chevron patt by 2 sts for each 8-row rep.

For Example: On the first rep, the Chevron patt in each wing will be (k1, yo, **k4**, sk2p, **k4**, yo) / (yo, **k4**, sk2p, **k4**, yo, k1) for Rows 17, 19, and 21 and (k1, yo, **k11**, yo) / (yo, **k11**, yo, k1) for Row 23. For the second rep, the Chevron patt in each wing will be (k1, yo, **k5**, sk2p, **k5**, yo) / (yo, **k5**, sk2p, **k5**, yo, k1) for Rows 17, 19, and 21 and (k1, yo, **k13**, yo) / (yo, **k13**, yo, k1) for Row 23, etc.

When the final repeat of Row 22 is worked, the stitch pattern in the wings will be (k1, yo, **k13**, sk2p, **k13**, yo) / (yo, **k13**, sk2p, **k13**, yo, k1) for Rows 17, 19, and 21.

Break MC yarn.

FLAMES

Join CC yarn; the remainder of the shawl will be worked with CC only.

Rep [Rows 23 and 24 of the Chevron section] 1 time—550 sts; 257 sts in each wing, 36 center sts.

Then rep [Rows 17–24 of the Chevron section] 4 more times—646 sts; 321 sts in each wing, 4 center sts. *Note: As you cont the reps, inc the sts in the wings chevron patt by 2*

sts for each 8-row rep as established.

With RS facing, loosely BO all sts knitwise.

FINISHING

Weave in ends. Wet block, using a t-pin to pin out each point of the bound-off edge to accentuate the wing tips. Allow to dry completely. Trim all ends.

"It was like a great shadow, in the middle of which was a dark form, of man-shape maybe, yet greater; and a power and terror seemed to be in it and to go before it."

—*The Lord of the Rings: The Fellowship of the Ring* by J.R.R. Tolkien

Schematic

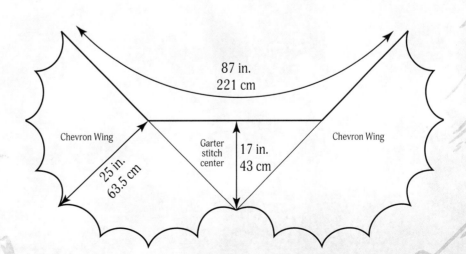

87 in.
221 cm

Chevron Wing

Garter stitch center

17 in.
43 cm

Chevron Wing

25 in.
63.5 cm

ONE RING COWL

DESIGNED BY JESSICA GODDARD

Created by Sauron in the fires of Mount Doom and infused with his soul, the One Ring was crafted with the intent of giving the wearer full power over Middle-earth. A deceptively simple golden band, when placed in fire, the inscription, "One Ring to rule them all, One Ring to find them, One Ring to bring them all and in the darkness bind them," was visible. In addition to the One Ring, nineteen other rings were forged and given to the Elves, Dwarves, and Men. With the lesser rings' powers linked to Sauron, he bequeathed them to the rulers of the other races to control them and make them bow to his reign.

One cowl to rule them all! Inspired by the all-powerful, golden One Ring and worked flat, this cowl is double knit, meaning the work has no visible wrong side, will have twice the thickness, and will have colors that invert. Begun with a provisional cast on, the cowl is worked back and forth in rows before the live edges are grafted together to form a seamless loop, much like a ring. The knitted text translates to "One Ring to rule them all," and you'll be the ruler of your domain while wearing it!

SIZES
One size

FINISHED MEASUREMENTS
Height: 7½ in. / 19 cm

Circumference: 38 in. / 96.5 cm

YARN
DK weight yarn, shown in Kim Dyes Yarn *Crumpets DK* (2-ply; 100% Falkland wool; 262 yd. / 240 m per 3½ oz. / 100 g hank)

Colorways:

- **Main Color (MC):** Dandelions, 1 hank
- **Contrast Color (CC):** Black, 1 hank

NEEDLES
US 6 / 4 mm straight knitting needles and set of 3 dpns or size needed to obtain gauge

NOTIONS
Locking stitch marker

G-6 / 4 mm crochet hook

Smooth waste yarn in 2 contrasting colors

Tapestry needle

GAUGE
23 sts and 29½ rows = 4 in. / 10 cm in 2-color double knitting, taken before blocking

Make sure to check your gauge.

PATTERN NOTES
The cowl is worked flat, from end to end, using the Double Knitting method. Charts are provided for the entirety of the double knitting work.

A provisional cast on is used to allow a seamless joining of the work in the round using Kitchener stitch.

Double knitting is a technique that produces a double thickness of fabric that looks like right-side stockinette stitch on both sides. The two sides of the knitting are inverse colors; the two sides mirror one another.

The stitch count does not change for the entire project.

All odd-numbered rows are RS rows and should be read from right to left; all even-numbered rows are WS rows and should be read from left to right.

Edge stitches are worked at each end of the chart rows to keep the edges neat; these stitches are not represented on the chart.

PATTERN INSTRUCTIONS

CAST ON & SETUP

*Using 1 color of waste yarn and the crochet hook, CO 43 sts using the Crochet Provisional cast on method onto 1 dpn.

Rep from * using a second color of waste yarn.

43 sts on each of 2 dpns (86 sts total). Clip a locking marker into the edge stitch of the front dpn. This indicator will be used during grafting; do not remove this marker until directed.

Holding the dpns parallel, work a slip stitch row (no stitches are knit) as follows: **Slip 1 st purlwise from front dpn to straight needle, slip 1 st purlwise from back dpn to same straight needle; rep from ** until all 86 sts are on one straight needle (sts are alternating in color).

BODY OF COWL

Work Rows 1–282 through Charts A, B, and C once, reading RS rows from right to left and WS rows from left to right, joining/breaking CCs as required, as follows:

RS Rows: Holding MC and CC yarns together, k2tog. Work across the 41 sts of the charted RS row using the Double Knitting method. Holding MC and CC yarns together, k2tog.

WS Rows: Holding MC and CC yarns together, p2tog.

Work across the 41 sts of the charted WS row using the Double Knitting method. Holding MC and CC yarns together, p2tog.

When finished, break MC and CC leaving a tail of each yarn approx. 4 times the width of the scarf.

GRAFTING

Hold the working needle in your left hand; hold 2 dpns in your right hand, parallel, one in front of the other.

Work a slip stitch row (no stitches are knit) as follows: *Slip 1 MC st purlwise from LHN to front dpn, slip 1 CC st purlwise from LHN to back dpn; rep from * until the front dpn holds 43 MC sts and the back dpn holds 43 CC sts.

Carefully remove the provisional CO waste yarn from cast on row with the locking marker and place the live sts onto a third dpn. The locking marker can be removed.

Fold the scarf into a loop so the live sts from the provisional CO are parallel to the dpn holding the CC sts. Graft these two sets of live sts using the CC tail and Kitchener stitch.

Carefully remove the remaining provisional CO waste yarn and place the live sts onto a dpn.

Holding the two remaining dpns parallel, graft these two sets of live sts using the MC tail and Kitchener stitch.

FINISHING

Weave in the ends carefully by inserting a tail into the tapestry needle and weaving the tail into the hollow of the double knitting. The original sample was not blocked, but if you would like to smooth out your stitches, you may wish to do a gentle steam block.

"Three Rings for the Elven-kings under the sky,
Seven for the Dwarf-lords in their halls of stone,
Nine for Mortal Men doomed to die,
One for the Dark Lord on his dark throne
In the Land of Mordor where the Shadows lie.
One Ring to rule them all, One Ring to find them,
One Ring to bring them all and in the darkness bind them
In the Land of Mordor where the Shadows lie."

—The Lord of the Rings: The Fellowship of the Ring by J.R.R. Tolkien

CHART A

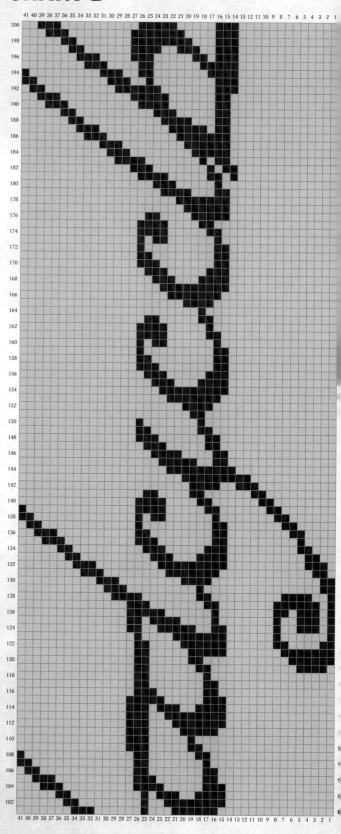

CHART B

CHART C

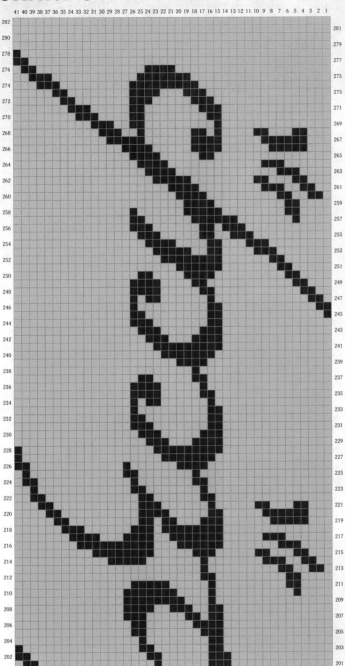

☐ MC
■ CC

THE EYE COWL

DESIGNED BY NICOLE COUTTS

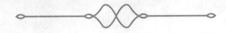

A shapeshifter, Sauron could infiltrate and corrupt different races and cultures with ease long before the Fellowship was formed. Using the power of the One Ring, he created Mount Doom in Mordor, his fortress of dark magic and wickedness, with the intention of ruling all of Middle-earth. As long as he had the Ring, he had power. Though Tolkien never goes into detail when describing him, in the books Sauron tells the Orcs to call him "Eye," so his real name is never spoken out loud or written down. He uses the Eye as his sigil, marking all those he controls. This is taken literally in the films, manifesting Sauron as a watchful, flame-wreathed eye hovering over Mount Doom in the tower of Barad-dûr. Calling the Ring home through their shared connection, if he can capture the Ring, he can regain physical form and power once more.

Inspired by the flame-wreathed all-seeing eye that misses nothing, this cowl will help you keep a 360-degree view on your surroundings, much like Sauron. Knit double tall in the round, then folded over with the cast on and live edge stitches grafted together, this cowl features stranded colorwork Eyes of Sauron that keep a lookout on everything, no matter how you wear it. With blazing tones of orange on a dark background, this is a bold accessory to add to your wardrobe as you plot the future of Middle-earth.

SIZES

One size

FINISHED MEASUREMENTS

Circumference: 25 in. / 63.5 cm

Height: 7¼ in. / 18.5 cm

YARN

Fingering weight yarn, shown in Jamieson's of Shetland *Shetland Spindrift* (2-ply; 100% pure Shetland wool; 115 yd. / 105 m per ¾ oz. / 25 g skein)

Colorways:

- **Main Color (MC):** #999 Black, 3 skeins
- **Contrast Color 1 (CC1):** #470 Pumpkin, 2 skeins
- **Contrast Color 2 (CC2):** #462 Ginger, 2 skeins
- **Contrast Color 3 (CC3):** #525 Crimson, 1 skein

NEEDLES

US 3 / 3.25 mm, 16 in. / 40 cm long circular needle

US 4 / 3.5 mm, 16 in. / 40 cm long circular needle, or size needed to obtain gauge

NOTIONS

Stitch marker

Row counter (optional)

Tapestry needle

GAUGE

33 sts and 39 rows = 4 in. / 10 cm in stranded colorwork pattern in the round, taken after blocking

Make sure to check your gauge.

PATTERN NOTES

The cowl is worked in the round, from bottom to top, using stranded colorwork.

This cowl is grafted together at the end to create the folded over / double thick fabric to provide structure for the cowl.

Written instructions are provided for the construction of the cowl; charts are provided for the colorwork pattern.

The larger needle is used to knit the outer layer of the cowl, and the smaller needle is used to knit the inner layer. The small needle should be 1 needle size smaller than the large needle when gauge is met.

PATTERN INSTRUCTIONS

CAST ON

Using MC and the larger needle, CO 208 sts using the Long Tail cast on method. Pm for BOR and join to work in the rnd, being careful not to twist the sts.

BODY OF COWL

Begin working from Chart A, reading all rows from right to left as for working in the rnd, joining the CCs as required (chart is worked 26 times across the rnd). Work [Rows 1–10] 7 times (70 rows total).

Using MC, knit 1 rnd (71 rows total).

Change to smaller needle.

Work [Rows 1–10] 7 more times. When complete, break all CCs (141 rows total).

Using MC, knit 1 rnd (142 rows total). Bind off all sts knitwise.

FINISHING

Turn the cowl inside out and secure all ends to the WS; trim excess ends.

Keeping the WS facing out, fold the cowl in half, WS together, bringing the cast on edge upward, parallel with the bind off edge. The first 71 rows of the cowl (worked with the larger needle) will be on the outside; the remaining 71 rows will be on the inside.

Using a tapestry needle and a long strand of MC (approx. 1¾ yd. / 1.5 m), seam the cast on and bind off edges together using the Horizontal Invisible Seaming method.

Weave the remaining ends of the grafting tail into the hollow of the seamed cowl.

Wet block and dry flat. Once dry, steam the cowl to ensure the grafted edge is flat and neat the whole way around.

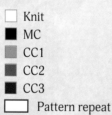

KEY

- ☐ Knit
- ■ MC
- ▨ CC1
- ▩ CC2
- ■ CC3
- ☐ Pattern repeat

CHART A

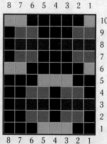

"The Eye was rimmed with fire, but was itself glazed, yellow as a cat's, watchful and intent, and the black slit of its pupil opened on a pit, a window into nothing."

–The Lord of the Rings: The Fellowship of the Ring by J.R.R. Tolkien

ENCHANTMENT SHAWL

DESIGNED BY SUSANNA IC

A land as diverse as the creatures living in it, Middle-earth is home to Elves, Men, Dwarves, Hobbits, Wizards, Ents, and many other beings living across plains, mountains, caves, rivers, and forests. The Middle-earth timeline is divided into three parts—Years of Lamps, Years of Trees, and Years of Sun. The Years of Sun is further divided into the Four Ages. It is in the Third Age that the Fellowship is formed to destroy the One Ring and restore peace across the lands.

As enchanting as the world of Middle-earth itself, this stunning beaded shawl will make you feel like Elven royalty. With the body of the shawl worked in one piece in stockinette stitch from end to end, the beaded motif is placed along the length of the shawl. After the body is finished, stitches are picked up along the bottom edge with the beaded lace leaf border worked outward. All the lace patterning is worked only on the right side, except for bead placement, with the wrong-side rows simply purled across. A good blocking will open the stunning lacework.

SIZES
One size

FINISHED MEASUREMENTS
Wingspan: 67 in. / 170 cm

Center Depth: 30 in. / 76 cm

YARN
Fingering weight yarn, shown in Freia Fine Handpaint Yarns *Fingering Shawl Ball Semi-Solid* (single ply; 100% US merino wool; 430 yd. / 393 m per 3½ oz. / 100 g ball), 1 ball in color Olivine (MC)

Fingering weight yarn, shown in Freia Fine Handpaint Yarns *Ombré Merino Fingering Shawl Ball* (single ply; 100% US merino wool; 430 yd. / 393 m per 3½ oz. / 100 g ball), 1 ball in color Hayride (CC)

NEEDLES
US 7 / 4.5 mm, 32 in. / 80 cm long circular needle or size needed to obtain gauge

US 8 / 5 mm, 32 in. / 80 cm long circular needle

US 9 / 5.5 mm double-pointed needle (1)

NOTIONS
Approx. 1900 beads, size 6/0 4 mm (optional)

US 10 / 0.75 mm crochet hook (or smaller as needed to fit through holes of beads, optional)

Stitch markers

Tapestry needle

T-pins / blocking pins

GAUGE
19 sts and 27 rows = 4 in. / 10 cm in stockinette stitch worked flat on smallest needles, taken after blocking

Make sure to check your gauge.

PATTERN NOTES

The shawl is worked in one piece. The upper half of the shawl is worked simply, in stockinette stitch, from end to end with a large, beaded crown motif.

When the upper half of the shawl is complete, stitches are picked up along the bottom edge and a deep lace border featuring leaf motifs and additional beads is worked to the bind off edge.

The shawl is finished by wet blocking, which opens up the lace fully.

Written instructions are provided for the construction of the shawl. Charts are provided for the bead placement and lace portions of the shawl.

All of the lace patterning is worked only on the right side of the project, and with the exception of bead placement, the wrong-side rows are rest rows and are largely purled.

Beads are added throughout the shawl; these beads are optional, and the project will look great without them. If you omit the bead placement, simply knit (on RS) or purl (on WS) the stitch where the "apply bead" is indicated.

Three different needle sizes are used for this shawl. The smallest needle is the gauge-size needle; it will be used for the majority of the shawl, including the first half of the border lacework. The middle size needle should be 1 US size larger than the gauge-size needle; it is used for the latter half of the border lacework. The largest needle should be 2 US sizes larger than the gauge-size needle and will be used only for the bind off; only 1 needle is needed. A dpn, straight or short circular needle will work equally well for this.

PATTERN INSTRUCTIONS

CAST ON

Using MC and the smallest needle, CO 6 sts using the Long Tail cast on method. Do not join to work in the rnd.
Setup Row (WS): P3, k3.

BODY OF SHAWL

Establish Seed Edging:
Row 1 (RS, inc): K1, k2tog, yo, k1, M1L, k2—7 sts.
Row 2 (WS): Sl1 wyif, p2, k1, k1tbl, k2.
Row 3 (inc): K1, k2tog, yo, k1, p1, M1L, k2—8 sts.
Row 4: Sl1 wyif, p3, k1, k1tbl, k2.
Row 5 (inc): K1, k2tog, yo, k1, p1, k1, M1L, k2—9 sts.
Row 6: Sl1 wyif, p2, k1, p1, k1, k1tbl, k2.
Row 7 (inc): K1, k2tog, yo, (k1, p1) 2 times, M1L, k2—10 sts.
Row 8: Sl1 wyif, p3, k1, p1, k1, k1tbl, k2.
Row 9 (inc): K1, k2tog, yo, (k1, p1) 2 times, k1, M1L, k2—11 sts.
Row 10: Sl1 wyif, p2, (k1, p1) 2 times, k1, k1tbl, k2.
Row 11 (inc): K1, k2tog, yo, (k1, p1) 3 times, M1L, k2—12 sts.
Row 12: Sl1 wyif, p1, pm, p1, pm, (p1, k1) 3 times, k1tbl, k2.
Increases:
Row 1 (RS, dec): K1, k2tog, yo, (k1, p1) 3 times, sm, knit to M, M1L, sm, k2—1 st inc.

Row 2 (WS): Sl1 wyif, p1, sm, purl to M, sm, (p1, k1) 3 times, k1tbl, k2.
Rep [Rows 1 and 2] 18 more times; 19 sts inc, 31 sts total (20 sts between M).
Place Crown Beads:
Begin Beaded Crown chart, reading all RS (odd-numbered) rows from right to left and all WS (even-numbered) rows from left to right. Work [Rows 1–116] 1 time. At chart completion, 31 sts rem (21 sts between M; leftmost M has moved 1 st to the left).
Decreases:
Row 1 (RS, dec): K1, k2tog, yo, (k1, p1) 3 times, sm, knit to 2 sts before M, k2tog, sm, k1—1 st dec.
Row 2 (WS): Sl1 wyif, sm, purl to M, sm, (p1, k1) 3 times, k1tbl, k2.
Rep [Rows 1 and 2] 18 more times; 19 sts dec, 12 sts rem (2 sts between M).
Decrease Seed Edging:
Row 1 (RS, dec): K1, k2tog, yo, (k1, p1) 3 times, rm, k2tog, rm, k1—11 sts.
Row 2 (WS): Sl1 wyif, p1, (p1, k1) 3 times, k1tbl, k2.
Row 3 (dec): K1, k2tog, yo, (k1, p1) 2 times, k1, k2tog, k1—10 sts.
Row 4: Sl1 wyif, (p1, k1) 3 times, k1tbl, k2.
Row 5 (dec): K1, k2tog, yo, (k1, p1) 2 times, k2tog, k1—9 sts.
Row 6: Sl1 wyif, p1, (p1, k1) 2 times, k1tbl, k2.
Row 7 (dec): K1, k2tog, yo, k1, p1, k1, k2tog, k1—8 sts.
Row 8: Sl1 wyif, (p1, k1) 2 times, k1tbl, k2.

Row 9 (dec): K1, k2tog, yo, k1, p1, k2tog, k1—7 sts.

Row 10: Sl1 wyif, p2, k1, k1tbl, k2.

Row 11 (dec): K1, k2tog, yo, k1, k2tog, k1—6 sts.

Row 12: Sl1 wyif, p2, p1tbl, p1, k1.

Break MC. Leave 6 live sts on the needle, ready to work the next RS row.

BORDER OF SHAWL

Join CC.

K6, pick up and knit 109 sts along the bottom edge (1 for each slipped stitch edge of the body of the shawl), then pick up and knit 6 sts from the CO edge—121 sts total.

Setup Row 1 (WS, inc): (P1, M1RP) 2 times, purl to last 2 sts, (M1RP, p1) 2 times—125 sts.

Setup Row 2 (RS): K2tog, yo, k9, pm, (k8, pm) 13 times, k8, yo, ssk.

Setup Row 3 (WS): K1, k1tbl, purl to last 2 sts, k1tbl, k1 (sm as encountered).

Begin Verdant Border chart, reading all RS (odd-numbered) rows from right to left and all WS (even-numbered) rows from left to right. Work [Rows 1–29] 1 time (patt rep is worked 13 times)—245 sts total.

Switch to middle size needle. Work [Rows 30–75] 1 time.

With the WS facing, and using the largest needle to work across the row, BO as follows: *K2tog, k1, sl2 sts purlwise back to LHN; rep from * until 2 sts rem, k2tog.

Break yarn and pull tail through rem st to secure.

FINISHING

Weave in all loose ends but do not trim. Wet block the shawl to measurements, using blocking pins to pin out the points of the shawl border. When completely dry, remove blocking pins and trim all yarn tails.

"Well, here at last, dear friends, on the shores of the sea comes the end of our fellowship in Middle-earth. Go in peace! I will not say: do not weep for not all tears are an evil."

–Gandalf, *The Lord of the Rings: The Return of the King* by J.R.R. Tolkien

VERDANT BORDER CHART

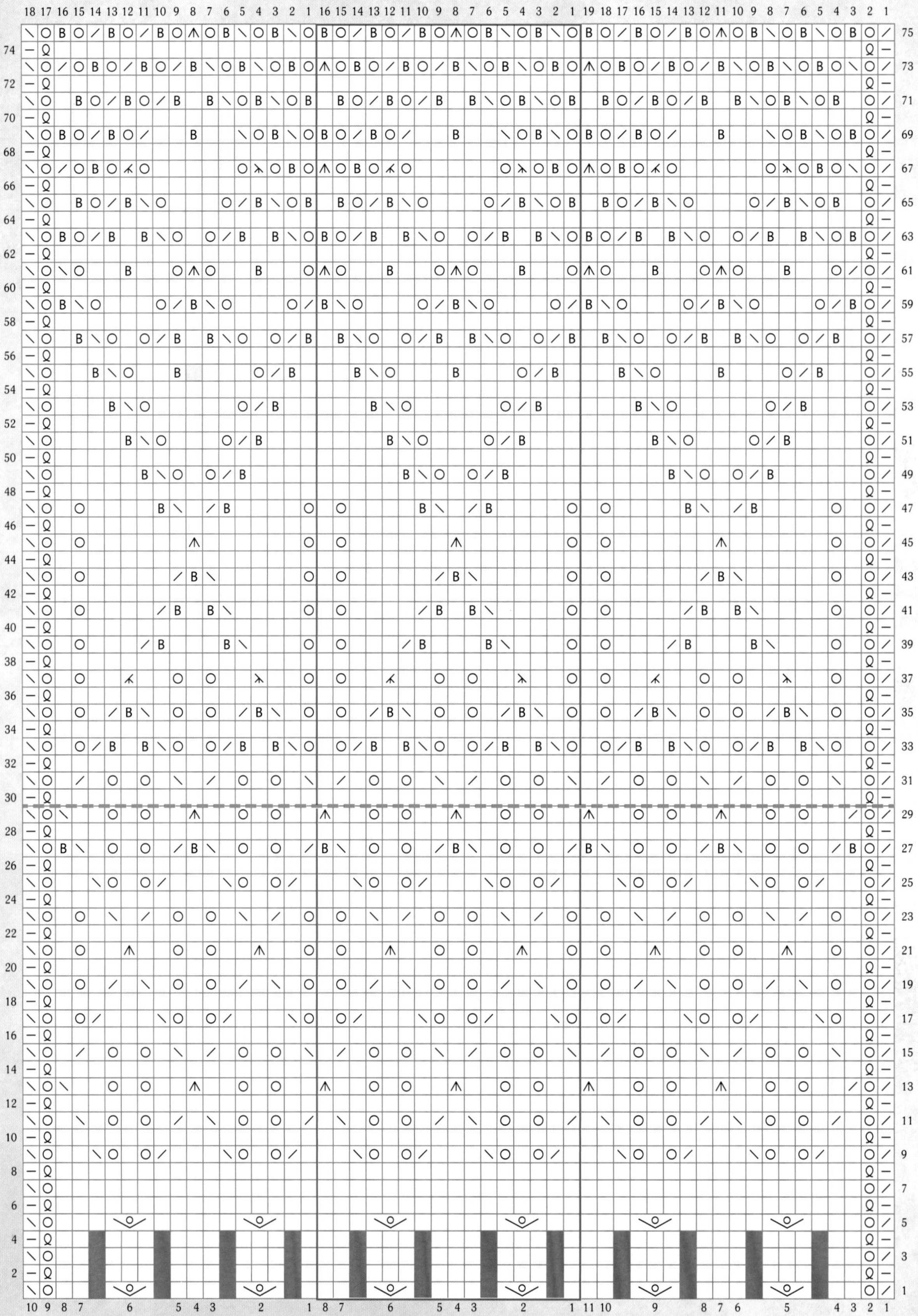

BEADED CROWN CHART

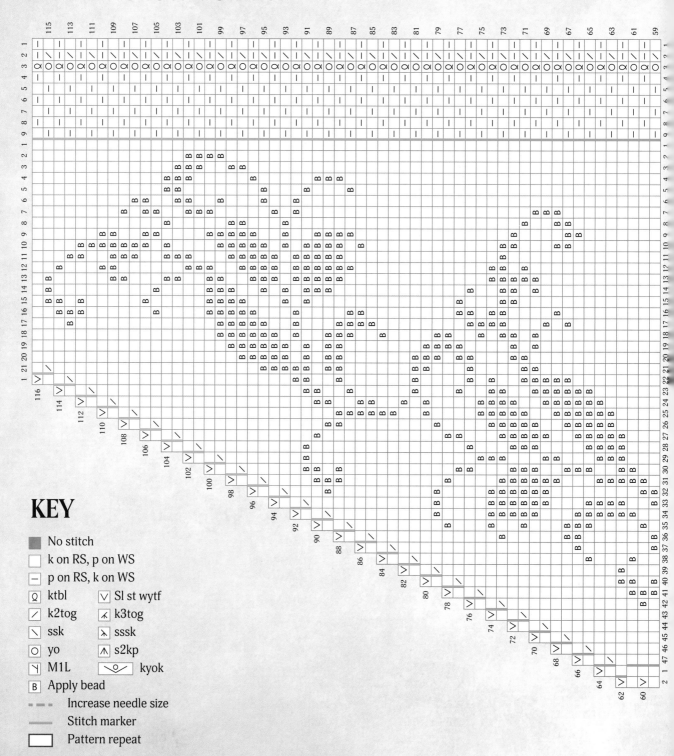

KEY

■	No stitch
□	k on RS, p on WS
−	p on RS, k on WS
Ω	ktbl
╱	k2tog
╲	ssk
O	yo
⋁	M1L
B	Apply bead
- - -	Increase needle size
——	Stitch marker
▭	Pattern repeat
⋁	Sl st wytf
⋏	k3tog
⋌	sssk
⋀	s2kp
⌣	kyok

BEADED CROWN CHART

ELVEN HERITAGE PULLOVER

DESIGNED BY RUTH NGUYEN

Reforged by the Elves in Rivendell with the pieces of Isildur's broken sword Narsil, Andúril was re-formed after Arwen pleads with her father, Elrond. Engraved with "*Anar. Nányë Andúril I né Narsil i macil Elendilo. Lercuvantan i móli Mordórëo. Isil,*" Elvish for "*Sun. I am Andúril who was once Narsil, sword of Elendil. The slaves of Mordor shall flee from me. Moon,*" it can only be wielded by Isildur's heir, Aragorn. It is this renamed sword in the hands of the rightful king of Gondor that calls upon the Army of the Dead for aid in battle.

This pullover pays tribute to the skills of the Elves, who are known for their artistry and craft, and to the markings on the hilt of Andúril. The sweater is worked in the round from the top down beginning with an i-cord cast on, with intricate cables on the yoke and sleeves to mimic a breastplate and vambraces, echoed by simple i-cord trim. German short rows gently raise the back neck for a better fit, and the body is finished neatly with a folded hem.

SIZES

1 (2, 3, 4, 5) [6, 7, 8, 9] {10, 11, 12, 13}

FINISHED MEASUREMENTS

Chest Circumference: 34½ (37½, 40, 43¼, 46½) [49½, 52, 55¼, 58½] {61½, 64, 67½, 70½} in. / 86.5 (95.5, 101.5, 110, 118) [126, 132, 140.5, 148.5] {156, 162.5, 171, 179} cm

Garment designed to be worn with 2 to 4 in. / 5 to 10 cm positive ease.

The garment is a size 2 modeled on a 36 in. / 91 cm bust.

YARN

DK weight yarn, shown in SweetGeorgia Yarns *Mohair Silk DK* (12-ply; 90% superwash merino, 5% super kid mohair, 5% silk; 218 yd. / 200 m per 3½ oz. / 100 g hank), 5 (5, 5, 5, 6) [6, 7, 7, 8] {8, 9, 10, 10} hanks in color Slate

NEEDLES

US 4 / 3.5 mm set of double-pointed needles

US 6 / 4 mm, 16 to 40 in. / 40 to 100 cm long circular needles and set of double-pointed needles or size needed to obtain gauge

NOTIONS

4 stitch markers (1 unique for BOR)

Cable needle

Waste yarn or stitch holders

Row counter (optional)

Tapestry needle

GAUGE

20 sts and 28 rnds = 4 in. / 10 cm in stockinette stitch in the round on larger needle, taken after blocking

Make sure you check your gauge.

PATTERN NOTES

This pullover is worked from the top down, in the round. A small amount of seaming (whipstitch) is used to secure the folded hem at the bottom of the garment.

The neckline edge is cast on using the i-cord cast on. Stitches are picked up along the edge of the i-cord and joined to work in the round. Once the yoke is complete, stitches are placed on hold for the sleeves and the body is completed. The sleeves are worked in the round, outward from the sweater, after the body is complete.

When the circumference of the yoke becomes too large for the shorter circular needle, switch to a longer needle as needed for comfort.

Throughout the yoke increases, the beginning of round will be behind the left shoulder. Before the short rows, the beginning of round moves to the center back. References to right and left are relative to how the garment is worn on the body, not how it appears laid flat.

Instructions are written for size 1 first, with additional sizes in parentheses, brackets, and braces. When only one number is provided, it applies to all sizes in that instruction.

Written instructions are provided for the construction of the garment; charts are provided for the yoke shaping/patterning and sleeve cable pattern.

PATTERN INSTRUCTIONS

CAST ON

Using smaller dpns, CO 4 sts using the Knitted cast on method. Do not join to work in the rnd.

Work a 4-stitch i-cord for 108 (112, 120, 120, 124) [124, 124, 128, 132] {132, 136, 136, 136} rows.

BO the i-cord knitwise. Do not break yarn.

With 16 in. / 40 cm circular needle, and beginning where the working yarn is attached to the bind off edge, pick up and knit 108 (112, 120, 120, 124) [124, 124, 128, 132] {132, 136, 136, 136} sts into the long edge of i-cord (1 st for every row). Pm (unique M) for BOR and join to work in the rnd. The BOR M will be at the back of the left shoulder.

YOKE

Sizes 1–5 ONLY:

Setup Rnd 1: *Work Rnd 1 of yoke Chart A across 40 sts, pm, k14 (16, 20, 20, 22) [-, -, -, -] {-, -, -, -}, pm; rep from * once more (the final marker will be the BOR M).

40 sts for each Front and Back

14 (16, 20, 20, 22) [-, -, -, -] {-, -, -, -} sts for each Sleeve.

Sizes 6–10 ONLY:

Setup Rnd 1 (inc): *Work Rnd 1 of yoke Chart B across 34 sts, pm, k- (-, -, -, -) [28, 28, 30, 32] {32, -, -, -}, pm; rep from * once

more (the final marker will be the BOR M)—8 sts inc;

- (-, -, -, -) [132, 132, 136, 140] {140, -, -, -} sts total:

38 sts for each Front and Back

- (-, -, -, -) [28, 28, 30, 32] {32, -, -, -} sts for each Sleeve.

Sizes 11–13 ONLY:

Setup Rnd 1 (inc): *Work Rnd 1 of yoke Chart B across 34 sts, pm, (k7, kfb, k8, kfb) 2 times, pm; rep from * once more (the final marker will be the BOR M)—16 sts inc; 152 sts total:

38 sts for each Front and Back

38 sts for each Sleeve.

All Sizes:

For the remainder of the charted yoke shaping, Sizes 1–5 will work yoke Chart A across the Front and Back of the yoke; sizes 6–13 will work yoke Chart B across the Front and Back of the yoke.

Rnd A: *Work next rnd of yoke chart for your size to M, sm, knit to M, sm; rep from * once more.

Rep [Rnd A] 0 (0, 0, 0, 0) [2, 2, 2, 2] {2, 2, 2, 2} more times, ending after Chart Rnd 2 (2, 2, 2, 2) [4, 4, 4, 4] {4, 4, 4, 4}—0 (0, 0, 0, 0) [28, 28, 28, 28] {28, 28, 28, 28} sts inc;

108 (112, 120, 120, 124) [160, 160, 164, 168] {168, 180, 180, 180} sts total:

40 (40, 40, 40, 40) [52, 52, 52, 52] {52, 52, 52, 52} sts for each Front and Back

14 (16, 20, 20, 22) [28, 28, 30, 32] {32, 38, 38, 38} sts for each Sleeve.

Sleeve Inc 1: *Work next rnd of yoke chart for your size to M, sm, k1 (0, 0, 0, 1) [2, 2, 2, 1] {0, 1, 1, 1}, [k2 (2, 2, 2, 2) [2, 2, 2, 2] {2, 2, 2, 1}, M1L, k2] 3 (4, 5, 5, 5) [6, 6, 7, 8] {8, 9, 9, 12} times, k1 (0, 0, 0, 1) [2, 2, 1, 0] {0, 1, 1, 1}, sm; rep from * once more—30 (32, 34, 34, 34) [28, 28, 30, 32] {32, 34, 34, 40} sts inc; 138 (144, 154, 154, 158) [188, 188, 194, 200] {200, 214, 214, 220} sts total: 52 (52, 52, 52, 52) [60, 60, 60, 60] {60, 60, 60, 60} sts for each Front and Back

17 (20, 25, 25, 27) [34, 34, 37, 40] {40, 47, 47, 50} sts for each Sleeve.

Rep [Rnd A] 1 (1, 1, 1, 5) [3, 3, 3, 3] {5, 5, 5, 5} time(s), ending after Chart Rnd 4 (4, 4, 4, 8) [8, 8, 8, 8] {10, 10, 10, 10}—0 (0, 0, 0, 16) [12, 12, 12, 12] {20, 20, 20, 20} sts inc; 138 (144, 154, 154, 174) [200, 200, 206, 212] {220, 234, 234, 240} sts total: 52 (52, 52, 52, 60) [66, 66, 66, 66] {70, 70, 70, 70} sts for each Front and Back

17 (20, 25, 25, 27) [34, 34, 37, 40] {40, 47, 47, 50} sts for each Sleeve.

Sleeve Inc 2: *Work next rnd of yoke chart for your size to M, sm, k1 (0, 0, 0, 1) [2, 2, 1, 0] {0, 1, 1, 1}, [k2, M1L, k3 (3, 3, 3, 2) [3, 3, 3, 3] {3, 3, 2, 2}] 3 (4, 5, 5, 6) [6, 6, 7, 8] {8, 9, 11, 12} times, k1 (0, 0, 0, 2) [2, 2, 1, 0] {0, 1, 2, 1}, sm; rep from * once more—14 (16, 18, 18, 24) [20, 20, 22, 24] {20, 22, 26, 28} sts inc; 152 (160, 172, 172, 198)

[220, 220, 228, 236] {240, 256, 260, 268} sts total: 56 (56, 56, 56, 66) [70, 70, 70, 70] {72, 72, 72, 72} sts for each Front and Back

20 (24, 30, 30, 33) [40, 40, 44, 48] {48, 56, 58, 62} sts for each Sleeve.

Rep [Rnd A] 3 (5, 5, 7, 7) [7, 7, 9, 9] {9, 9, 11, 11} times, ending after Chart Rnd 8 (10, 10, 12, 16) [16, 16, 18, 18] {20, 20, 22, 22}—8 (20, 20, 20, 12) [16, 16, 20, 20] {28, 28, 28, 28} sts inc; 160 (180, 192, 192, 210) [236, 236, 248, 256] {268, 284, 288, 296} sts total: 60 (66, 66, 66, 72) [78, 78, 80, 80] {86, 86, 86, 86} sts for each Front and Back

20 (24, 30, 30, 33) [40, 40, 44, 48] {48, 56, 58, 62} sts for each Sleeve.

Sleeve Inc 3: *Work next rnd of yoke chart for your size to M, sm, k1 (0, 0, 0, 0) [2, 2, 2, 1] {1, 4, 3, 3}, [k3 (3, 3, 2, 2) [2, 2, 2, 2] {2, 2, 2, 2}, M1L, k3 (3, 3, 3, 2) [3, 3, 3, 3] {3, 2, 2, 2}] 3 (4, 5, 6, 8) [7, 7, 8, 9] {9, 12, 13, 14} times, k1 (0, 0, 0, 1) [3, 3, 2, 2] {2, 4, 3, 3}, sm; rep from * once more—18 (8, 10, 16, 20) [18, 18, 28, 30] {18, 24, 26, 28} sts inc; 178 (188, 202, 208, 230) [254, 254, 276, 286] {286, 308, 314, 324} sts total: 66 (66, 66, 68, 74) [80, 80, 86, 86] {86, 86, 86, 86} sts for each Front and Back

23 (28, 35, 36, 41) [47, 47, 52, 57] {57, 68, 71, 76} sts for each Sleeve.

Rep [Rnd A] 7 (7, 7, 9, 9) [9, 9, 11, 11] {11, 11, 13, 13} times, ending after Chart Rnd 16 (18, 18, 22, 26)

[26, 26, 30, 30] {32, 32, 36, 36}—12 (16, 16, 12, 24) [16, 16, 28, 28] {28, 28, 32, 32} sts inc; 190 (204, 218, 220, 254) [270, 270, 304, 314] {314, 336, 346, 356} sts total: 72 (74, 74, 74, 86) [88, 88, 100, 100] {100, 100, 102, 102} sts for each Front and Back

23 (28, 35, 36, 41) [47, 47, 52, 57] {57, 68, 71, 76} sts for each Sleeve.

Sleeve Inc 4: *Work next rnd of yoke chart for your size to M, sm, k1 (0, 0, 0, 0) [2, 2, 2, 1] {1, 4, 3, 3}, [k4 (4, 4, 3, 2) [3, 3, 3, 3] {3, 3, 3, 3}, M1L, k3 (3, 3, 3, 3) [3, 3, 3, 3] {3, 2, 2, 2}] 3 (4, 5, 6, 8) [7, 7, 8, 9] {9, 12, 13, 14} times, k1 (0, 0, 0, 1) [3, 3, 2, 2] {2, 4, 3, 3}, sm; rep from * once more—10 (8, 10, 12, 16) [14, 14, 16, 18] {18, 24, 26, 28} sts inc; 200 (212, 228, 232, 270) [284, 284, 320, 332] {332, 360, 372, 384} sts total: 74 (74, 74, 74, 86) [88, 88, 100, 100] {100, 100, 102, 102} sts for each Front and Back

26 (32, 40, 42, 49) [54, 54, 60, 66] {66, 80, 84, 90} sts for each Sleeve.

Rep [Rnd A] 7 (7, 9, 9, 9) [9, 9, 13, 13] {13, 13, 15, 15} times, ending after Chart Rnd 24 (26, 28, 32, 36) [36, 36, 44, 44] {46, 46, 52, 52}—0 (24, 24, 24, 4) [28, 28, 40, 40] {40, 40, 36, 36} sts inc; 200 (236, 252, 256, 274) [312, 312, 360, 372] {372, 400, 408, 420} sts total: 74 (86, 86, 86, 88) [102, 102, 120, 120] {120, 120, 120,

120} sts for each Front and Back

26 (32, 40, 42, 49) [54, 54, 60, 66] {66, 80, 84, 90} sts for each Sleeve.

Sleeve Inc 5: *Work next rnd of yoke chart for your size to M, sm, k1 (0, 0, 0, 0) [2, 2, 2, 1] {0, 4, 3, 3}, [k4 (4, 4, 4, 2) [4, 4, 4, 4] {3, 3, 3, 3}, M1L, k4 (4, 4, 3, 2) [3, 3, 3, 3] {3, 3, 3, 3}] 3 (4, 5, 6, 12) [7, 7, 8, 9] {11, 12, 13, 14} times, k1 (0, 0, 0, 1) [3, 3, 2, 2] {0, 4, 3, 3}, sm; rep from * once more—30 (8, 10, 12, 24) [14, 14, 16, 18] {22, 24, 26, 28} sts inc; 230 (244, 262, 268, 298) [326, 326, 376, 390] {394, 424, 434, 448} sts total: 86 (86, 86, 86, 88) [102, 102, 120, 120] {120, 120, 120, 120} sts for each Front and Back

29 (36, 45, 48, 61) [61, 61, 68, 75] {77, 92, 97, 104} sts for each Sleeve.

Rep [Rnd A] 9 (11, 11, 13, 13) [13, 13, 13, 13] {13, 13, 9, 9} times, ending after Chart Rnd 34 (38, 40, 46, 50) [50, 50, 58, 58] {60, 60, 62, 62}—0 (4, 28, 28, 24) [36, 36, 0, 0] {0, 0, 0, 0} sts inc; 230 (248, 290, 296, 322) [362, 362, 376, 390] {394, 424, 434, 448} sts total: 86 (88, 100, 100, 100) [120, 120, 120, 120] {120, 120, 120, 120} sts for each Front and Back

29 (36, 45, 48, 61) [61, 61, 68, 75] {77, 92, 97, 104} sts for each Sleeve.

Sizes 12 & 13 ONLY:

Rnd B: *Knit to M, sm; rep from * 3 more times.

Rep [Rnd B] 5 more times.

Sizes 1–11 ONLY:

Sleeve Inc 6: *Work next rnd of yoke chart for your size to M, sm, k1 (0, 0, 0, 3) [0, 0, 1, 1] {1, 2, -, -}, [k5 (3, 5, 2, 2) {30, 30, 6, 4} {2, 6, -, -}, M1L, k4 (3, 4, 2, 3) [30, 30, 5, 4] {3, 5, -, -}] 3 (6, 5, 12, 11) [1, 1, 6, 9] {15, 8, -, -} time(s), k1 (0, 0, 0, 3) [1, 1, 1, 2] {1, 2, -, -}, sm; rep from * once more—10 (36, 10, 24, 22) [2, 2, 12, 18] {30, 16, -, -} sts inc; 240 (284, 300, 320, 344) [364, 364, 388, 408] {424, 440, -, -} sts total:

88 (100, 100, 100, 100) [120, 120, 120, 120] {120, 120, -, -} sts for each Front and Back

32 (42, 50, 60, 72) [62, 62, 74, 84] {92, 100, -, -} sts for each Sleeve.

Rep [Rnd A] 21 (17, 15, 9, 5) [11, 11, 3, 3] {1, 1, -, -} time(s), ending after Chart Rnd 56 (56, 56, 56, 56) [62, 62, 62, 62] {62, 62, -, -}—24 (0, 0, 0, 0) [0, 0, 0, 0] {0, 0, -, -} sts inc; 264 (284, 300, 320, 344) [364, 364, 388, 408] {424, 440, -, -} sts total:

100 (100, 100, 100, 100) [120, 120, 120, 120] {120, 120, -, -} sts for each Front and Back

32 (42, 50, 60, 72) [62, 62, 74, 84] {92, 100, -, -} sts for each Sleeve.

Proceed to Finish Yoke.

Sizes 12 & 13 ONLY:

Sleeve Inc 6: *Knit to M, sm, k- (-, -, -, -) [-, -, -, -] {-, -, 3, 4}, [k3, M1L, k3] - (-, -, -, -) [-, -, -, -] {-, -, 15, 16} times, k4, sm; rep from * once more— - (-, -, -, -) [-,

-, -, -] {-, -, 30, 32} sts inc; - (-, -, -, -) [-, -, -, -] {-, -, 464, 480} sts total:

- (-, -, -, -) [-, -, -, -] {-, -, 120, 120} sts for each Front and Back

- (-, -, -, -) [-, -, -, -] {-, -, 112, 120} sts for each Sleeve.

FINISH YOKE

All Sizes:
If necessary, work in St st (knit every rnd), rm all M except BOR M, until the Yoke measures 8 (8, 8, 8½, 8½) [9, 10, 10½, 11] {11½, 12, 12¼, 12½} in. / 20.5 (20.5, 20.5, 21.5, 21.5) [23, 25.5, 26.5, 28] {29, 30.5, 31, 32} cm from the picked-up edge of the i-cord collar, or to desired length.

SHORT ROWS

Setup Rnd: Remove BOR M, k50 (50, 50, 50, 50) [60, 60, 60, 60] {60, 60, 60, 60}, pm for new BOR. BOR is now at center back.

Short Row 1 (RS): K23 (24, 25, 28, 29) [30, 30, 34, 35] {35, 29, 31, 30}, turn.

Short Row 2 (WS): DS, purl to BOR M, p23 (24, 25, 28, 29) [30, 30, 34, 35] {35, 29, 31, 30}, turn.

Short Row 3: DS, knit to BOR M, sm, knit to prev DS, kDS, k21 (23, 25, 26, 28) [30, 30, 32, 34] {35, 27, 28, 30}, turn.

Short Row 4: DS, purl to BOR M, sm, purl to prev DS, pDS, p21 (23, 25, 26, 28) [30, 30, 32, 34] {35, 27, 28, 30}, turn.

Rep [Short Rows 3 and 4] 1 (1, 1, 1, 1) [1, 1, 1, 1] {1, 2,

2, 2} more time(s).

Next Row (RS): Knit to BOR.

Next Rnd: Knit, processing rem DS as kDS when encountered.

SEPARATE SLEEVES & BODY

K41 (44, 47, 50, 53) [56, 57, 61, 65] {68, 71, 75, 78}, place the next 50 (54, 56, 60, 66) [70, 68, 72, 74] {76, 78, 82, 84} sts on waste yarn or stitch holder for the right sleeve, CO 4 (6, 6, 8, 10) [12, 16, 16, 16] {18, 18, 18, 20} sts using the Backward Loop cast on method, k82 (88, 94, 100, 106) [112, 114, 122, 130] {136, 142, 150, 156}, place the next 50 (54, 56, 60, 66) [70, 68, 72, 74] {76, 78, 82, 84} sts on waste yarn or stitch holder for the left sleeve, CO 4 (6, 6, 8, 10) [12, 16, 16, 16] {18, 18, 18, 20} sts using the Backward Loop cast on method, knit to BOR—172 (188, 200, 216, 232) [248, 260, 276, 292] {308, 320, 336, 352} sts rem.

BODY

Cont in St st until the body measures 14 in. / 35.5 cm from the underarm, or to desired length.

Purl 1 rnd.
Knit 6 rnds.
BO all sts loosely knitwise.

SLEEVES (MAKE 2 THE SAME)

Read carefully through the following instructions before beginning.

Place the 50 (54, 56, 60, 66) [70, 68, 72, 74] {76, 78, 82, 84} sts of one sleeve onto the set of larger dpns and distribute evenly.

Starting at the center of the underarm CO sts, join the working yarn and pick up and knit 2 (3, 3, 4, 5) [6, 8, 8, 8] {9, 9, 9, 10} sts, k15 (17, 18, 20, 23) [25, 24, 26, 27] {28, 29, 31, 32} live sts, pm, k20, pm, k15 (17, 18, 20, 23) [25, 24, 26, 27] {28, 29, 31, 32} rem live sts, then pick up and knit 2 (3, 3, 4, 5) [6, 8, 8, 8] {9, 9, 9, 10} more sts, pm for BOR and join to work in the rnd—54 (60, 62, 68, 76) [82, 84, 88, 90] {94, 96, 100, 104} sts total. *The top of sleeve markers placed will indicate the Sleeve chart panel location.*

Knit 17 (13, 13, 11, 9) [8, 8, 7, 7] {7, 7, 7, 7} rnds even, sm as encountered.

Dec Rnd: K1, k2tog, knit to last 3 sts (sm as encountered), ssk, k1—2 sts dec.

Cont in St st until the sleeve measures 18 in. / 46 cm, or to desired length, repeating the Dec Rnd every 15 (11, 11, 9, 7) [6, 6, 5, 5] {5, 5, 5, 5}th rnd 6 (9, 9, 11, 15) [17, 18, 19, 19] {20, 20, 21, 22} more times—14 (20, 20, 24, 32) [36, 38, 40, 40] {42, 42, 44, 46} total sts dec; 40 (40, 42, 44, 44) [46, 46, 48, 50] {52, 54, 56, 58} sts rem.

AT THE SAME TIME, when the sleeve measures 12 in. / 30.5 cm from the underarm (or 6 in. / 15 cm short of the desired total length), begin working the Sleeve chart as follows:

Sleeve Chart Rnd: Work est patt to M, sm, work Sleeve chart over the next 20 sts, sm, work est patt to end of rnd.

Rep the Sleeve Chart Rnd until all 42 sleeve chart rnds are complete.

Switch to smaller dpns and BO all sts using I-Cord bind off method.

FINISHING

Using the tapestry needle and remaining tails, whipstitch the ends of any i-cords together.

Weave in all rem ends. Wet block to dimensions, noting that the body length from the underarm will be 1 in. / 2.5 cm longer than specified on the schematic. Once dry, trim all ends.

Thread the tapestry needle with a length of yarn approx. 2 times the bottom circumference of the sweater. Fold the hem at the purl ridge and whipstitch bound-off edge to inside of garment.

Schematic

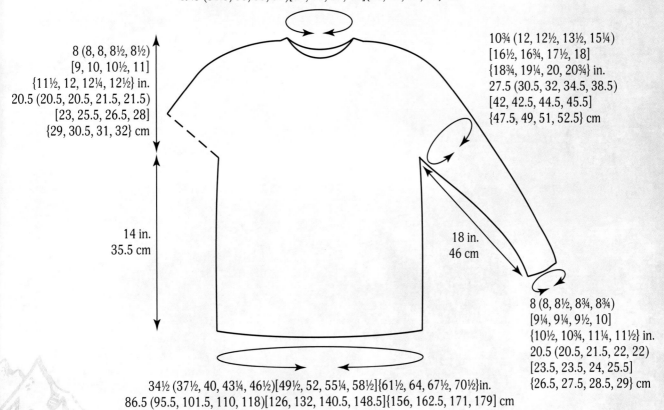

19½ (20¼, 21¾, 21¾, 22½)[22½, 22½, 23¼, 24]{24, 24¾, 24¾, 24¾} in.
49.5 (51.5, 55, 55, 57)[57, 57, 59, 61]{61, 63, 63, 63} cm

8 (8, 8, 8½, 8½)
[9, 10, 10½, 11]
{11½, 12, 12¼, 12½} in.
20.5 (20.5, 20.5, 21.5, 21.5)
[23, 25.5, 26.5, 28]
{29, 30.5, 31, 32} cm

10¾ (12, 12½, 13½, 15¼)
[16½, 16¾, 17½, 18]
{18¾, 19¼, 20, 20¾} in.
27.5 (30.5, 32, 34.5, 38.5)
[42, 42.5, 44.5, 45.5]
{47.5, 49, 51, 52.5} cm

14 in.
35.5 cm

18 in.
46 cm

8 (8, 8½, 8¾, 8¾)
[9¼, 9¼, 9½, 10]
{10½, 10¾, 11¼, 11½} in.
20.5 (20.5, 21.5, 22, 22)
[23.5, 23.5, 24, 25.5]
{26.5, 27.5, 28.5, 29} cm

34½ (37½, 40, 43¼, 46½)[49½, 52, 55¼, 58½]{61½, 64, 67½, 70½}in.
86.5 (95.5, 101.5, 110, 118)[126, 132, 140.5, 148.5]{156, 162.5, 171, 179] cm

"Very bright was that sword when it was made whole again; the light of the sun shone redly in it, and the light of the moon shone cold, its edge was hard and keen. And Aragorn gave it a new name and called it Andúril, Flame of the West."

— The Lord of the Rings: The Fellowship of the Ring by J.R.R. Tolkien

KEY

■ No stitch	M1L	k2tog
□ purl	M1LP	ssk
− k tbl	M1R	p2tog
Q 1/1 LC	M1RP	p2tog tbl
1/1 RC	1/1 LPT	1/1 LT
1/2 LT	1/1 RPT	1/1 RT
1/2 RC	1/2 LPT	
1/2 RC	1/2 RPT	
2/1 LC	2/1 LPC	
2/1 RC	2/1 RPC	
2/2 LC	2/2 LPC	
2/2 RC	2/2 RPC	
2/3 LC	2/3 LPC	
2/3 RC	2/3 RPC	

SLEEVE CHART

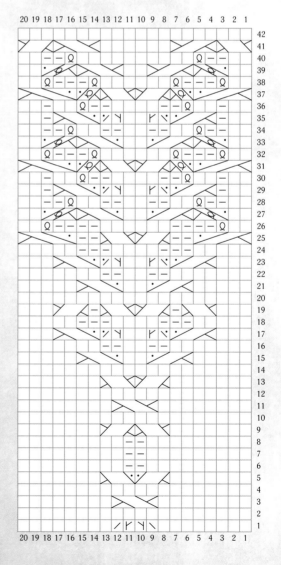

CHART A

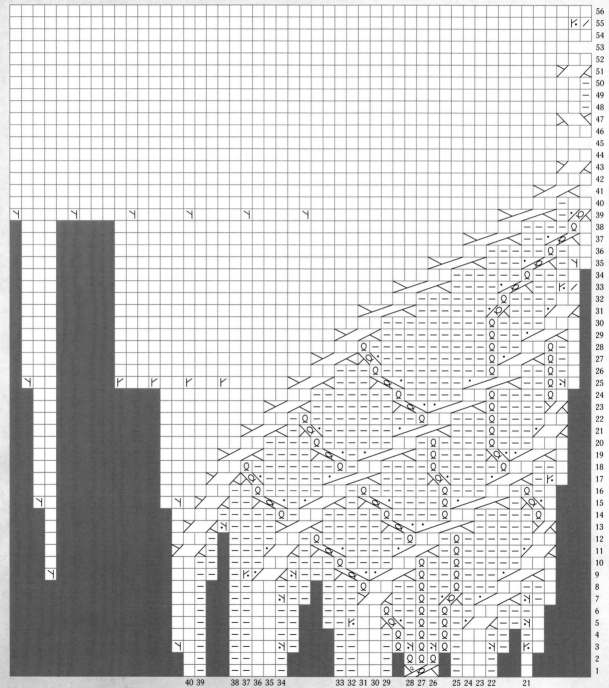

CHART A

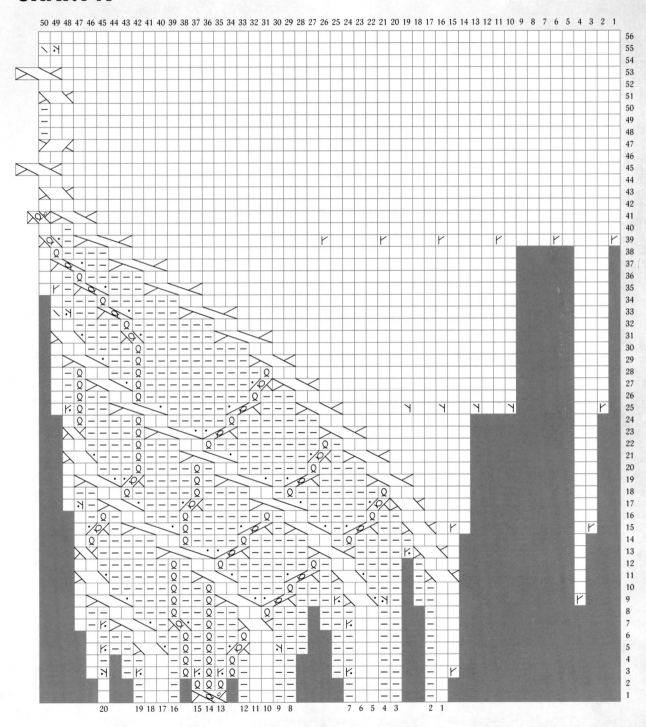

CHART B

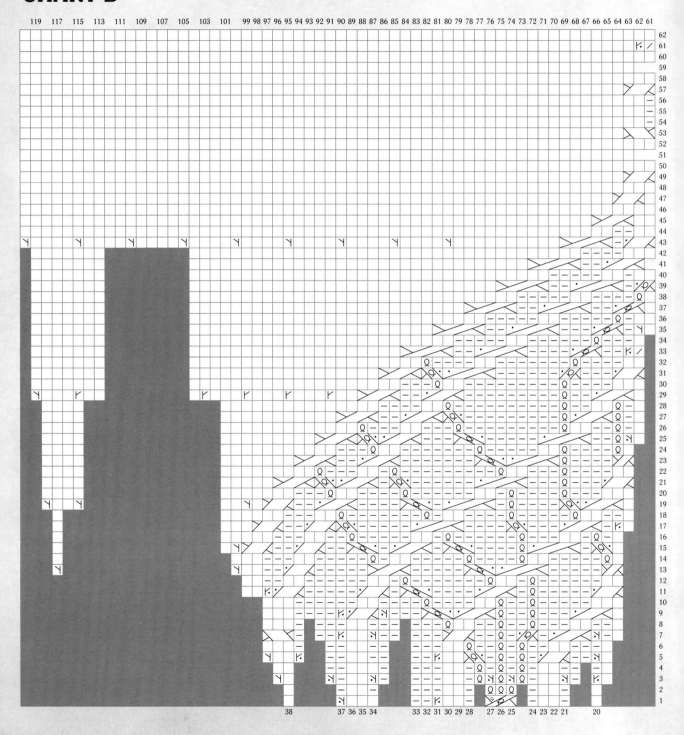

HART B

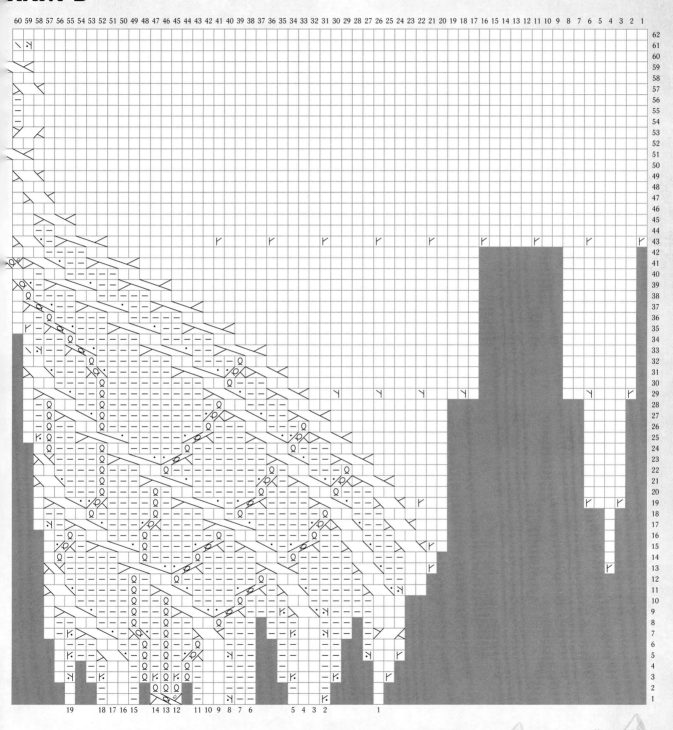

WOODLAND REALM COWL

DESIGNED BY TANIS GRAY

Legolas, one of the nine members of the Fellowship, is a Silvan Elf. From a kingdom located in Mirkwood in the Woodland Realm, Silvan Elves are descendants of Avarin and Nandorin Elves and are considered the most dangerous type of Elf. A master archer and prince, Legolas (Silvan for "greenleaf") brings his skills with a bow and arrow, lightness of foot, exceptional eyesight, and superb hearing to the Fellowship, often leading the group as its "eyes and ears." Despite their fathers' dislike for each other, Legolas and Gimli become unlikely friends, traveling together until their final journey many years later to the Undying Lands.

Wrap a bit of Mirkwood flora around your neck when wearing this botanically inspired cowl. Twisted stitches and buds on a backdrop of reverse stockinette dance across this cowl, which is worked in the round seamlessly and flanked by garter edges. Woodland buds are created by cabling and decreasing simultaneously. It's easy to add more height with additional repeats. Wear this cowl on your next adventure!

> "Legolas Greenleaf, long under tree, in joy thou hast lived. Beware of the Sea! If thou hearest the cry of the gull on the shore, thy heart shall then rest in the forest no more."
>
> —Galadriel's message to Legolas, *The Lord of the Rings: The Two Towers* by J.R.R. Tolkien

SIZES
One size

FINISHED MEASUREMENTS
Circumference: 31½ in. / 80 cm

Height: 7¾ in. / 19.5 cm

YARN
Fingering weight yarn, shown in Miss Babs Hand-Dyed Yarns *Estrellita* (92% superwash merino wool, 8% Lurex; 400 yd. / 365 m per 4 oz. / 115 g hank), 1 hank in color Rock Sparrow

NEEDLES
US 1 / 2.25 mm, 24 in. / 60 cm long circular needle

US 3 / 3.25 mm, 24 in. / 60 cm long circular needle or size needed to obtain gauge

NOTIONS
Stitch markers (1 unique for BOR; 26 optional for separating stitch pattern repeats)

Cable needle

Tapestry needle

GAUGE
31 sts and 42 rnds = 4 in. / 10 cm in stitch pattern in the round on larger needles, blocked

Make sure to check your gauge.

PATTERN NOTES
The cowl is worked in the round, seamlessly, from bottom to top.

Garter stitch top and bottom edging is worked on the smaller needles (2 US sizes smaller than gauge).

The branching stitch pattern is worked on the larger, gauge-size needles and makes up the body of the cowl.

Written instructions are provided for the entirety of the pattern; an optional chart is provided for the stitch pattern in the body of the cowl.

It may be helpful to place a marker between each chart repeat in the body of the cowl. Use a unique marker for the BOR.

The stitch counts fluctuate as the charted stitch pattern is worked. Stitch counts are provided at the end of the increase and decrease rounds in the written Branch Pattern instructions.

PATTERN STITCHES

Branch Pattern (worked over a multiple of 9 sts)

Rnds 1 and 2: *P4, k1tbl, p1, k1tbl, p2; rep from * to end.

Rnd 3 (inc): *P4, kyok, p1, k1tbl, p2; rep from * to end—297 sts.

Rnd 4: *P4, sl3 wyib, p1, k1tbl, p2; rep from * to end.

Rnd 5 (dec): *P2, 2/3 RPCDEC, p1, k1tbl, p2; rep from * to end—243 sts.

Rnd 6: *P4, k1tbl, p1, k1tbl, p2; rep from * to end.

Rnd 7 (inc): *P4, k1tbl, p1, kyok, p2; rep from * to end—297 sts.

Rnd 8: *P4, k1tbl, p1, sl3 wyib, p2; rep from * to end.

Rnd 9 (dec): *P4, k1tbl, p1, 2/3 LPCDEC; rep from * to end—243 sts.

Rnd 10: *P4, k1tbl, p1, k1tbl, p2; rep from * to end.

Rep Rnds 1–10 for patt.

PATTERN INSTRUCTIONS

CAST ON & BOTTOM EDGING

Using smaller needle, CO 243 sts using the Long Tail cast on method. Pm for BOR and join to work in the rnd, being careful not to twist the sts.

Rnd 1: Knit.
Rnd 2: Purl.
Rep [Rnds 1 and 2] 2 more times (6 rnds total).

BODY OF COWL

Switch to larger needles.
Begin Chart A (or work from written Branch Pattern instructions), reading all rows from right to left as for working in the rnd. Work [Rows 1–10] 7 times total (chart is repeated 27 times across each rnd).

TOP EDGING

Switch to smaller needles.
Rnd 1: Knit.
Rnd 2: Purl.
Rep [Rnds 1 and 2] 1 more time (4 rnds total).
Next Rnd: Knit.
BO all sts purlwise.

FINISHING

Weave in ends to the WS. Wet block the cowl to allow the sts to relax.

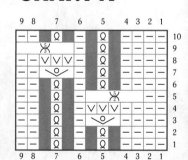

KEY

■	No stitch
−	purl
Q	ktbl
∨	Sl st purlwise wyib
⌣	kyok
⤬	2/3 LPCDEC
⤫	2/3 RPCDEC
☐	Pattern repeat

CHART A

LIGHT OF THE TWO TREES PULLOVER

DESIGNED BY DRAGON HOARD DESIGNS

Born in the Undying Lands in the Years of Trees, Galadriel rules over Lothlórien with her husband Celeborn. Astute and graceful, Galadriel has long golden hair that glows with the light of one of the Two Trees of Valinor. Said to have been the only source of light other than the stars at the beginning of creation, the Two Trees—Laurelin (gold) and Telperion (silver)—eventually became the sun and moon. The trees also divided the Elves in two groups—those who had seen the light and those who had not. Those who had seen the trees themselves are highly regarded and powerful Elves.

Shining with the grace and elegance fit for an Elven ruler, this Laurelin and Telperion inspired pullover is worked in the round from the top down, beginning with a tree canopy lace and bobbled neckline. German short rows raise the back neck up for a better fit. The sleeves are then put on waste yarn while the stockinette shaped torso is completed with a twisted rib, lace, and bobbled sapling motif at the bottom edge. The sleeves are then worked in stockinette and finished off with a matching cuff motif.

SIZES

1 (2, 3, 4, 5) [6, 7, 8, 9] {10, 11, 12, 13}

FINISHED MEASUREMENTS

Chest Circumference: 26½ (30¼, 33¾, 37¼, 40¾) [44½, 48, 51½, 55] {58½, 62¼, 65¾, 69¼} in. / 67.5 (77, 85.5, 94.5, 103.5) [113, 122, 131, 139.5] {148.5, 158, 167, 176} cm

The pullover is designed to be worn with 0 to 4 in. / 0 to 10 cm positive ease.

YARN

DK weight yarn, shown in Dragon Hoard Yarn *Storytime DK* (100% superwash Polwarth wool; 246 yd. / 225 m per 3½ oz. / 100 g hank), 4 (4, 5, 5, 6) [6, 7, 7, 8] {8, 9, 10, 10} hanks in color Feather

NEEDLES

US 4 / 3.5 mm, 24 to 40 in. / 60 to 100 cm long circular needles and needles of the same size for your preferred method of small circumference knitting

US 6 / 4 mm, 24 to 40 in. / 60 to 100 cm long circular needles and needles of the same size for your preferred method of small circumference knitting or size needed to obtain gauge

GAUGE

18 sts and 26½ rows = 4 in. / 10 cm in St st in the round on larger needles, taken after blocking

Make sure to check your gauge.

NOTIONS

Stitch markers (2; 1 unique for BOR)

Smooth waste yarn or stitch holders

Row counter (recommended)

Tapestry needle

PATTERN NOTES

This yoke-style sweater is knit top down in the round. When the yoke is complete, the sleeve stitches are put on hold and the rest of the body is completed. Once the body is complete, the sleeves are worked in the round, outward from the body, from the underarm to the cuff.

When the circumference of the yoke becomes too large for the shorter circular needle, switch to a longer needle as needed for comfort.

The smaller needle should be 2 sizes smaller than the larger needle when gauge is met. The smaller needles will be used for the lacework at the collar, hem, and cuff; the gauge-size / larger needles are used for the yoke, body, and sleeves.

Instructions are written for size 1 first, with additional sizes in parentheses, brackets, and braces. When only one number is provided, it applies to all sizes in that instruction.

Written instructions are provided for the construction of the garment; charts are provided for the lace collar, hem, and cuffs.

PATTERN INSTRUCTIONS

CAST ON

Using the smaller 24 in. / 60 cm long circular needle, CO 128 (128, 144, 144, 144) [160, 160, 160, 176] {176, 176, 176, 176} sts using Long Tail cast on method. Pm for BOR and join to work in the rnd, being careful not to twist your sts. *The BOR M is at the center back of the yoke.*

BEGIN YOKE

Cont with smaller needles. Begin Chart A, reading all rows from right to left as for working in the rnd. Work [Rows 1–13] 1 time (the chart is worked 8 (8, 9, 9, 9) [10, 10, 10, 11] {11, 11, 11, 11} times across each rnd).

Switch to larger needles. *Adjust needle length for comfort as the circumference of the yoke increases.*

Knit 1 rnd.

Inc Rnd #1

Size 1 ONLY: *K5, M1R; rep from * to last 3 sts, k3—153 sts.

Size 2 ONLY: *K4, M1R; rep from * to end of rnd—160 sts.

Size 3 ONLY: *K4, M1R; rep from * to end of rnd—180 sts.

Size 4 ONLY: *K3, M1R; rep from * to end of rnd—192 sts.

Size 5 ONLY: *K2, M1R, k3, M1R; rep from * to last 4 sts, k2, M1R, k2—201 sts.

Size 6 ONLY: *K2, M1R, k3, M1R; rep from * to end of rnd—224 sts.

Size 7 ONLY: *K2, M1R; rep from * to end of rnd—240 sts.

Size 8 ONLY: *K1, M1R, k2, M1R; rep from * to last 4 sts, k4—264 sts.

Size 9 ONLY: *K1, M1R, (k2, M1R) 2 times; rep from * to last st, k1—281 sts.

Sizes 10–13 ONLY: *K1, M1R, k2, M1R; rep from * to last st, k1, M1R—293 sts.

SHORT ROWS

Short Row 1 (RS): K47 (48, 54, 58, 61) [68, 72, 80, 85] {88, 88, 88, 88}, turn.

Short Row 2 (WS): DS, purl to M, sm, p47 (48, 54, 58, 61) [68, 72, 80, 85] {88, 88, 88, 88}, turn.

Short Row 3: DS, knit to prev DS, kDS, k10, turn.

Short Row 4: DS, purl to prev DS, pDS, p10, turn.

Short Row 5: DS, knit to prev DS, kDS, k8, turn.

Short Row 6: DS, purl to prev DS, pDS, p8, turn.

Short Row 7: DS, knit to prev DS, kDS, k6, turn.

Short Row 8: DS, purl to prev DS, pDS, p6, turn.

Short Row 9: DS, knit to BOR M.

Next Rnd (RS): Knit to end of rnd, working all rem DS as kDS.

Work 1½ in. / 4 cm in St st.

FINISH YOKE

Inc Rnd #2

Size 1 ONLY: *K10, M1R; rep from * to last 3 sts, k3—168 sts.

Size 2 ONLY: *K6, M1R, (k7, M1R) 2 times; rep from * to end of rnd—184 sts.

Size 3 ONLY: *K9, M1R; rep from * to end of rnd—200 sts.

Size 4 ONLY: *K8, M1R; rep from * to end of rnd—216 sts.

Size 5 ONLY: *(K5, M1R) 12 times, k7, M1R; rep from * to end of rnd—240 sts.

Size 6 ONLY: *K5, M1R, k6, M1R; rep from * to last 4 sts, k4—264 sts.

Size 7 ONLY: *K5, M1R, (k4, M1R) 3 times; rep from * to last 2 sts, k2—296 sts.

Size 8 ONLY: *K5, M1R, k6, M1R; rep from * to end of rnd—312 sts.

Size 9 ONLY: *(K5, M1R) 8 times, k6, M1R; rep from * to last 5 sts, k5, M1R—336 sts.

Size 10 ONLY: *(K5, M1R) 13 times, k4, M1R; rep from * to last 17 sts, (k5, M1R) 3 times, k2—352 sts.

Sizes 11–13 ONLY: *K4, M1R, k3, M1R; rep from * to last 6 sts, k4, M1R, k2—376 sts.

Work in St st until the yoke measures 5¼ (5¾, 6¼, 6½, 6¾) [7, 7¼, 7½, 7¾] {8, 8¼, 8½, 9} in. / 13.5 (14.5, 16, 16.5, 17) [18, 18.5, 19, 19.5] {20.5, 21, 21.5, 23} cm from the CO edge, or to desired length, before proceeding to the final inc rnd / separation of sleeves and body.

Inc Rnd #3

Sizes 1–11 ONLY: Proceed to Separate Sleeves & Body.

Size 12 ONLY: *(K19, M1R) 4 times, k18, M1R; rep from * to end of rnd—396 sts.

Size 13 ONLY: *(K10, M1R) 2 times, (k9, M1R) 3 times; rep from * to end of rnd—416 sts.

Sizes 12 & 13 ONLY: Knit 1 rnd. Proceed to Separate Sleeves & Body.

SEPARATE SLEEVES & BODY

Remove BOR M, k24 (27, 30, 33, 37) [40, 44, 47, 51] {54, 58, 62, 66}, place the next 36 (38, 40, 42, 46) [52, 60, 62, 66] {68, 72, 74, 76} sts on waste yarn or stitch holder for the right sleeve, CO 6 (7, 8, 9, 9) [10, 10, 11, 11] {12, 12, 12, 12} sts using the Backward Loop cast on method, pm for new BOR, CO 6 (7, 8, 9, 9) [10, 10, 11, 11] {12, 12, 12, 12} more sts, k48 (54, 60, 66, 74) [80, 88, 94, 102] {108, 116, 124, 132}, place the next 36 (38, 40, 42, 46) [52, 60, 62, 66] {68, 72, 74, 76} sts on waste yarn or stitch holder for the left sleeve, CO 6 (7, 8, 9, 9) [10, 10, 11, 11] {12, 12, 12, 12} sts using the Backward Loop cast on method, pm (SSM), CO 6 (7, 8, 9, 9) [10, 10, 11, 11] {12, 12, 12, 12} sts, knit to new BOR—120 (136, 152, 168, 184) [200, 216, 232, 248] {264, 280, 296, 312} sts rem. *The BOR M is now at the right underarm.*

BODY

Cont in St st until the body measures approx. 8¼ in. / 21 cm from the underarm (or 7¾ in. / 19.5 cm short of the desired total length).

BODY SHAPING

Inc Rnd: *K1, M1L, knit to 1 st before M, M1R, k1, sm; rep from * once more—4 sts inc.

Knit 12 rnds.

Rep from ** once more—128 (144, 160, 176, 192) [208, 224, 240, 256] {272, 288, 304, 320} sts total. Remove SSM.

HEM

Switch to smaller needles. Begin Chart B, reading all rows from right to left as for working in the rnd. Work [Rows 1–27] 1 time (the chart is worked 8 (9, 10, 11, 12) [13, 14, 15, 16] {17, 18, 19, 20} times across each rnd).

BO all sts loosely knitwise.

SLEEVES (MAKE 2 THE SAME)

Place the 36 (38, 40, 42, 46) [52, 60, 62, 66] {68, 72, 74, 76} sts of one sleeve onto the larger needles

KEY

- Knit
- Purl
- B MB3
- ktbl
- yo
- k2tog
- ssk
- k3tog
- k3tog tbl
- Pattern repeat

CHART A

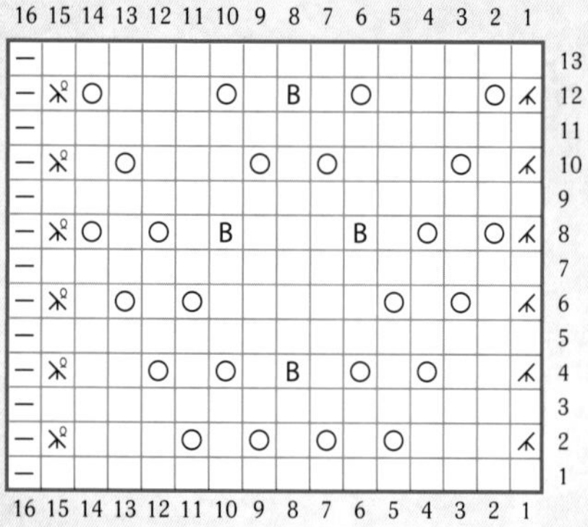

CHART B

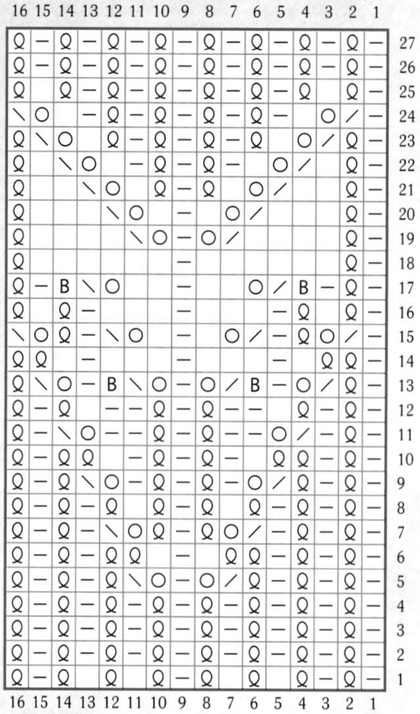

CHART C

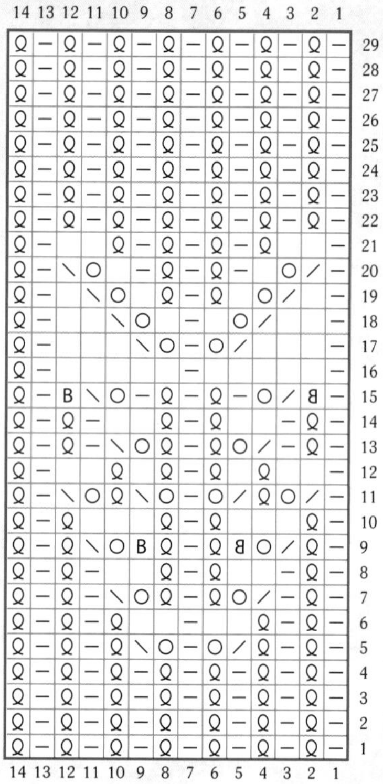

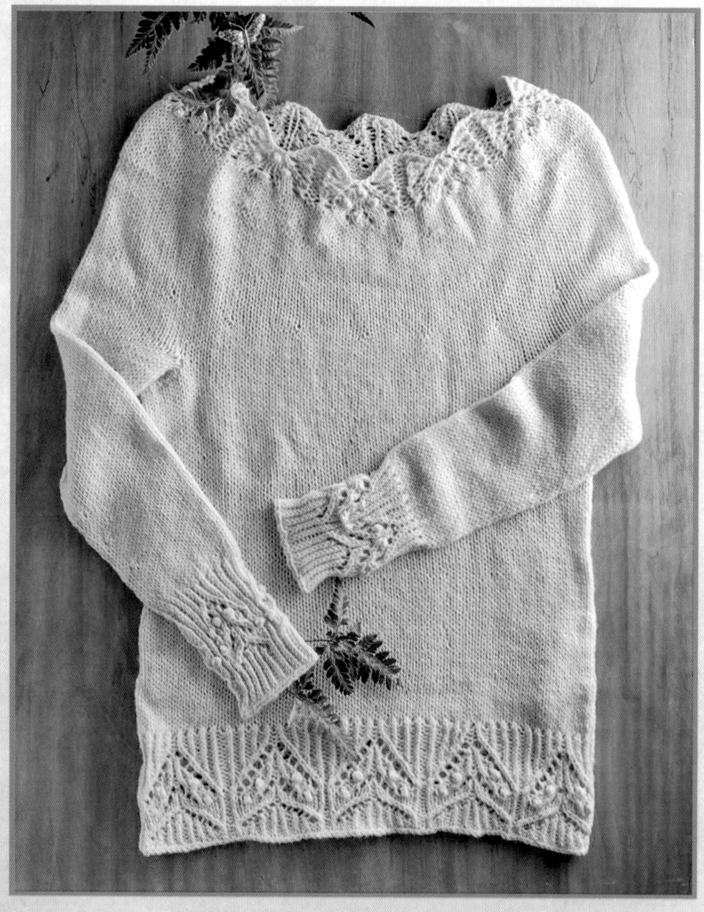

"Instead of a Dark Lord, you would have a queen, not dark but beautiful and terrible as the dawn! Tempestuous as the sea, and stronger than the foundations of the earth! All shall love me and despair!"

—Galadriel, *The Lord of the Rings: The Fellowship of the Ring* film in your preferred method of small circumference knitting.

Starting at the center of the underarm CO sts, join yarn and pick up and knit 6 (7, 8, 9, 9) [10, 10, 11, 11] {12, 12, 12, 12} sts, knit across the live 36 (38, 40, 42, 46) [52, 60, 62, 66] {68, 72, 74, 76} sts, pick up and knit 6 (7, 8, 9, 9) [10, 10, 11, 11] {12, 12, 12, 12} more sts, pm for BOR and join to work in the rnd—48 (52, 56, 60, 64) [72, 80, 84, 88] {92, 96, 98, 100} sts total.

Knit 20 (14, 10, 8, 7) [5, 6, 6, 5] {6, 5, 5, 5} rnds.

Dec Rnd: K1, k2tog, knit to last 3 sts, ssk, k1—2 sts dec.

Cont in St st until the sleeve measures 12 in. / 30.5 cm (or 5 in. / 12.5 cm short of the desired length), repeating the Dec Rnd every 19 (13, 9, 7, 6) [4, 5, 5, 4] {4, 3, 3, 3}th/rd rnd 2 (4, 6, 8, 10) [14, 11, 13, 15] {17, 19, 20, 21} more times—6 (10, 14, 18, 22) [30, 24, 28, 32] {36, 40, 42, 44} total sts dec; 42 (42, 42, 42, 42) [42, 56, 56, 56] {56, 56, 56, 56} sts rem.

Switch to smaller needles.

Begin Chart C, reading all rows from right to left as for working in the rnd. Work [Rows 1–29] 1 time (the chart is worked 3 (3, 3, 3, 3) [3, 4, 4, 4] {4, 4, 4, 4} times across each rnd).

BIND OFF

BO all sts loosely knitwise. Weave in all ends. Wet block to dimensions on schematic. Once dry, trim all ends.

Schematic

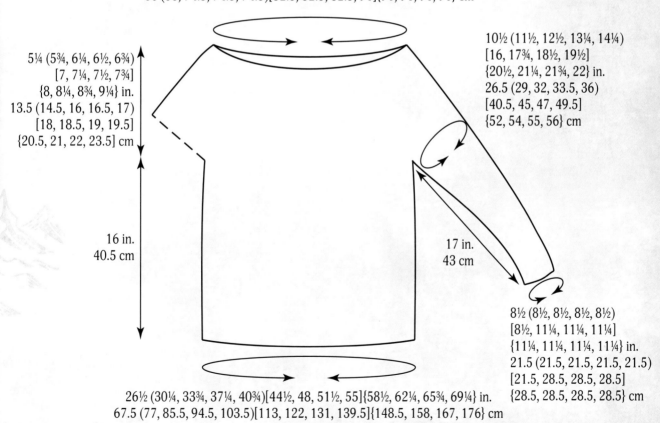

26 (26, 29¼, 29¼, 29¼) [32½, 32½, 32½, 35¾] {35¾, 35¾, 35¾, 35¾} in.
66 (66, 74.5, 74.5, 74.5) [82.5, 82.5, 82.5, 91] {91, 91, 91, 91} cm

5¼ (5¾, 6¼, 6½, 6¾) [7, 7¼, 7½, 7¾] {8, 8¼, 8¾, 9¼} in.
13.5 (14.5, 16, 16.5, 17) [18, 18.5, 19, 19.5] {20.5, 21, 22, 23.5] cm

10½ (11½, 12½, 13¼, 14¼) [16, 17¾, 18½, 19½] {20½, 21¼, 21¾, 22} in.
26.5 (29, 32, 33.5, 36) [40.5, 45, 47, 49.5] {52, 54, 55, 56} cm

16 in.
40.5 cm

17 in.
43 cm

8½ (8½, 8½, 8½, 8½) [8½, 11¼, 11¼, 11¼] {11¼, 11¼, 11¼, 11¼} in.
21.5 (21.5, 21.5, 21.5, 21.5) [21.5, 28.5, 28.5, 28.5] {28.5, 28.5, 28.5, 28.5} cm

26½ (30¼, 33¾, 37¼, 40¾) [44½, 48, 51½, 55] {58½, 62¼, 65¾, 69¼} in.
67.5 (77, 85.5, 94.5, 103.5) [113, 122, 131, 139.5] {148.5, 158, 167, 176} cm

CHAPTER FOUR

SCARVES & SOCKS

FOOD FOR THE JOURNEY SCARF

DESIGNED BY TANIS GRAY

Galadriel gifts the remaining members of the Fellowship Lembas Bread, Elven fare made with a secret recipe and rarely consumed by anyone other than Elves. Said to sustain any creature for lengthy periods, this thin, triangle-shaped bread is wrapped in leaves and can stay fresh for months. It is what keeps Sam and Frodo alive as they continue their quest to Mordor. Evil creatures like Gollum will not consume it, even when starving. In *The Lord of the Rings: The Return of the King*, Gollum creates mistrust between the two, framing Sam by sprinkling Lembas crumbs on him after the Hobbits agreed to ration the remaining food. In doing so, he drives a wedge between the friends and leads Frodo to the giant spider Shelob, hoping to reclaim the Ring. This scene is pivotal, and the only time Frodo allows his faith in Sam to waver.

This beautiful scarf is inspired by the energy-giving cuisine. Grab your own Lembas Bread and get knitting! Worked back and forth in rows, this lace scarf mimics the patterning on the Elvish bread. Lace is worked only on the right-side rows, with all the wrong-side resting rows worked across in purl stitch. Garter borders and selvage stitches allow the scarf to lie flat. It's easy to make it longer or shorter by adding or removing full repeats of the lace pattern.

SIZES

One size

FINISHED MEASUREMENTS

Width: 8½ in. / 21½ cm
Length: 58 in. / 147½ cm

YARN

Fingering weight yarn, shown in Spindrift Fibers *Fingering* (single ply; 70% superwash merino, 30% silk; 438 yd. / 400 m per 3½ oz. / 100 g hank), 1 hank in color Spring Thaw

NEEDLES

US 4 / 3.5 mm, 16 in. / 40 cm long circular needle

US 6 / 4 mm, 16 in. / 40 cm long circular needle or size needed to obtain gauge

NOTIONS

Stitch markers (optional)

Tapestry needle

GAUGE

26 sts and 25½ rows = 4 in. / 10 cm in Food for the Journey Pattern on larger needle, taken after blocking

Make sure to check your gauge.

PATTERN NOTES

The scarf is worked flat, back and forth in rows, from the bottom up.

All wrong-side rows are purled/resting rows. The first and last 2 stitches of every row are worked as a garter stitch selvage (knit on RS and WS).

If desired, place stitch markers between the pattern repeats. If placed, on Rows 7, 13, 21, and 23, the markers will move by 1 stitch.

PATTERN STITCHES

Food for the Journey Pattern
(worked over a multiple of 12 + 19 sts)

Row 1 (RS): K5, k2tog, yo, k1, yo, ssk, k2, (yo, ssk, k3, k2tog, yo, k1, yo, ssk, k2) 3 times, yo, ssk, k5.

Row 2 (and all WS rows): K2, purl to last 2 sts, k2.

Row 3: K4, k2tog, yo, k3, yo, ssk, k1, (k1, yo, ssk, k1, k2tog, yo, k3, yo, ssk, k1) 3 times, k1, yo, ssk, k4.

Row 5: K3, k2tog, yo, k2, k2tog, yo, k1, yo, ssk, (k2, yo, k3tog, yo, k2, k2tog, yo, k1, yo, ssk) 3 times, k2, yo, ssk, k3.

Row 7: K2, k2tog, yo, k2, k2tog, yo, k3, yo, (ssk, k1, k2tog, yo, k2, k2tog, yo, k3, yo) 3 times, ssk, k1, k2tog, yo, k3.

Row 9: K5, k2tog, yo, k5, (yo, k3tog, yo, k2, k2tog, yo, k5) 3 times, yo, k3tog, yo, k4.

Row 11: K4, k2tog, yo, k6, (k2tog, yo, k2, k2tog, yo, k6) 3 times, k2tog, yo, k5.

Row 13: K3, k2tog, yo, k1, yo, ssk, k3, k2tog, (yo, k2, k2tog, yo, k1, yo, ssk, k3, k2tog) 3 times, yo, k6.

Row 15: K2, k2tog, yo, k3, yo, ssk, k1, k2tog, yo, (k2, k2tog, yo, k3, yo, ssk, k1, k2tog, yo) 3 times, k2, k2tog, yo, k3.

Row 17: K4, yo, ssk, k2, yo, sk2p, yo, k1, (k1, k2tog, yo, k1, yo, ssk, k2, yo, sk2p, yo, k1) 3 times, k1, k2tog, yo, k4.

Row 19: K5, yo, ssk, k2, yo, ssk, k1, (k2tog, yo, k3, yo, ssk, k2, yo, ssk, k1) 3 times, k2tog, yo, k5.

Row 21: K6, yo, ssk, k2, yo, sk2p, (yo, k5, yo, ssk, k2, yo, sk2p) 3 times, yo, k6.

Row 23: K7, yo, ssk, k2, yo, (ssk, k6, yo, ssk, k2, yo) 3 times, ssk, k6.

Row 24: K2, purl to last 2 sts, k2.

Rep Rows 1–24 for patt.

PATTERN INSTRUCTIONS

CAST ON & BOTTOM EDGING

Using smaller needle, CO 55 sts using the Long Tail cast on method. Do not join to work in the rnd.
Knit 4 rows.
Switch to larger needles.
Next Row (RS): Knit.
Next Row (WS): K2, purl to last 2 sts, k2.

BODY OF SCARF

Begin working from Food for the Journey chart or written instructions.
Work [Rows 1–24] 15 times, or to desired length, ending with Row 24. The patt rep is worked 3 times across each row.

TOP EDGING & BIND OFF

Row 1 (RS): Knit.
Row 2 (WS): K2, purl to last 2 sts, k2.
Switch to smaller needles.
Knit 4 rows.
With RS facing, and using larger needle, BO all sts knitwise.

FINISHING

Weave in all loose ends to the WS with tapestry needle. Wet block the scarf well to allow the sts to relax and the lacework to open up. Once dry, trim all ends.

KEY

- ▢ Knit on RS, purl on WS
- − Purl on RS, knit on WS
- ◯ yo
- ╱ k2tog
- ⼂ k3tog
- ╲ ssk
- ⼈ sk2p
- ▭ Pattern repeat

FOOD FOR THE JOURNEY PATTERN

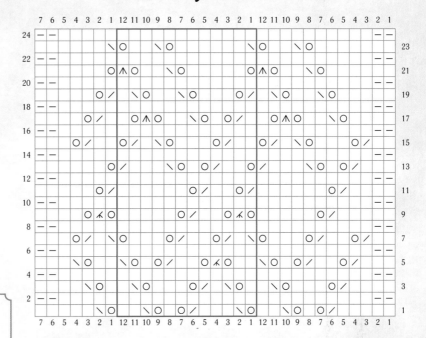

Legolas: "Lembas Bread, one bite is enough to fill the stomach of a grown man."

Merry: "How many did you eat?"

Pippin: "Four."

—The Lord of the Rings: The Fellowship of the Ring film

CLOAK PIN SOCKS

DESIGNED BY MEAGHAN SCHMALTZ

In the film adaptation of *The Lord of the Rings: The Fellowship of the Ring*, Galadriel gives each remaining member of the Fellowship a gift before they leave Lothlórien. The gifts are vital to the characters they are given to as the Fellowship begins to break up into smaller groups, and for some, like Frodo, the gift proves lifesaving. Legolas is given a Galadhrim bow strung with Elf hair and arrows; Merry and Pippin are bequeathed daggers; Aragorn a sheath for his sword that makes it unbreakable; Frodo the Light of Eärendil—the Elves' most treasured star; Gimli receives three strands of hair from Galadriel—the most beautiful creature he's ever seen; Sam is given rope—an essential tool while traversing the mountains to Mordor; and because she knows his fate, Boromir receives nothing. In addition to these gifts, the Fellowship is also gifted boats, Lembas Bread, and camouflaged cloaks gathered at the neck with a Lórien leaf clasp depicting beech tree leaves.

Inspired by the Elven leaf brooches given by Galadriel, these socks will allow you to bring a bit of Lothlórien to your needles. Worked identically in the round from the cuff down using the Magic Loop method, the socks begin with a 2x2 rib. A Lórien leaf-shaped cable motif grows on a background of reverse stockinette on the front and back of the leg. The toes are grafted together for a seamless join.

SIZES

1 (2, 3)

FINISHED MEASUREMENTS

Sock Circumference: 8 (9, 10) in. / 20.5 (23, 25.5) cm

The sock is designed to be worn with 0 to 1 in. / 0 to 2.5 cm of negative ease.

The sock is a size 1 modeled on an 8 in. / 20.5 cm circumference foot.

YARN

Fingering weight yarn, shown in Ewe Ewe Yarns *Fluffy Fingering* (3-ply; 100% Australian fine merino superwash; 200 yd. / 183 m per 1¾ oz. / 50 g skein), 3 skeins in color 53 Forest Fern

NEEDLES

US 1.5 / 2.5 mm, 32 in. / 80 cm long circular needle or size needed to obtain gauge

NOTIONS

Locking stitch marker (1, optional)

Cable needle

Row counter (optional)

Tapestry needle

GAUGE

33½ sts and 46 rows = 4 in. / 10 cm over reverse St st worked in the round, taken after blocking

Make sure to check your gauge.

PATTERN NOTES

These socks are worked from the cuff down using the Magic Loop method.

These socks feature a Fleegle heel (no pickups!), and Kitchener stitch is used to graft the toe closed.

The socks are worked identically to one another; make two to complete a pair.

Instructions are provided for size 1 with sizes 2 and 3 in parentheses. When only one set of instructions is provided, it applies to all sizes.

Only charted instructions are provided for cable design of the socks. Separate charts are provided for each size. Work all charts starting on Row 1, reading from right to left as for working in the round.

SPECIAL TECHNIQUE

Start of Cable—creating 4 stitches

With RS facing: With working yarn in front from previous purl stitch, move the working yarn to the back over the RHN (creating a new stitch). Before first stitch on LHN, M1L (2 new stitches). Slip both new stitches back to the LHN purlwise and Cable cast on 1 stitch between the yo and M1L stitch leaving the new stitch on the RHN (1 stitch increased, 2 new stitches on LHN and 1 new stitch on RHN). Into the first stitch on the LHN, work kfbS (1 stitch increased). Slip next stitch purlwise to RHN; 4 new stitches now on RHN.

PATTERN INSTRUCTIONS

CAST ON & CUFF

CO 64 (72, 80) sts using the Twisted German cast on method. Divide the sts evenly, placing the first 32 (36, 40) sts on the FN— these will be the Front/ Instep sts. The remaining 32 (36, 40) sts will be the Back/Sole sts and will be worked on the BN. If desired, clip a locking marker to indicate BOR; otherwise use the cast on tail as the indicator.

Rib Rnd: K1, p2, *k2, p2; rep from * to last st, k1.

Rep Rib Rnd until the Cuff measures 1¼ in. / 3 cm, or desired length.

LEG

Setup Rnd A (inc): *Kfb, p29 (33, 37), pfb, k1; rep from * across BN—68 (76, 84) sts.

Setup Rnd B: *K1, p32 (36, 40), k1; rep from * across BN.

Setup Rnd C (inc): *K1, p6 (8, 10), work Start of Cable, p20, work Start of Cable, p6 (8, 10), k1; rep from * across BN—84 (92, 100) sts total.

Work Rows 1–59 of Chart A once per the Leg Rnd, below. The chart will be worked 1 time across the FN and 1 time across the BN.

Leg Rnd: *K1, p2 (4, 6), work Leg chart over the next 36 sts, p2 (4, 6), k1; rep from * across BN.

Stitch count after Row 59: 68 (76, 84) sts total; 34 (38, 42) sts each on FN & BN.

HEEL GUSSET

As the Heel Gusset is worked, stitches will inc on the BN only; written instructions are provided for this. Work the chart for your size across the FN once. Begin on Row 1 and move up the chart on each consecutive round.

Gusset Rnd 1 (FN): Work as per Chart B (C, D).

Gusset Rnd 1 (BN, inc): Kfb, purl to the last 2 sts, pfb, k1—2 sts inc.

Gusset Rnd 2 (FN): Work as per Chart B (C, D).

Gusset Rnd 2 (BN): K1, purl to last st, k1.

Rep [Gusset Rnds 1 and 2] 7 (8, 9) more times—50 (56, 62) sts on the BN.

Chart B (C, D) is now complete.

Gusset Rnd 3 (FN): Knit.

Gusset Rnd 3 (BN, inc): Kfb, purl to the last 2 sts, pfb, k1—2 sts inc.

Gusset Rnd 4 (FN): Knit.

Gusset Rnd 4 (BN): K1, purl to last st, k1.

Rep [Gusset Rnds 3 and 4] 6 (7, 8) more times—64 (72, 80) sts on the BN.

The stitch count on the FN will not change—98 (110, 122) sts total.

TURN THE HEEL

Knit across all sts on the FN. The remainder of the Heel will be worked flat on the BN only, beginning on the RS. From this point forward, the fabric will be St st.

Row 1 (RS, dec): K35 (39, 43), k2tog, k1, turn—1 st dec.

Row 2 (WS, dec): Sl1 wyif, p7, p2tog, p1, turn—1 st dec.

Row 3 (dec): Sl1 wyib, knit to 1 st before gap, ssk across gap, k1, turn—1 st dec.

Row 4 (dec): Sl1 wyif, purl to 1 st before gap, p2tog across gap, p1, turn—1 st dec.

Rep Rows 3 and 4 until 37 (41, 45) sts rem on BN, ending with Row 3. Do NOT turn work to WS. Resume working in the rnd.

FINISH THE HEEL

Rnd 1 (FN): Knit.
Rnd 1 (BN, dec): K1, k2tog, knit to last 2 sts, ssk—35 (39, 43) sts on BN.
Rnd 2 (FN): Knit.
Rnd 2 (BN, dec): K2tog, knit to end—34 (38, 42) sts on each FN & BN.

FOOT

Work in St st (knit every rnd) until the foot is 1½ (1¾, 2) in. / 4 (4.5, 5) cm short of the desired total length.

TOE SHAPING

Rnd 1 (FN, dec): K1, ssk, knit to last 3 sts, k2tog, k1—2 sts dec.
Rnd 1 (BN, dec): K1, ssk, knit to last 3 sts, k2tog, k1—2 sts dec.
Rnd 2 (FN & BN): Knit.
Rep [Rnds 1 and 2] 8 (9, 10) more times—32 (36, 40) sts rem; 16 (18, 20) sts on each FN & BN.

FINISHING

Break yarn leaving a 12 in. / 30.5 cm tail. Using Kitchener stitch, graft closed the toe of your sock. Weave in the ends.

Make a second sock identical to the first.

Wet block your socks and allow to dry completely before wearing. Trim ends.

Schematic

6.75 in.
17 cm

8 (9, 10) in.
20.5 (23, 25.5) cm

Adjustable

KEY

- ■ No stitch
- □ Knit
- − Purl
- ⋀ s2kp
- ╱ k2tog
- ╱ p2tog
- ⋁ Slip st purlwise wyib
- ╲ 1/1 LPC
- ╱ 1/1 RPC
- ╲ 2/1 LC
- ╲ 2/1 RC
- ╲ 2/1 LPC
- ╱ 2/1 RPC
- ╲ 2/2 LC
- ╲ 2/2 RC
- ╲ 2/2 LPC
- ╱ 2/2 RPC
- ▭ Pattern repeat

"May it be a light to you in dark places, when all other lights go out."

–Galadriel, *The Lord of the Rings: The Fellowship of the Ring* film

CHART A - Leg: All Sizes

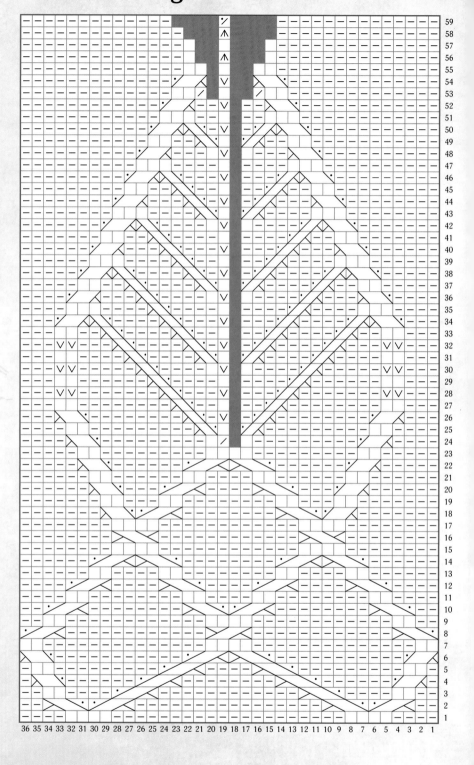

CHART B - Heel Gusset: Size 1 (FN Only)

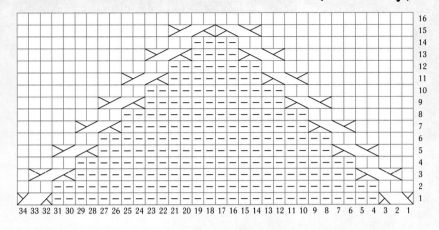

CHART C - Heel Gusset: Size 2 (FN Only)

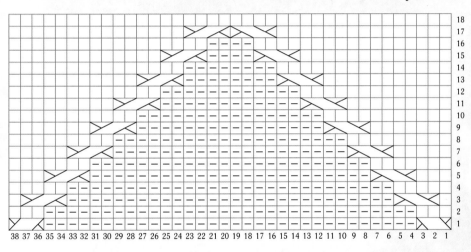

CHART D - Heel Gusset: Size 3 (FN Only)

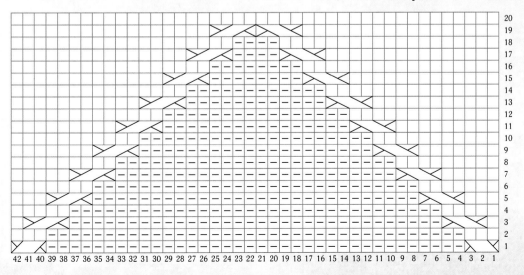

FOLIAGE SOCKS

DESIGNED BY NATALIE SHELDON

After being Hobbit-napped and mistaken for ring-bearer Frodo at Amon Hen by Uruk-hai and Orcs, Merry and Pippin found themselves in grave danger. Although Saruman told his henchmen to keep the Halflings alive, hungry Orcs always kept a close eye on them as a possible next meal. While being carried across Middle-earth toward Saruman, Pippin freed the leaf brooch given to him by Galadriel and dropped it as a way for the Fellowship to find them. The leaves of Lórien brooch came in handy a second time when Aragorn told Faramir about the fate of his brother giving his life to save the Hobbits.

Inspired by the legendary Lórien leaves, these beautiful socks will have you running for your needles to cast on the same way Gimli, Legolas, and Aragorn ran toward their friends after finding Pippin's brooch. Knit in the round from the cuff down, a slightly sparkly variegated yarn paired with a solid brings a bit of Elvish mystique to the wearer. Eight stranded colorwork leaves gently fall down the body of the leg, representing each leaf cloak pin given by Galadriel to the remaining members of the Fellowship in *The Lord of the Rings: The Fellowship of the Ring*. "Not idly do the leaves of Lórien fall" is stitched into the sole of the sock. A forethought heel is placed while knitting the body of the sock, then picked up after the toe stitches are grafted together to finish the heel.

SIZES

1 (2, 3, 4, 5)

FINISHED MEASUREMENTS

Sock Circumference: 6¼ (7, 7¾, 8½, 9¼) in. / 16 (18, 19.5, 21.5, 23.5) cm

Minimum Foot Length: 7 (8, 9, 10, 11) in. / 18 (20.5, 23, 25.5, 28) cm

Adjustable foot length (can be made longer than the minimum foot length)

The sock is designed to be worn with ½ in. / 1 cm of negative ease.

The sock is a size 3 modeled on a 7¼ in. / 18.5 cm circumference foot.

YARN

Fingering weight yarn, shown in Leading Men Fiber Arts *Show Stopper* (75% superwash merino, 25% nylon; 463 yd. / 423 m per 3½ oz. / 100 g hank), 1 hank in color Bare Necessities (MC)

Fingering weight yarn, shown in Leading Men Fiber Arts *Sparkle Sock* (75% superwash merino, 20% nylon, 5% Lurex; 437 yd. / 400 m per 3½ oz. / 100 g hank), 1 hank in color Envy (CC)

NEEDLES

US 1 / 2.25 mm set of 4 double-pointed needles

US 2 / 2.75 mm, 9 in. / 23 cm circular needle or size needed to obtain gauge

NOTIONS

Stitch marker (optional)

Tapestry needle

Smooth fingering weight waste yarn in contrasting color

GAUGE

Size 1: 46 sts and 51 rounds = 4 in. / 10 cm in stranded colorwork in the round on larger needle, taken after blocking

Size 2: 41 sts and 45 rounds = 4 in. / 10 cm in stranded colorwork in the round on larger needle, taken after blocking

Size 3: 37 sts and 41 rounds = 4 in. / 10 cm in stranded colorwork in the round on larger needle, taken after blocking

Size 4: 34 sts and 37 rounds = 4 in. / 10 cm in stranded colorwork in the round on larger needle, taken after blocking

Size 5: 31 sts and 34 rounds = 4 in. / 10 cm in stranded colorwork in the round on larger needle, taken after blocking

Make sure to check your gauge.

PATTERN NOTES

To honor the original design of the socks and ensure a wider range of available fit, rather than compromise on the stitch pattern, these socks have been graded using different gauges for each size. To achieve the gauge for your finished size of socks, adjust your needle size as needed.

These socks are worked in the round from the cuff down with a forethought heel placed while working the colorwork Leg chart. When slipping stitches for the placement of the forethought heel, slip all stitches purlwise.

The smaller needles will be used for the cuff, heel, and toe; the larger needles are used for the leg and foot of the sock (the colorwork portions of the sock). The small needle should be 1 needle size smaller than the large needle when gauge is met.

Written instructions are provided for the construction of the socks; charts are provided for the colorwork leg and foot.

The socks are worked identically to one another; make two to complete a pair.

PATTERN INSTRUCTIONS

CAST ON & CUFF

Using MC and the smaller needles, CO 72 sts using the Long Tail cast on method. Distribute the sts evenly over the dpns. Pm for BOR (if desired) and join to work in the rnd, being careful not to twist the sts.

Rib Rnd: *K2, p2; rep from * to end of rnd.

Rep [Rib Rnd] 19 more times.

LEG

Switch to larger needle.

Begin Leg chart, reading all rows from right to left as for working in the rnd, joining CC as required.

Work Rows 1–48 once.

Row 49 (place Forethought Heel lifeline): Work 41 sts in patt as per Row 49 of the chart; drop (don't cut) MC and CC yarns. Slip the last 35 just-worked sts from RHN to LHN. Join the contrast waste yarn and knit across the 35 slipped sts. Cut the waste yarn. Pick up CC and MC and work rem 31 sts as per Row 49.

FOOT

Begin Foot chart, reading all rows from right to left as for working in the rnd, joining CC as required.

Work Rows 1–49 once. When complete, break CC. The remainder of the sock is worked with MC only.

TOE

Cont with larger needle, rm (BOR M), knit 6 sts, pm for new BOR. *This centers the toe over the foot motif.*

Switch to smaller needles.

Starting at the new BOR M, arrange sts as follows on the smaller needles: 36 sts on the first dpn (N1) and 18 sts on each of 2 additional dpns (N2 and N3).

Rnd 1: Knit.

Rnd 2 (N1, dec): K1, skp, knit to last 3 sts of N1, k2tog, k1—2 sts dec.

Rnd 2 (N2, dec): K1, skp, knit to end of N2—1 st dec.

Rnd 2 (N3, dec): Knit to last 3 sts of N3, k2tog, k1—1 st dec; 4 total sts dec for the rnd; 68 sts rem.

Rep Rnd 1 only until the total foot length is 3 (3½, 4, 4½, 5) in. / 7.5 (9, 10, 11.5, 12.5) cm short of the desired total foot length when measured from the waste yarn for the forethought heel.

Then, beg with Rnd 2, rep [Rnds 1 and 2] 11 times, ending with Rnd 1.

48 total sts dec; 24 sts rem (12 sts on N1; 6 sts on each of N2 and N3).

Slip all sts from N3 to N2; N1 and N2 each hold 12 sts.

Break yarn leaving a 12 in. / 30.5 cm tail. Using Kitchener stitch, graft closed the toe of your sock. Weave in the ends.

FORETHOUGHT HEEL

With the cuff of the sock closest to you, and the sole of the sock facing up (so you can see the waste yarn), use 1 small dpn to pick up the right leg of each stitch below the waste yarn (picking up from right to left)—35 sts on N1.

Rotate the sock 180 degrees so that the toe is closest to you; the sole is still facing up. Using a second small dpn, pick up the right leg of each stitch below the waste yarn (picking up from right to left)—35 sts on N2; 70 sts total. Distribute these 35 sts over 2 dpns: 17 sts on N2 and 18 sts on N3.

Rotate the sock again so the cuff is closest to you (N1 should be the closest needle). Join MC yarn to the right edge of the live sts of N1.

Rnd 1: Knit.

Rnd 2 (N1, dec): K1, skp, knit to last 3 sts of N1, k2tog, k1—2 sts dec.

Rnd 2 (N2, dec): K1, skp, knit to end of N2—1 st dec.

Rnd 2 (N3, dec): Knit to last 3 sts of N3, k2tog, k1—1 st dec; 4 total sts dec for the rnd.

Rep [Rnds 1 and 2] 10 more times, ending with Rnd 2. 44 total sts dec; 26 sts rem (13 sts on N1; 6 sts on N2 and 7 sts on N3).

Slip all sts from N3 to N2; N1 and N2 each hold 13 sts.

Break yarn leaving a 12 in. / 30.5 cm tail. Using Kitchener stitch, graft closed the heel of your sock. Weave in the ends.

FINISHING

Make a second sock identical to the first.

Using MC yarn, sew up any gaps at the sides of the heels.

Wet block your socks and allow to dry completely. Trim ends.

Schematic

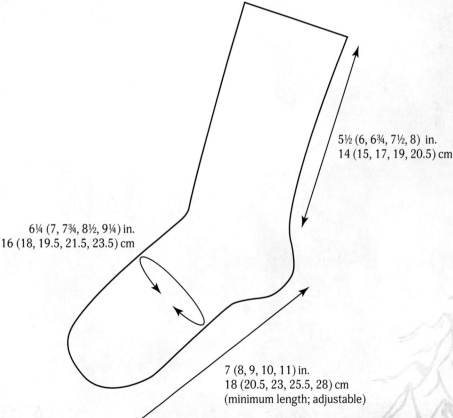

6¼ (7, 7¾, 8½, 9¼) in.
16 (18, 19.5, 21.5, 23.5) cm

5½ (6, 6¾, 7½, 8) in.
14 (15, 17, 19, 20.5) cm

7 (8, 9, 10, 11) in.
18 (20.5, 23, 25.5, 28) cm
(minimum length; adjustable)

KEY

☐ Knit
☐ MC
■ CC

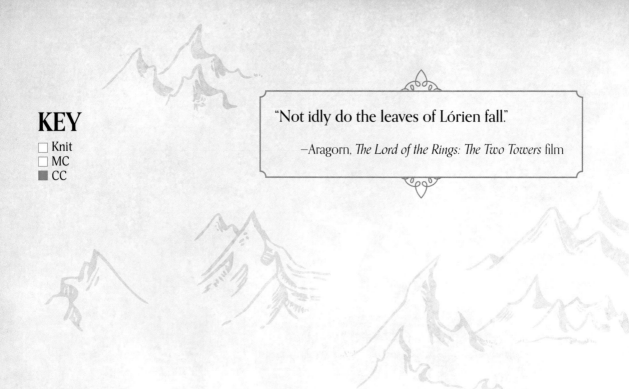

"Not idly do the leaves of Lórien fall."

—Aragorn, *The Lord of the Rings: The Two Towers* film

LEG CHART

FOOT CHART

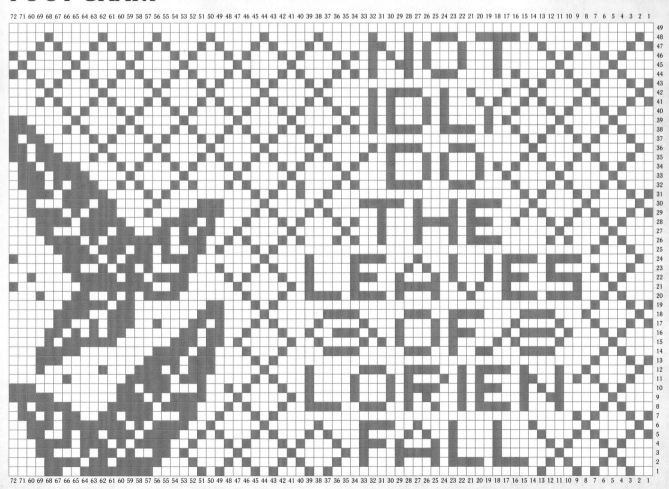

SECOND BREAKFAST SOCKS & MITTENS

DESIGNED BY SPILLYJANE

Hobbits are renowned for their jovial nature and frequent mealtimes. No Hobbit custom is more emblematic of these two qualities than second breakfast, which falls after breakfast, but before elevensies, luncheon, afternoon tea, dinner, and supper. Hobbits eat and drink frequently, enjoying the fruits of their labor coming from their agrarian culture. Short and stout, they are known for having well-stocked pantries, throwing excellent parties, and being more than willing to share. Bilbo stated in his diary:

> *"It has been remarked by some that Hobbits' only real passion is for food. A rather unfair observation as we have also developed a keen interest in the brewing of ales and the smoking of pipe weed. But where our hearts truly lie is in peace and quiet and good tilled earth. For all Hobbits share a love of all things that grow."*

These mittens and socks depict a table filled with Hobbit staples just waiting for their guests to sit down and dig in! Tankards of ale, apples, mushrooms, and seedcakes—all Hobbiton favorites—are created in stranded colorwork. The golden yellow background evokes the cozy glow of both candlelight and the contentment of a full stomach. The mittens are worked beginning at the cuff with an afterthought thumb placed while working on the body. The stitches are then picked up once the body of the mitt is finished, and the thumb is worked. The socks are worked from the cuff down with an afterthought heel completed once the body of the sock is finished. Tiny details are duplicate stitched post-knitting on both the mittens and socks to avoid using more than two colors per round. Let's eat!

SIZES

Socks

Small (Medium, Large)

Mittens

Small (Medium, Large)

FINISHED MEASUREMENTS

Socks

Finished Foot Circumference: 7½ (8¼, 9) in. / 19 (21, 23) cm

Minimum Foot Length: 8½ (9½, 10¼) in. / 21.5 (24, 26) cm

Adjustable foot length (can be made longer than the minimum foot length)

The socks are designed to be worn with ½ to 1 in. / 1 to 2.5 cm of negative ease.

The sock is a size Small modeled on an 8 in. / 20.5 cm circumference foot.

Mittens

Finished Hand Circumference: 7½ (8¼, 9) in. / 19 (21, 23) cm

Finished Length (cuff to fingertip): 10 (10¾, 11¾) in. / 25.5 (27.5, 30) cm

Finished Thumb Circumference: 3¼ (3½, 4) in. / 8.5 (9, 10) cm

The mittens are designed to be worn with 0 in. / 0 cm of ease.

YARN

Socks

Fingering weight yarn, shown in Emma's Yarn *Practically Perfect Sock* (2-ply; 80% superwash merino, 20% nylon; 400 yd. / 366 m per 3½ oz. / 100 g hank)

Colorways:

- **Main Color (MC):** Yellow Submarine, 1 hank
- **Contrast Color 1 (CC1):** Beach Please, 1 hank

Fingering weight yarn, shown in Emma's Yarn *Practically Perfect Smalls* (2-ply; 80% superwash merino, 20% nylon; 81 yd. / 74 m per ¾ oz. / 20 g hank)

Colorways:

- **Contrast Color 2 (CC2):** Wish You Were Beer, 1 hank
- **Contrast Color 3 (CC3):** Freshly Cut, 1 hank
- **Contrast Color 4 (CC4):** Stiletto, 1 hank
- **Contrast Color 5 (CC5):** Morel of the Story, 1 hank
- **Contrast Color 6 (CC6):** Kisses, 1 hank
- **Contrast Color 7 (CC7):** Barking Up the Wrong Tree, 1 hank
- **Contrast Color 8 (CC8):** After Dark, 1 hank

Mittens

Fingering weight yarn, shown in Emma's Yarn *Practically Perfect Sock* (2-ply; 80% superwash merino, 20% nylon; 400 yd. / 366 m per 3½ oz. / 100 g hank) in color Yellow Submarine (MC), 1 hank

Fingering weight yarn, shown in Emma's Yarn *Practically Perfect Smalls* (2-ply; 80% superwash merino, 20% nylon; 81 yd. / 74 m per ¾ oz. / 20 g hank)

Colorways:

- **Contrast Color 1 (CC1):** Beach Please, 1 mini skein
- **Contrast Color 2 (CC2):** Wish You Were Beer, 1 hank
- **Contrast Color 3 (CC3):** Freshly Cut, 1 hank
- **Contrast Color 4 (CC4):** Stiletto, 1 hank
- **Contrast Color 5 (CC5):** Morel of the Story, 1 hank
- **Contrast Color 6 (CC6):** Kisses, 1 hank
- **Contrast Color 7 (CC7):** Barking Up the Wrong Tree, 1 hank
- **Contrast Color 8 (CC8):** After Dark, 1 hank

NEEDLES

US 2 / 2.75 mm set of 5 double-pointed needles or size needed to obtain gauge

NOTIONS

Stitch marker (optional)

Fingering weight smooth waste yarn (approx. 1 yd. / 1 m per project)

Tapestry needle

GAUGE

Small: 34 sts and 37 rnds = 4 in. / 10 cm in stranded colorwork pattern, taken after steam blocking

Medium: 31 sts and 34 rnds = 4 in. / 10 cm in stranded colorwork pattern, taken after steam blocking

Large: 28½ sts and 31 rnds = 4 in. / 10 cm in stranded colorwork pattern, taken after steam blocking

Make sure to check your gauge.

PATTERN NOTES

Socks

To honor the original design of the socks and ensure a wider range of available fit, rather than compromise on the stitch pattern, these socks have been graded using different gauges for each size. To achieve the gauge for your finished size of socks, adjust your needle size as needed.

These socks are worked top down in the round from cuff to toe. The cuff, heel, and toe are worked in the MC alone; colorwork knitting is done across the leg and foot.

Waste yarn is used to place an afterthought heel once the leg is complete and before the foot begins. The afterthought heel is worked once the sock is completed.

A stitch marker is used to indicate the beginning of round, if desired.

These socks are identical to each other. Make 2 the same to complete a pair.

Instructions are provided for size small first, with additional sizes in parentheses. When only one number is given, it applies to all sizes.

The basic shapes of the top-of-foot design are worked into the construction of the sock using colorwork/stranded knitting. Additional details such as iron bands on the tankards, stems on the apple, and seeds on top of the Hobbit seedcakes are added after the sock is finished by means of duplicate stitch or straight embroidery. While adding these details, be sure to keep your embroidery loose enough so that the socks retain their elasticity. You may wish to use a separate length of yarn as you embellish each separate motif; while there may be more ends to weave in this way, the resulting sock will be more easily worn.

Contrast Color 8 (CC8) is only used to embellish the tankards. If you prefer to substitute in a yarn from your stash, as so little is used, you will need approximately 1 yd. / 1 m of a very dark brown/black fingering weight yarn.

Colorwork will be easier and faster to work if the MC is held with the right hand while the CC is held with the left. This will also improve the look of the resulting colorwork.

You may wish to check that the length of sock is correct before beginning the toe. To do this, transfer the heel stitches from above and below the waste yarn placed for the afterthought heel to a spare set of dpns and then carefully try the sock on. When tried on in this manner, the foot of the sock should measure approximately 2¼ (2½, 2¾) in. / 5.5 (6.5, 7) cm less than the length of your foot (the heel will be exposed when tried on).

Mittens

To honor the original design of the mittens and ensure a wider range of available fit, rather than compromise on the stitch pattern, these mittens have been graded using different gauges for each size. To achieve the gauge for your finished size of mittens, adjust your needle size as needed.

These mittens are worked from the bottom up in the round from the cuff to fingertips. The pattern uses a peasant thumb (afterthought thumb) to interrupt the colorwork as little as possible. The peasant thumb will be worked after the body of the mitten has been completed.

A stitch marker is used to indicate the beginning of round, if desired.

These mitts are nearly identical to each other; the position of the thumb differentiates the two. Take care to follow the thumb placement for the opposing mittens to ensure both wear as intended.

Instructions are provided for size small first, with additional sizes in parentheses. When only one number is given, it applies to all sizes.

The basic shapes of the top-of-mitten design are worked into the construction of the mitten using colorwork/stranded knitting. Additional details such as iron bands on the tankards, stems on the apple, and seeds on top of the Hobbit seedcakes are added after the mitten is finished by means of duplicate stitch or straight embroidery. While adding these details, be sure to keep your embroidery loose enough so that the mittens retain their elasticity. You may wish to use a separate length of yarn as you embellish each separate motif; while there may be more ends to weave in this way, the resulting mitten will be more easily worn.

Contrast Color 8 (CC8) is only used to embellish the tankards. If you prefer to substitute in a yarn from your stash, as so little is used, you will need approximately 1 yd. / 1 m of a very dark brown/black fingering weight yarn.

Colorwork will be easier and faster to work if the MC is held with the right hand while the CC is held with the left. This will also improve the look of the resulting colorwork.

PATTERN INSTRUCTIONS

SOCKS

CAST ON & CUFF

Using MC, CO 64 sts using the Long Tail cast on method. Distribute sts evenly across 4 needles—16 sts per needle. Pm for BOR (if desired) and join to work in the rnd, being careful not to twist the sts.

Rib Rnd: *K2tbl, p2; rep from * to end of rnd.

Rep Rib Rnd 9 more times for a total of 10 rnds.

Next 2 Rnds: Knit.

LEG

Begin Chart A, reading all rows from right to left as for working in the rnd, joining CCs as required. Work Rows 1–39 once (chart is worked 2 times across each rnd). Once complete, break all yarns except MC and CC1.

AFTERTHOUGHT HEEL PLACEMENT

With waste yarn, knit 32 sts. Slide all sts back to the other end of the needles ready to start at the BOR again. With MC, knit across these just-worked waste yarn sts, and then knit to end of rnd; 1 rnd is completed with a half-round of waste yarn placed for the afterthought heel.

FOOT

Begin Chart B, reading all rows from right to left as for working in the rnd, joining CCs as required. Work Rnds 1–44 once (chart is worked once across each rnd). Once complete, break all yarns except MC.

Knit 1 rnd.

To ensure proper fit, it is recommended to try on the sock before working the toe. To do this, transfer the heel sts from above and below the waste yarn placed for the afterthought heel (per the Afterthought Heel section) to a spare set of dpns, then carefully try the sock on. When tried on in this manner, the foot of the sock should measure approximately 2¼ (2½, 2¾) in. / 5.5 (6.5, 7) cm less than the length of your foot before starting the toe (the heel will be exposed). If the foot is still short of this target length, continue to work in stockinette st (knit every rnd) in MC only until this target length is reached.

TOE

Rnd 1 (N1, dec): K1, ssk, knit to end—1 st dec.

Rnd 1 (N2, dec): Knit to last 3 sts, k2tog, k1—1 st dec.

Rnd 1 (N3, dec): K1, ssk, knit to end—1 st dec.

Rnd 1 (N4, dec): Knit to last 3 sts, k2tog, k1—1 st dec; 4 total sts dec for the rnd.

Rnd 2: Knit.

Rep [Rnds 1 and 2] 10 more times.

44 total sts dec; 20 sts rem (5 sts on each dpn).

Slipping sts purlwise, slip all sts from N2 to N1 and all sts from N4 to N3; 10 sts now on each of 2 dpns held parallel.

Break yarn leaving a 12 in. / 30.5 cm tail. Using Kitchener stitch, graft closed the toe of your sock. Weave in the ends to the WS.

AFTERTHOUGHT HEEL

With the sole of the sock facing up and the toe pointed away from you, using 1 dpn, carefully pick up the right leg of each of the 32 sts below the waste yarn. Repeat with a second dpn for the sts above the waste yarn; 64 sts total over 2 needles.

Carefully remove and discard waste yarn. Distribute these sts evenly across 4 needles—16 sts per needle.

Pm for BOR (if desired) at the right edge of the picked up sts (with the toe pointed away from you). Join MC at the BOR and *pick up and knit 1 st in the gap between N1 and N4. Knit across N1 and N2 and pick up and knit 1 st in the gap between N2 and N3; rep from * once more across N3 and N4—68 sts total; 17 sts on each needle.

Setup Rnd: Knit.

Rnd 1 (N1, dec): K1, ssk, knit to end—1 st dec.

Rnd 1 (N2, dec): Knit to last 3 sts, k2tog, k1—1 st dec.

Rnd 1 (N3, dec): K1, ssk, knit to end—1 st dec.

Rnd 1 (N4, dec): Knit to last 3 sts, k2tog, k1—1 st dec; 4 total sts dec for the rnd.

Rnd 2: Knit.

Rep [Rnds 1 and 2] 7 more times.

32 sts dec; 36 sts rem (9 sts on each dpn).

Slipping sts purlwise, slip all sts from N2 to N1 and all sts from N4 to N3; 18 sts now on each of 2 dpns held parallel.

Break yarn leaving a 16 in. / 40.5 cm tail. Using Kitchener stitch, graft closed the toe of your sock. Weave in the ends to the WS.

FINISHING

Weave in all ends.

Working from the Duplicate Stitch chart, and using a tapestry needle, add additional details to the table, tankard, and apple motifs. Using CC6 and short straight stitches, add a scattering of "seeds" to the top of the Hobbit seedcake motifs, using the Duplicate Stitch chart as a reference for placement. Weave in all ends from the duplicate stitch process. Steam block and press if desired.

MITTENS

CAST ON & CUFF

Using MC, CO 64 sts using the Long Tail cast on method. Distribute sts evenly across 4 needles—16 sts per needle. Pm for BOR (if desired) and join to work in the rnd, being careful not to twist the sts.

Rib Rnd: *K2tbl, p2; rep from * to end of rnd.

Rep Rib Rnd 9 more times for a total of 10 rnds.

Next 2 Rnds: Knit.

BODY

Begin Mittens chart, reading all rows from right to left as for working in the rnd, joining CCs as required. Work Rnds 1–31 once (Rnd 32 of chart, where there are marks for thumb placement, will be worked in tandem with written instructions that differ for each mitten).

THUMB PLACEMENT AND BODY (CONT'D)

For Left Mitten: Using MC only, knit all sts on N1, N2, and N3 (per Row 32 of the chart). Knit the first 2 sts on N4. Drop MC. Using waste yarn, knit the next 12 sts on N4. Drop the waste yarn. Sl these 12 sts back onto the LHN and knit across 12 sts again using MC. Knit the last 2 sts on N4.

For Right Mitten: Using MC only, knit all sts on N1 and N2 (per Row 32 of the chart). Knit the first 2 sts on N3. Drop MC. Using waste yarn, knit the next 12 sts on N3. Drop the waste yarn. Sl these 12 sts back onto the LHN and knit across 12 sts again using MC. Knit rem 2 sts on N3,

and all sts on N4.

Both Mittens: Cont working Mittens chart up to the end of Row 80, noting that the top-of-mitten shaping begins on Row 71 for N1 and N3 and Row 72 for N2 and N4. When complete, break all CCs—26 sts rem.

Slipping sts purlwise, slip all sts from N2 to N1 and all sts from N4 to N3; 13 sts now on each of 2 dpns held parallel.

Break yarn leaving a 16 in. / 40.5 cm tail. Using Kitchener stitch, graft closed the top of your mitten. Weave in the ends to the WS.

PEASANT (AFTERTHOUGHT) THUMB

With 1 dpn, carefully pick up the right leg of each of the 12 sts below the waste yarn—12 sts on the needle. Rep with a second dpn for the 12 sts above the waste yarn—24 sts total over 2 dpns.

Carefully remove and discard waste yarn. Distribute the sts evenly across 4 needles—6 sts on each dpn.

Pm for BOR (if desired) at the right edge of the picked up sts (with the top of mitten pointed away from you). Join MC at the BOR and *pick up and knit 1 st in the gap between N1 and N4. Knit across N1 and N2 and pick up and knit 1 st in the gap between N2 and N3; rep from * once more across N3 and N4—28 sts total; 7 sts on each needle.

Knit 23 rnds, or until the fabric covers the wearer's thumb all the way to the tip. Then begin the thumb shaping as follows:

Rnd 1 (N1, dec): K1, ssk, knit to end—1 st dec.

Rnd 1 (N2, dec): Knit to last 3 sts, k2tog, k1—1 st dec.

Rnd 1 (N3, dec): K1, ssk, knit to end—1 st dec.

Rnd 1 (N4, dec): Knit to last 3 sts, k2tog, k1—1 st dec; 4 total sts dec for the rnd.

Rnd 2: Knit.

Rep [Rnds 1 and 2] 4 more times.

20 sts dec; 8 sts rem (2 sts on each dpn).

Slipping sts purlwise, slip all sts from N2 to N1 and all sts from N4 to N3; 4 sts now on each of 2 dpns held parallel.

Break yarn leaving a 6 in. /

15 cm tail. Using Kitchener stitch, graft closed the top of your thumb. Weave in the ends to the WS.

FINISHING

Weave in all ends.

Working from the Duplicate Stitch chart, and using a tapestry needle, add additional details to the table, tankard, and apple motifs. Using CC6 and short straight stitches, add a scattering of "seeds" to the top of the Hobbit seedcake motifs, using the Duplicate Stitch chart as a reference for placement. Weave in all ends from the duplicate stitch process. Steam block and press if desired.

COLORWORK KEY

- ■ No stitch
- □ Knit
- ☑ k2tog
- ◲ ssk MC
- ■ CC1
- ■ CC2
- ■ CC3
- ■ CC4
- ■ CC5
- ■ CC6
- ■ CC7
- ▯ Right thumb
- ▯ Left thumb
- ▮ Needle divider
- ▭ Pattern repeat

DUPLICATE STITCH KEY

- ▢ Existing MC
- ■ Existing CC1
- ■ Existing CC2
- ■ Existing CC3
- ■ Existing CC4
- ■ Existing CC6
- ■ Existing CC7
- ☒ Duplicate stitch with CC3
- ◪ Straight embroider with CC6
- ☒ Duplicate stitch with CC7
- ☒ Duplicate stitch with CC8

SOCKS: CHART A

"Hobbits really are amazing creatures, as I have said before. You can learn all that there is to know about their ways in a month, and yet after a hundred years, they can still surprise you at a pinch."

–Gandalf, *The Lord of the Rings: The Fellowship of the Ring* film

SOCKS: CHART B

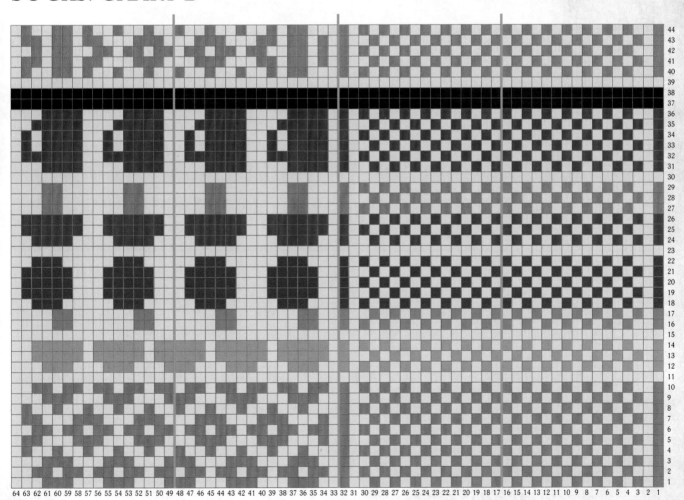

MITTENS

DUPLICATE STITCH

Above Mitten Cuff

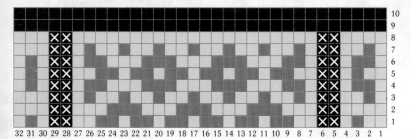

Foot of Sock

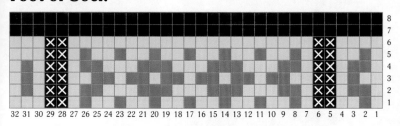

Seedcakes

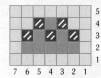

Apples

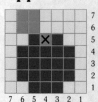

Tankards

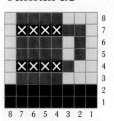

CHAPTER FIVE

HOME & TOYS

THE GREY WIZARD PILLOW

DESIGNED BY KRISTÍN ÖRNÓLFSDÓTTIR

Known by many names—Olórin, Muithrandir, or "Grey Pilgrim" by the Elves; Incánus by Southern Middle-earth dwellers; Tharkûn by the Dwarves; and Gandalf by Men—Gandalf the Grey was a powerful and wise Wizard from the Istari Order. Although he appeared to be an old man with a long beard, pointy hat, and ornate staff, he was tenacious and mighty. A wanderer for hundreds of years, he was sent to aid in the defeat of Sauron and sat on the White Council alongside Elrond, Galadriel, and fellow Wizard Saruman. Fond of Hobbits, he joined the Fellowship after realizing Bilbo's ring was the One Ring, acting as a guide for the group. Despite Saruman's betrayal and his fall into the abyss at the Bridge of Khazad-dûm, he is reborn as Gandalf the White, rejoining the Fellowship on their quest in Fangorn Forest.

Inspired by the wandering Wizard, you'll have your very own sorcerer to snuggle with this mystical home accessory. Gandalf the Grey with his magical staff, pointed hat, and iconic beard circles around this pillow in stranded colorwork, knit in the round as a tube. Once the desired height is reached, a pillow form is placed inside, and the top and bottom edges are mattress stitched together. Prefer Gandalf the White? Switch the charcoal yarn to white for a transformation!

SIZES
One size

FINISHED MEASUREMENTS
Width: 16 in. / 40.5 cm

Height: 16 in. / 40.5 cm

YARN
Worsted weight yarn, shown in Berroco *Comfort* (50% superfine nylon, 50% superfine acrylic; 210 yd. / 193 m per 3½ oz. / 100 g skein)

Colorways:

- **Main Color (MC):** #9785 Falseberry Heather, 2 skeins
- **Contrast Color 1 (CC1):** #9701 Ivory, 1 skein
- **Contrast Color 2 (CC2):** #9713 Dusk, 1 skein

NEEDLES
US 7 / 4.5 mm, 24 in. / 60 cm long circular needle or size needed to obtain gauge

NOTIONS
Stitch marker

Tapestry needle

16 by 16 in. / 40.5 by 40.5 cm pillow form (1)

GAUGE
21 sts and 23 rows = 4 in. / 10 cm over stranded colorwork in the round, taken after steam blocking

Make sure to check your gauge.

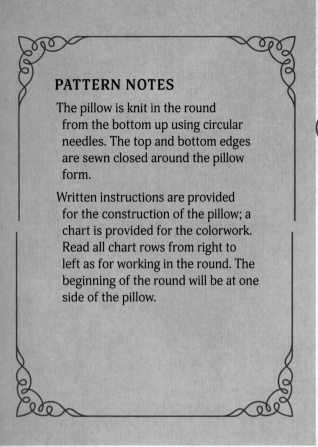

PATTERN NOTES

The pillow is knit in the round from the bottom up using circular needles. The top and bottom edges are sewn closed around the pillow form.

Written instructions are provided for the construction of the pillow; a chart is provided for the colorwork. Read all chart rows from right to left as for working in the round. The beginning of the round will be at one side of the pillow.

PATTERN INSTRUCTIONS

CAST ON

Using MC, CO 170 sts using the Long Tail cast on method. Pm for BOR and join to work in the rnd, being careful not to twist the sts.

PILLOW COVER

Begin working from Chart A, reading all rows from right to left as for working in the rnd. Work [Rows 1–24] 3 times, then [Rows 1–23] 1 more time (95 rows total); the chart is worked 17 times across each rnd. As you work the charted patt reps, join/use MC and CC1 for Rows 1–12, then break CC1; join/use MC and CC2 for Rows 14–21, then break CC2. This avoids carrying unused colors up the inside unnecessarily.

When the charted rows are complete, break CCs.

BO knitwise using MC. Break yarn, leaving a tail approx. 48 in. / 122 cm long; this tail will be used for seaming the top edge of the pillow.

FINISHING

Weave in all ends to the WS of the pillow (except the long tail of MC at the top of the pillow).

Thread the tapestry needle with a length of MC yarn approx. 48 in. / 122 cm long; sew the bottom of the pillow closed using the Horizontal Invisible Seaming method. Weave in rem ends to the WS.

Steam block the pillow cover gently.

Insert the pillow form.

Thread the tapestry needle with the long tail rem at the top of the pillow; sew the top of the pillow cover closed using the Horizontal Invisible Seaming method. Carefully weave the rem end to the inside of the pillow cover.

KEY

- ☐ Knit
- ■ MC
- ☐ CC1
- ■ CC2
- Pattern repeat

CHART A

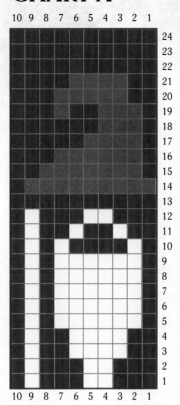

"Gandalf was shorter in stature than the other two; but his long white hair, his sweeping beard, and his broad shoulders made him look like some wise king of ancient legend. In his aged face under great snowy brows his eyes were set like coals that could suddenly burst into fire."

—*The Lord of the Rings: The Fellowship of the Ring*
by J.R.R. Tolkien

LITTLE FOLK TOY

DESIGNED BY SARA KELLNER

Close to the Brandywine River, the Shire is home to the Hobbits—mortal creatures small in stature, with curly hair, pointed ears, and large hairy feet. Generations of Hobbits are nestled into the hillsides in their Hobbit holes. Lovers of good food, drink, and pipe weed, they are a peaceful farming society mostly left untouched by the evils of Mordor. Generally shy and preferring to live quiet, predictable lives, they refer to people living outside the Shire as "outsiders" and have a love/hate relationship with Gandalf after Bilbo and Frodo develop a sense of adventure because of him. Courageous, brave, and steadfast of heart, these small, unsuspecting creatures are essential in saving Middle-earth.

This adorable pocket Hobbit is inspired by Bilbo Baggins of Bag End! Worked in the round in one piece, the body of this adorable fellow is knit from the neck down to the hairy feet with cleverly placed short rows and filled with craft stuffing. Moss stitch is worked intarsia-style to form his curls, with facial expressions embroidered on post-knitting. Clothing items are each knit separately and full of the little quirks which define an amiable Hobbit—breeches with a buttoned flap, a dashing waistcoat, and an overcoat to keep him warm in his Hobbit hole. Make an additional set of clothes in different colors or switch up the hair or skin color—make him your own!

SIZES

One size

FINISHED MEASUREMENTS

Height: 13 in. / 33 cm

Width (from hand to hand): approx. 8 in. / 20.5 cm

YARN

Worsted weight yarn, shown in Cascade Yarns *Cascade 220 Solids & Heathers* (3-ply; 100% Peruvian Highland wool; 220 yd. / 200 m per 3½ oz. / 100 g hank)

Colorways:

- **Color A:** #8021 Beige, 1 hank
- **Color B:** #8686 Brown, 1 hank
- **Color C:** #9448 Olive Heather, 1 hank
- **Color D:** #2415 Sunflower, 1 hank
- **Color E:** #2431 Chocolate Heather, 1 hank

Alternate Garment Colors:

- **Color C (breeches):** #2431 Chocolate Heather, 1 hank
- **Color D (waistcoat):** #9489 Red Wine Heather, 1 hank
- **Color E (overcoat):** #9448 Olive Heather, 1 hank

NEEDLES

US 3 / 3.25 mm set of 4 double-pointed needles, or size needed to obtain gauge

US 4 / 3.5 mm, 16 in. / 40 cm long circular needle (optional), pair of straight needles and set of 4 double-pointed needles

NOTIONS

Stitch marker

Locking stitch markers

Smooth waste yarn

Light red or pink waste yarn for the mouth (approx. 6 in. / 15 cm)

4 in. / 10 cm dowel or spare dpn to provide structure for the neck (optional)

Row counter (optional)

Tapestry needle

Polyester stuffing; approx. 5 oz. / 142 g)

Two ⁵⁄₁₆ in. / 7.5 mm gold shank buttons for breeches

Three ¼ in. / 6.5 mm black shank buttons for waistcoat

Three ³⁄₈ in. / 9.5 mm gold shank buttons for overcoat

GAUGE

24 sts and 30 rows = 4 in. / 10 cm in St st worked flat on smaller needles, unblocked

Gauge is not critical for this project; however, a difference in gauge may affect the required yardage and finished size of the toy. The ideal fabric for the body is dense enough to keep the stuffing from showing through.

PATTERN NOTES

The body is worked in the round, in one piece, from his neck down to his hairy feet. His head is worked separately and seamed to the neck to complete the body. His clothing items are each knit separately and are full of the little quirks which define an amiable Hobbit— breeches with a buttoned flap, a dashing waistcoat, and an overcoat to keep him warm in his underground home.

Be aware of needle size changes. All body parts, except for the head, are worked using the gauge-size needle. The head and all three articles of clothing are worked using a needle 1 size larger.

References to right and left are relative to the character's right and left, not the position when laid flat.

Increases in the waistcoat are made by casting on stitches. Use the Backward Loop cast on method for these increases unless otherwise noted.

While the body of the toy remains unblocked, blocking the waistcoat will be required to prevent rolling. It is optional to block the breeches and overcoat; the samples show them blocked.

To customize the colors of your toy: Colors A and B are for the body and hair, respectively. Colors C, D, and E are for the breeches, waistcoat, and overcoat, respectively. Your choice of color can be used for the eyes, though the samples show the eyes worked with Color B.

Stuffing: When to stuff the body is left up to the knitter. It can be done a little at a time as the body is constructed, or it can be stuffed after all four of the limbs have been completed via the hole between the legs. The latter option makes the toy easier to construct, but it becomes necessary to use a dpn to shift the stuffing down the body from the outside of the toy. Stuff mindfully, rounding out his fat tummy, and paying special attention to the shape of his knobby knees, muscular calves, ankles, heels, and elbows. The feet and hands are stuffed only sparingly and should be flatter than rounder.

PATTERN INSTRUCTIONS

TORSO

Work begins at the neckline; the first st of the rnd is at the center/back of neck.

Using Color A and the smaller dpns, CO 15 sts using the Long Tail cast on method. Join to work in the rnd by slipping the first CO st purlwise from the LHN to RHN; then pass the second st on the RHN (the last st cast on) up and over the slipped st from right to left and off the needle—14 sts rem. Pm for BOR (if desired) and distribute sts evenly for comfort over the dpns.

Rnds 1 and 2: Knit.

Rnd 3 (inc): (K1, LR1) 4 times, k4, (k1, LR1) 4 times, k2—22 sts.

Rnd 4 (and all even-numbered rnds of this section unless otherwise noted): Knit.

Rnd 5 (inc): K2, LR1, k1, LR1, k3, LR1, k1, LR1, k7, LR1, k1, LR1, k3, LR1, k1, LR1, k3—30 sts.

Rnd 7 (inc): K3, LR1, k1, LR1, k5, LR1, k1, LR1, k9, LR1, k1, LR1, k5, LR1, k1, LR1, k4—38 sts.

Rnd 9 (inc): K4, LR1, k9, LR1, k11, LR1, k9, LR1, k5—42 sts.

Rnd 11 (inc): K5, LR1, k9, LR1, k13, LR1, k9, LR1, k6—46 sts.

Rnd 13 (inc): K6, LR1, k9, LR1, k15, LR1, k9, LR1, k7—50 sts.

Rnd 15 (inc): K7, LR1, k9, LR1, k17, LR1, k9, LR1, k8—54 sts.

Rnd 17 (inc): K8, LR1, k9, LR1, k19, LR1, k9, LR1, k9—58 sts.

Rnd 19 (inc): K9, LR1, k9, LR1, k21, LR1, k9, LR1, k10—62 sts.

Rnd 20 (dec): K11, place next 8 sts on waste yarn for right arm, k24, place next 8 sts on waste yarn for left arm, k11—46 sts.

Rnds 21–23: Knit.

Rnd 24 (inc): K17, (LR1, k4) 3 times, LR1, k17—50 sts.

Rnds 25 and 26: Knit.

Rnd 27 (inc): K16, (LR1, k6) 3 times, LR1, k16—54 sts.

Rnds 28 and 29: Knit.

Rnd 30 (inc): K15, (LR1, k8) 3 times, LR1, k15—58 sts.

Rnds 31–40: Knit.

Rnd 41 (dec): K1, (k5, k2tog) 8 times, k1—50 sts.

Rnd 43 (dec): (K3, k2tog) 10 times—40 sts.

Rnd 44: Knit.

RIGHT LEG AND FOOT

Cont with smaller dpns.

Setup Rnd (inc): K20, place the next 20 sts on waste yarn for the left leg. At the end of the live sts, CO 4 sts using the Backward Loop cast on method—24 sts. Distribute sts evenly over 3 dpns. Join to work in the rnd again. Rm (if placed), k4, pm for new BOR. The BOR is now at the back of the right leg.

Rnds 1–6: Knit.

Rnd 7 (dec): K2tog, k20, ssk—22 sts.

Rnds 8–10: Knit.

Rnd 11 (dec): K2tog, k18, ssk—20 sts.

Rnds 12–14: Knit.

Rnd 15 (dec): K2tog, k2, ssk, k2tog, k4, ssk, k2tog, k2, ssk—14 sts.

Rnd 16: Knit.

The following 5 rows are worked flat, using short rows to shape the knee. Work in the round resumes on Rnd 22.

Short Row 17 (RS): K9, w&t.

Short Row 18 (WS): P4, w&t.

Short Row 19: K5, w&t.

Short Row 20: P6, w&t.

Short Row 21: K10 (BOR). Resume working in the rnd.

Rnd 22 (dec): K2tog, k10, ssk—12 sts.

Rnd 23: Knit.

Rnd 24 (inc): K1, LR1, k10, LR1, k1—14 sts.

Rnd 25: Knit.

Rnd 26 (inc): K2, LR1, k10, LR1, k2—16 sts.

Rnd 27: Knit.

Rnd 28 (inc): K3, LR1, k10, LR1, k3—18 sts.

Rnds 29–31: Knit.

Rnd 32 (dec): (K2tog) 2 times, k10, (ssk) 2 times—14 sts.

Rnds 33 and 34: Knit.

Rnd 35 (dec): K2tog, k10, ssk—12 sts.

Rnds 36–38: Knit.

The following 9 rows are worked flat, using short rows to shape the ankle. Work in the round resumes on Rnd 48.

Short Row 39: K1, w&t.

Short Row 40: P2, w&t.

Short Row 41: K3, w&t.

Short Row 42: P4, w&t.

Short Row 43: K5, w&t.

Short Row 44: P6, w&t.

Short Row 45: K7, w&t.

Short Row 46: P8, w&t.

Short Row 47: K4 (BOR). Resume working in the rnd.

Rnds 48 and 49: Knit.

Rnd 50 (inc): K1, LR1, k10, LR1, k1—14 sts.

Rnds 51 and 52: Knit.

Rnd 53 (inc): K1, LR1, k12, LR1, k1—16 sts.

Rnds 54–57: Knit.

Rnd 58 (dec): K4, ssk, k4, k2tog, k4—14 sts.

Rnd 59: Knit.

Rnd 60 (dec): K3, ssk, k4, k2tog, k3—12 sts.

Graft the Foot

Rm (if placed), k3. Distribute sts evenly over 2 dpns (6 sts per needle) and hold parallel.

Break yarn leaving an 8 in. / 20.5 cm tail. Using Kitchener stitch, graft closed the end of the foot.

LEFT LEG AND FOOT

Place the live 20 sts of the left leg onto a set of smaller dpns. Rejoin Color A yarn at the first st (at the front of the body).

Setup Rnd (inc): K20, CO 4 sts using the Backward Loop cast on method—24 sts. Distribute sts evenly over 3 dpns. Join to work in the rnd. K16, pm for new BOR (if desired). The BOR is now at the back of the left leg.

Work Rnds 1–60 as for the Right Leg and Foot section. Graft the Foot in the same manner.

Leave the hole between legs unseamed until all work on the body of the toy is completed in order to adjust the amount of stuffing if necessary.

RIGHT ARM AND HAND

Place the live 8 sts of the right arm onto 1 smaller dpn. Using a second smaller dpn, rejoin Color A at the bottom center of the opening.

Setup Rnd: Pick up and knit 3 sts along the left edge. K8 live sts. Using a third smaller dpn, pick up and knit 3 sts along the right edge—14 sts total. Pm for BOR (if desired) and join to work in the rnd. Redistribute sts over dpns for comfort as desired.

Rnds 1–15: Knit.

The following 5 rows are worked flat, using short rows to shape the elbow. Work in the round resumes on Rnd 21.

Short Row 16 (RS): K6, w&t.

Short Row 17 (WS): P3, w&t.

Short Row 18: K4, w&t.

Short Row 19: P5, w&t.

Short Row 20: K12 (BOR). Resume working in the rnd.

Rnd 21 (dec): K10, ssk, k2tog—12 sts.

Rnds 22–31: Knit.

Rnd 32 (dec): K2tog, k8, ssk—10 sts.

Rnd 33: Knit.

Rnd 34 (inc): K3, LR1, k4, LR1, k3—12 sts.

Rnds 35–41: Knit.

Rnd 42 (dec): (K2tog, k2) 3 times—9 sts.

Rnd 43 (dec): (K2tog, k1) 3 times—6 sts.
Break yarn; thread tail through rem live sts and cinch closed. Weave in tail to inside of hand.

LEFT ARM AND HAND

Work as for Right Arm and Hand up to the end of Rnd 15.
The following 5 rows are worked flat, using short rows to shape the elbow. Work in the round resumes on Rnd 21.
Short Row 16 (RS): K11, w&t.
Short Row 17 (WS): P3, w&t.
Short Row 18: K4, w&t.
Short Row 19: P5, w&t.
Short Row 20: K7 (BOR). Resume working in the rnd.
Rnd 21 (dec): K1, ssk, k2tog, k9—12 sts.
Rnds 22–43: Work as for Rnds 22–43 of the Right Arm and Hand.
Break yarn; thread tail through rem live sts and cinch closed. Weave in tail to inside of hand.

HEAD

Color A is held single; two strands of Color B are held double to work the hair. When changing between Colors A and B, bring the new yarn over the old one to prevent a gap from forming between them.

Setup for Color B: Prepare 2 double-strand balls of Color B. Each of the 4 strands of yarn should be about 10 arm lengths (approx. 5 yd. / 4.5 m). Using the Long Tail cast on method, CO the following number of sts using the specified colors onto 1 larger dpn (14 sts total):
Color B: CO 4 sts.
Color A: CO 6 sts.
Color B: CO 4 sts.
Row 1 (WS): With Color B, (k1, p1) 2 times; with Color A, p6; with Color B, (k1, p1) 2 times.
Row 2 (RS, inc): With Color B, (kfb) 4 times; with Color A, (LR1, k1) 6 times; with Color B, (kfb) 4 times—28 sts.
Row 3: With Color B, (p1, k1) 4 times; with Color A, p12; with Color B, (k1, p1) 4 times.
Row 4: With Color B, (p1, k1) 4 times, k1; with Color A, k10; with Color B, k1, (k1, p1) 4 times.
Row 5: With Color B, (p1, k1) 4 times, k1; with Color A, p10; with Color B, k1, (k1, p1) 4 times.
Rows 6 and 7: Rep [Rows 3 and 4] 1 time.
Row 8: With Color B, (p1, k1) 5 times; with Color A, k8; with Color B, (k1, p1) 5 times.
Row 9: With Color B, (p1, k1) 5 times; with Color A, p8; with Color B, (k1, p1) 5 times.
Rows 10 and 11: Rep [Rows 3 and 4] 1 time.
Row 12: With Color B, (p1, k1) 5 times, k1; with Color A, k6; with Color B, k1, (k1, p1) 5 times.

Row 13: With Color B, (p1, k1) 5 times, k1; with Color A, p6; with Color B, k1, (k1, p1) 5 times.
Break Color A and the second ball of Color B. The remainder of the head is worked with only one of the Color B balls.
Row 14 (RS): (P1, k1) 5 times, p1, k6, p1, (k1, p1) 5 times.
Row 15 (WS): (P1, k1) 8 times, (k1, p1) 6 times.
Row 16: (P1, k1) 6 times, p2, (k1, p1) 7 times.
Row 17: (P1, k1) 7 times, p2, (k1, p1) 6 times.
Row 18 (dec): (Ssk, p1) 4 times, (k1, p1) 2 times, (p1, k2tog) 4 times—20 sts.
Row 19: (K1, p1) 4 times, (p1, k1) 6 times.
Row 20 (dec): (Ssk) 5 times, (k2tog) 5 times—10 sts.
Without breaking the yarn, distribute the sts over 3 dpns and join to work in the rnd.
Rnd 21 (dec): (K2tog) 5 times—5 sts.
Break yarn, leaving a tail approx. 8 in. / 20.5 cm long. Thread tail though remaining live sts and cinch closed.
Using the long tail, seam the back of the head closed from the top down to the original 14 CO sts. Stuff fully.

FINISH THE HEAD/FACE

Using the photos as a reference for placement:
Embroider a nose with Color A by making 7 vertical lines on top of each other over 2 rows.

Embroider eyes with Color B by making 2 horizontal lines on top of each other over 1 st.
Embroider mouth with pale red or pink waste yarn by making 1 horizontal line over 3 sts.
Embroider ears with Color A by making 2 vertical lines on top of each other at sides of head.
Seam the cast on edge of the head to the cast on edge of the neck using Color A, adding enough stuffing to the neck before closing to make it stiff enough to keep head from falling to one side. A 4 in. / 10 cm long dowel or spare dpn can be inserted down through the head and into body for additional stabilization, if needed. Carefully weave all ends to the inside of the head/neck.

BREECHES

Work begins at waistline; the first st in the rnd is at the center/back of waist.
Using Color C and the larger dpns, CO 53 sts using the Long Tail cast on method. Join to work in the rnd by slipping the first CO st purlwise from the LHN to RHN; then pass the second st on the RHN (the last st cast on) up and over the slipped st from right to left and off the needle—52 sts rem. Pm for BOR (if desired) and distribute sts evenly for comfort over the dpns.

Rnd 1: Purl.

Rnd 2: Knit.

Rnds 3 and 4: Rep [Rnds 1 and 2] 1 time.

Rnd 5: Purl.

Rnds 6–9: Knit.

Rnd 10 (dec): K23, BO 6 sts knitwise, knit to end of rnd—46 sts.

Note: 23 sts rem on each side of the BO sts. Rows 11–18 are worked flat on each side of the bound-off sts. Sts are cast on to the end of Row 19 and knitting resumes in the rnd.

Row 11 (RS, inc): K1, (LR1, k4) 5 times, k2, turn—51 sts.

Row 12 (WS): Purl to end of live sts, turn.

Row 13 (inc): K6, (LR1, k4) 4 times, LR1, k29, turn—56 sts.

Row 14: Purl to end of live sts, turn.

Row 15: Knit to end of live sts, turn.

Rows 16 and 17: Rep [Rows 14 and 15] 1 time.

Row 18: Purl to end of live sts, turn.

Row 19 (inc): Knit to end of live sts, CO 6 sts using the Backward Loop cast on method—62 sts.

Join to work in the rnd.

Rnd 20: K28 (at original BOR).

Rnds 21–25: Knit.

Right Leg

Setup Rnd: K31, place next 31 sts on waste yarn for the left leg. At the end of the live sts, CO 1 st using the Backward Loop cast on method—32 sts. Distribute sts for comfort over 3 dpns. Join to work in the rnd again. Rm (if placed),

k8, pm for new BOR. The BOR is now at the back of the right leg.

Rnd 1: Knit.

Rnd 2 (dec): K1, k2tog, k2, k2tog, k18, ssk, k2, ssk, k1—28 sts.

Rnds 3 and 4: Knit.

Rnd 5 (dec): K1, k2tog, k2, k2tog, k14, ssk, k2, ssk, k1—24 sts.

Rnds 6 and 7: Knit.

Rnd 8 (dec): K1, k2tog, k2, k2tog, k10, ssk, k2, ssk, k1—20 sts.

Rnds 9–16: Knit.

BO all sts loosely knitwise.

Left Leg

Place the live 31 sts of the left leg onto 1 larger dpn. Rejoin Color C at the start of the live sts at the front of the leg (adjacent to the hole).

Setup Rnd: Knit across all live sts. At the end of the live sts, CO 1 st using the Backward Loop cast on method—32 sts. Distribute sts for comfort over 3 dpns. Join to work in the rnd. K24, pm for BOR (if desired). The BOR is now at the back of the left leg.

Work Rnds 1–16 as for the Right Leg. BO all sts loosely knitwise.

Flap

With RS facing, using a larger dpn and Color C, pick up and knit 8 sts along the bottom edge of the hole in the front of the breeches, making sure to center them with the hole.

Row 1 (WS): Purl.

Row 2 (RS, inc): K1, LR1, k6, LR1, k1—10 sts.

Row 3: Purl.

Row 4 (inc): K1, LR1, k8,

LR1, k1—12 sts.

Rows 5–11: Work 7 rows in reverse St st (knit on WS, purl on RS).

With RS facing, bind off all sts knitwise.

Hold the flap against the breeches to cover the hole and clip a locking marker to each of the corners to indicate the button placement. These markers should fall below the waistband on each side. Sew the $5/16$ in. / 7.5 mm gold buttons onto the front of the breeches at each of these markers. Pull up flap and push buttons through the corner sts of the flap on each side. All 3 sides of flap are left unseamed.

Thread the tapestry needle with approx. 6 in. / 15 cm of Color C yarn. Whipstitch the hole between the legs closed.

WAISTCOAT

The waistcoat is worked flat in 3 pieces—right front, left front, and back— then seamed together at sides and shoulders. The fronts are worked from the top down; the back is worked from the bottom up. Remember to use the Backward Loop cast on method for all increases in this section.

Right Front

Using Color D and 1 larger dpn, CO 6 sts using the Long Tail cast on method. Do not join to work in the rnd.

Row 1 (WS): Purl.

Row 2 (RS): Knit.

Row 3: Purl.

Row 4 (inc): Knit to last st, CO1, k1—1 st inc.

Rows 5–18: Rep [Rows 3 and 4] 7 more times—14 sts.

Row 19 (inc): P14, CO4—18 sts.

Row 20: Knit.

Row 21: Purl.

Rows 22–25: Rep [Rows 20 and 21] 2 more times.

Row 26 (dec): K16, k2tog—17 sts.

Row 27: Purl.

Row 28 (dec): K15, k2tog—16 sts.

Row 29: P12, w&t.

Row 30 (dec): K10, k2tog—15 sts.

Row 31: P8, w&t.

Row 32 (dec): K6, k2tog—14 sts.

Row 33: P4, w&t.

Row 34 (dec): K2, k2tog—13 sts.

Row 35 (dec/BO): P2tog, p1, pass first st over second st from right to left and off the needle (1 st BO), bind off rem sts purlwise.

Break yarn and pull through final loop to secure.

Left Front

Using Color D and 1 larger dpn, CO 6 sts using the Long Tail cast on method. Do not join to work in the rnd.

Row 1 (WS): Purl.

Row 2 (RS): Knit.

Row 3: Purl.

Row 4 (inc): K1, CO1, knit to end—1 st inc.

Rows 5–18: Rep [Rows 3 and 4] 7 more times—14 sts.

Row 19 (inc): CO4, p14—18 sts.

Row 20: Knit.

Row 21: Purl.

Rows 22–25: Rep [Rows 20 and 21] 2 more times.

Row 26 (dec): K2tog, k16—17 sts.

Row 27: Purl.

Row 28 (dec): K2tog, k11, w&t—16 sts.

Row 29: P12.

Row 30: K2tog, k7, w&t—15 sts.

Row 31: P8.

Row 32: K2tog, k3, w&t—14 sts.

Row 33: P4.

Row 34 (dec/BO): K2tog, k1, pass first st over second st from right to left and off the needle (1 st BO), bind off rem sts knitwise. Break yarn and pull through final loop to secure.

Back

Using Color D and 1 larger dpn, CO 26 sts using the Long Tail cast on method. Do not join to work in the rnd.

Row 1 (WS): Purl.

Row 2 (RS): Knit.

Rows 3–8: Rep [Rows 1 and 2] 3 times.

Row 9: Purl.

Row 10 (dec): (Ssk) 2 times, k18, (k2tog) 2 times—22 sts.

Row 11: Purl.

Row 12 (dec): (Ssk) 2 times, k14, (k2tog) 2 times—18 sts.

Rows 13–28: Rep [Rows 1 and 2] 8 times.

Row 29: Purl.

With RS facing, bind off all sts knitwise.

With Color D, seam shoulders of front pieces to back piece using whipstitch or the Horizontal Invisible Seaming method. Seam sides of front pieces up to the armholes to back piece using whipstitch or mattress stitch.

Weave in the ends. Wet block and pin out gently (or place a large, heavy object on top to prevent rolling).

Sew three ¼ in. / 6.5 mm buttons to the left front edge, evenly spaced, referencing the photos for placement. After dressing the toy, push buttons through the adjacent sts on right front side to secure the waistcoat.

OVERCOAT

The body of the overcoat is worked flat from the top down. The sleeves are placed on hold and the body is completed. A shawl collar is worked flat, using picked up sts along the front edges and back neck edge of the sweater. The sleeves are then worked outward from the body in the round.

Using Color E and the larger straight needles, CO 14 sts using the Long Tail cast on method. Do not join to work in the rnd.

Row 1 (WS, and all WS rows of this section unless otherwise noted): Purl.

Row 2 (RS, inc): (K1, LR1) 4 times, k4, (k1, LR1) 4 times, k2—22 sts.

Row 4 (inc): K2, LR1, k1, LR1, k3, LR1, k1, LR1, k7, LR1, k1, LR1, k3, LR1, k1, LR1, k3—30 sts.

Row 6 (inc): K3, LR1, k1, LR1, k5, LR1, k1, LR1, k9, LR1, k1, LR1, k5, LR1, k1, LR1, k4—38 sts.

Row 8 (inc): K4, LR1, k1, LR1, k7, LR1, k1, LR1, k11, LR1, k1, LR1, k7, LR1, k1, LR1, k5—46 sts.

Row 10 (inc): K5, LR1, k1, LR1, k9, LR1, k1, LR1, k13, LR1, k1, LR1, k9, LR1, k1, LR1, k6—54 sts.

Row 12 (inc): K6, LR1, k13, LR1, k15, LR1, k13, LR1, k7—58 sts.

Row 14 (inc): K7, LR1, k13, LR1, k17, LR1, k13, LR1, k8—62 sts.

Row 16 (inc): K8, LR1, k13, LR1, k19, LR1, k13, LR1, k9—66 sts.

Row 18 (inc): K22, LR1, k21, LR1, k23—68 sts.

Row 20 (inc): K22, LR1, k23, LR1, k23—70 sts.

Row 22 (inc): K22, LR1, k25, LR1, k23—72 sts.

Row 24 (inc): K22, LR1, k27, LR1, k23—74 sts.

Row 26 (dec): K10, place next 12 sts on waste yarn for left sleeve, k30, place next 12 sts on waste yarn for the right sleeve, k10—50 sts.

Row 28 (inc): K10, LR1, k30, LR1, k10—52 sts.

Rows 30 and 32: Knit.

Row 34 (inc): K10, LR1, k32, LR1, k10—54 sts.

Rows 36 and 38: Knit.

Row 40 (inc): K10, LR1, k34, LR1, k10—56 sts.

Rows 42, 44, 46, and 48: Knit.

Rows 49–53: Knit (including WS rows).

With RS facing, BO all sts knitwise to the last st. Do not break yarn (1 live st rem).

Button Band and Collar

With RS facing, rotate the work so the right edge of the overcoat is facing; 1 st rem on your working needle. Transfer live st to either 1 larger dpn or the larger circular needle for your preferred method of working the collar. Cont with the working yarn, pick up and knit 91 sts along the front and back neck edges of the coat as follows (distributing sts across dpns for comfort as needed):

3 sts in the garter stitch border (4 sts incl the rem live st), then

35 sts up the right front edge (approx. 3 sts for every 4 rows; 39 sts total), then

14 sts across the back neck (1 st for every CO st; 53 sts total), then

35 sts down the left front edge (approx. 3 sts for every 4 rows; 88 sts total), then

4 sts in the garter edge border (92 sts total).

Row 1 (WS): Purl.

Row 2 (RS): Knit.

Row 3: P72, *clip a locking M to the last st worked, p6; rep from * once more, clip a locking M to the last st worked (3 total locking markers placed), purl to end.

Note: These locking markers will help place the buttons for the button band; do not remove until instructed.

Row 4: Knit.

Rows 5–8: Rep [Rows 1 and 2] 2 more times.

Short Row 9: P65, w&t.

Short Row 10: K38, w&t.

Short Row 11: P34, w&t.

Short Row 12: K30, w&t.

Short Row 13: P61 (EOR).

With RS facing, BO all sts knitwise. Weave in all rem ends to the WS.

Using the locking markers for placement, sew three 3/8 in. / 9.5 mm gold shank buttons to the RS of the button band. The buttons should be in the third row from the picked-up edge, between sts 72 and 73, sts 78 and 79, and sts 84 and 85. Once each button is placed, remove the locking marker.

Secure any ends from sewing on the buttons to the WS.

Fold the button band / collar in half, lengthwise, so that the BO edge is aligned with the picked-up edge (WS together; RS facing out). Secure the BO edge to the picked-up edge using whipstitch and Color E. The folded collar (at the back neck as well as about 2 in. / 5 cm down from the shoulders on each side) is then folded in half again, toward the outside, tacked to the coat with Color E. The overcoat is left open.

SLEEVES (WORK 2 THE SAME)

Place the live 12 sts of one sleeve onto 2 larger dpns. Using a third larger dpn, rejoin Color E at the center of the underarm.

Setup Rnd: Pick up and knit 4 sts along the left edge. K12 live sts. Pick up and knit 4 sts along the right edge— 20 sts total. Pm for BOR (if desired) and join to work in the rnd. Redistribute sts over dpns for comfort as desired.

Rnds 1–14: Knit.

Rnd 15: Purl.

Rnd 16: Knit.

Rnd 17: Purl.

Rnd 18: Knit.

Rnd 19: Purl.

BO all sts knitwise.

Rep for second sleeve.

Weave in all ends.

FINISHING THE PROJECT

Add or remove stuffing to body as needed from hole between legs, using a dpn to move stuffing if needed. Whipstitch the hole closed from front to back with Color A.

Add the Foot Hair:

Step 1: Cut a length of Color B yarn approx. 12 in. / 30.5 cm long. Thread this length into the tapestry needle.

Step 2: Tie a knot at the tail end (i.e., the end not threaded through the needle).

Step 3: Insert the tapestry needle through the bottom of the foot and out the top, being careful not to split any strands. Tug the knot so that it pulls through the bottom of the foot, but not out the top. The knot will remain inside the foot.

Step 4: Cut the yarn approx. 1/2 in. / 1 cm above the top of the foot and separate the plies.

Rep [Steps 2–4] 3 or 4 more times. Trim all hairs to make even.

"Even the smallest person can change the course of the future."

—Galadriel, *The Lord of the Rings: The Fellowship of the Ring* film

MY PRECIOUS TOY

DESIGNED BY SUSAN CLAUDINO

Once a Hobbit named Sméagol, Gollum's mind and body were poisoned by the One Ring after he stole it from his cousin, Déagol. Driven mad by its power, he hid in a cave under the Misty Mountains with his "Precious," as the Ring's fourth captive. His life extended hundreds of years by the Ring, he survived off raw blind fish and bats, losing his taste for the food Hobbits so love to enjoy. Despite the maliciousness brought on by his constant desire to be reunited with the One Ring, readers and viewers caught occasional glimpses of helpful Sméagol aiding Sam and Frodo on their quest.

Inspired by Sam and Frodo's guide through the marshlands surrounding Mordor, this knitted Gollum is the perfect companion to keep guard over anything you find precious! This little toy is knit in the round using the Magic Loop method with simple stockinette to create a sinister yet cute look. All the pieces are knit in the round for minimal finishing except for his loincloth, which is worked flat. It's up to you if you end up with a plotting Gollum or a helpful Sméagol . . .

SIZES

One size

FINISHED MEASUREMENTS

Height: 13 in. / 33 cm

YARN

Worsted weight yarn, shown in Cascade Yarns *Cascade 220 Solids & Heathers* (3-ply; 100% Peruvian Highland wool; 220 yd. / 200 m per 3½ oz. / 100 g hank)

Colorways:

- **Main Color (MC):** #8021 Beige, 1 hank
- **Contrast Color (CC):** #9656 Burnt Sienna Heather, 1 hank

NEEDLES

US 5 / 3.75 mm, 40 in. / 100 cm long circular needle or size needed to obtain gauge

NOTIONS

Stitch marker (optional)

3 yd. / 2.75 m dark brown worsted weight yarn (for hair)

Polyester stuffing (approx. 8 oz. / 227 g)

21 mm safety eyes (2)

Fabric glue (for hair, optional)

Blocking pins

Row counter (optional)

Tapestry needle

GAUGE

20 sts and 28 rows = 4 in. / 10 cm over stockinette stitch worked in the round, unblocked

Gauge is not critical for this project; however, a difference in gauge may affect the required yardage and finished size of the toy. The ideal fabric for the body is dense enough to keep the stuffing from showing through.

PATTERN NOTES

The doll's head and body are worked as one continuous piece, in the round, from the bottom up, using the Magic Loop method.

Stuffing is added as the toy is constructed.

During the head construction, the fabric is marked with purl stitches to indicate eye and ear placement locations.

The ears are worked in the round, separate from the body, and are sewn onto the head.

The hands and arms are worked in the round, separate from the body, starting at the hand, working up the length of the arm. They are sewn onto the body in mirror orientation.

The feet and legs are worked in the round, separate from the body, with mirrored foot directions. Follow instructions carefully to ensure the feet are anatomically correct. The legs are sewn to the body once completed.

References to right and left are relative to the character's right and left, not the position when laid flat.

The loincloth is worked flat, as two separate pieces that are blocked and then sewn onto the body after the doll is completed.

Gauge is not critical for this project; however, a difference in gauge may affect the required yardage and finished size of the toy. The ideal fabric for the body is dense enough to keep the stuffing from showing through.

Written instructions are provided for the entirety of the project.

PATTERN INSTRUCTIONS

CAST ON & BODY

Using MC, CO 4 sts using the Long Tail cast on method. Pm for BOR (if desired) and join to work in the rnd, being careful not to twist the sts.

Rnd 1 (inc): (Kfb) 4 times—8 sts.

Rnd 2 (inc): (K1, kfb) 4 times—12 sts.

Rnd 3 (inc): (K2, kfb) 4 times—16 sts.

Rnd 4 (inc): (K3, kfb) 4 times—20 sts.

Rnd 5 (inc): (K4, kfb) 4 times—24 sts.

Rnd 6 (inc): (K5, kfb) 4 times—28 sts.

Rnd 7 (inc): (K6, kfb) 4 times—32 sts.

Rnd 8 (inc): (K7, kfb) 4 times—36 sts.

Rnds 9–17: Knit.

Rnd 18 (dec): (Ssk, k16) 2 times—34 sts.

Rnd 19 (dec): (K15, k2tog) 2 times—32 sts.

Rnd 20: Knit.

Rnd 21 (dec): (Ssk, k14) 2 times—30 sts.

Rnd 22 (dec): (K13, k2tog) 2 times—28 sts.

Rnd 23: Knit.

Rnd 24 (dec): (Ssk, k12) 2 times—26 sts.

Rnd 25 (dec): (K11, k2tog) 2 times—24 sts.

Rnd 26: Knit.

Using polyfil, begin stuffing the body. Continue to add stuffing as you finish the body.

Rnd 27 (dec): (Ssk, k10) 2 times—22 sts.

Rnd 28 (dec): (K9, k2tog) 2 times—20 sts.

Rnd 29: Knit.

Rnd 30 (dec): (Ssk, k8) 2 times—18 sts.

Rnd 31 (dec): (K7, k2tog) 2 times—16 sts.

Rnds 32–36: Knit.

Rnd 37 (dec): (Ssk, k4, k2tog) 2 times—12 sts.

HEAD

Rnd 38 (inc): (Kfb) to end of rnd—24 sts.

Rnd 39 (inc): (Kfb) to end of rnd—48 sts.

Rnd 40 (inc): (K3, kfb) to end of rnd—60 sts.

Rnds 41–47: Knit.

The un-bolded purl sts in Rnds 48–51 will mark the ear placement; the bolded purl sts in Rnd 49 will mark the eye placement.

Rnd 48: K31, p1, k26, p1, k1.

Rnd 49: K8, **p1**, k12, **p1**, k9, p1, k26, p1, k1.

Rnds 50 and 51: Rep [Rnd 48] 2 times.

Rnds 52–60: Knit.

Rnd 61 (dec): (K3, k2tog) to end of rnd—48 sts.

Rnd 62: Knit.

Rnd 63 (dec): (K2, k2tog) to end of rnd—36 sts.

Rnd 64: Knit.

Using the purl sts in Rnd 49 for placement, attach the safety eyes.

Continue to add stuffing as you finish the head.

Rnd 65 (dec): (K1, k2tog) to end of rnd—24 sts.

Rnd 66: Knit.

Rnd 67 (dec): (K2tog) to end of rnd—12 sts.

Rnd 68 (dec): (K2tog) to end of rnd—6 sts.

Break yarn. Thread the tapestry needle with the yarn tail and weave tail through rem live sts and cinch closed. Weave in all ends to inside of head and body.

EARS (MAKE 2 THE SAME)

Using MC, CO 14 sts using the Long Tail cast on method. When casting on, leave a 12 in. / 30.5 cm tail for joining/attaching the ears to the head. Pm for BOR (if desired) and join to work in the rnd, being careful not to twist the sts.

Rnds 1–3: Knit.

Rnd 4: Ssk, k4, (kfb) 2 times, k4, ssk.

Rnds 5 and 6: Rep [Rnd 4] 2 times.

Rnd 7 (dec): (S2kp, k1, k3tog) 2 times—6 sts.

Rnd 8 (dec): S2kp, k3tog—2 sts.

Break yarn. Thread the tapestry needle with the yarn tail and weave tail through rem live sts and cinch closed.

HANDS & ARMS (MAKE 2 THE SAME)

Using MC, CO 4 sts using the Long Tail cast on method. Pm for BOR (if desired) and join to work in the rnd, being careful not to twist the sts.

Rnd 1 (inc): (Kfb) 4 times—8 sts.

Rnd 2 (inc): (K1, kfb) 4 times—12 sts.

Rnds 3–6: Knit.

Rnd 7: K5, SB, k6.

Rnd 8: K5, k1tbl, k6.

Rnd 4 (inc): (K3, kfb) 4 times—20 sts.

Rnd 5 (inc): (K4, kfb) 4 times—24 sts.

Rnd 6: Knit.

Left Foot Only:

Rnd 7: K1, (SB, k1) 3 times, SB, k2, LB, k13.

Right Foot Only:

Rnd 7: K1, LB, k2, (SB, k1) 3 times, SB, k13.

Both Feet:

Rnd 8: Knit all sts tbl.

Rnds 9–11: Knit.

Rnd 12 (dec): (Ssk, k10) 2 times—22 sts.

Rnd 13 (dec): (K9, k2tog) 2 times—20 sts.

Rnd 14 (dec): (Ssk, k8) 2 times—18 sts.

Rnd 15 (dec): (K7, k2tog) 2 times—16 sts.

Rnd 16 (dec): (Ssk, k6) 2 times—14 sts.

Rnd 17 (dec): (K5, k2tog) 2 times—12 sts.

Using polyfil, stuff the foot (the legs will not be stuffed).

Rnd 18 (dec): (Ssk, k2, k2tog) 2 times—8 sts.

Rnds 19–36: Knit.

Rnd 37 (inc): K1, (kfb) 2 times, k5—10 sts.

Rnd 38: Knit.

Rnd 39 (dec): K1, ssk, k2tog, k5—8 sts.

Rnd 40: Knit.

Left Leg Only:

Rnd 41 (dec): (Ssk, k2) 2 times—6 sts.

Right Leg Only:

Rnd 41 (dec): (K2, k2tog) 2 times—6 sts.

Both Legs:

Rnds 42–55: Knit.

BO all sts knitwise. Break yarn leaving an 8 in. / 20.5 cm tail for sewing the arm to the body.

Rnd 9 (dec): K4, k2tog, ssk, k4—10 sts.

Rnd 10 (dec): Ssk, k6, k2tog—8 sts.

Rnds 11–18: Knit.

Rnd 19 (dec): Ssk, k4, k2tog—6 sts.

Rnds 20–33: Knit.

BO all sts knitwise. Break yarn leaving an 8 in. / 20.5 cm tail for sewing the arm to the body.

FEET AND LEGS (MAKE 2)

The left and right legs are made nearly identically, the exception being Rnds 7 and 41. Follow instructions carefully to ensure you have left- and right-facing feet.

Using MC, CO 4 sts using the Long Tail cast on method.

Pm for BOR (if desired) and join to work in the rnd, being careful not to twist the sts.

Both Feet:

Rnd 1 (inc): (Kfb) 4 times—8 sts.

Rnd 2 (inc): (K1, kfb) 4 times—12 sts.

Rnd 3 (inc): (K2, kfb) 4 times—16 sts.

LOINCLOTH (MAKE 2 THE SAME)

Using CC, CO 17 sts using the Long Tail cast on method. When casting on, leave a 12 in. / 30.5 cm tail for joining/attaching the loincloths. Do not join to work in the rnd.

Row 1 (WS): Knit.

Row 2 (RS, dec): Ssk, k13, k2tog—15 sts.

Row 3 (and all WS rows in this section unless otherwise noted): Purl.

Row 4 (dec): Ssk, k11, k2tog—13 sts.

Row 6 (dec): Ssk, k9, k2tog—11 sts.

Row 8 (dec): Ssk, k7, k2tog—9 sts.

Row 10 (dec): Ssk, k5, k2tog—7 sts.

Row 12 (dec): Ssk, k3, k2tog—5 sts.

Row 14 (dec): Ssk, k1, k2tog—3 sts.

Row 16 (dec): S2kp—1 st.

Break yarn. Pull tail through rem live st and cinch closed.

FINISHING

Use the purl sts from Rnds 48–51 for placement of the ears. Position the ear so that all the purl sts are covered and sew the ears to the head using the long tails from the cast on using the Horizontal Invisible Seaming method.

Sew the limbs to the body.

Wet block the loincloth halves, pinning the edges to keep them flat; do not overstretch.

Sew the loincloth ends together using the long tails from the cast on; using the same tail, sew onto the body using the photos as a reference for placement. Weave in ends.

Using the MC for the facial features, thread a tapestry needle with a length of yarn and create wrinkles around the eyes and on the forehead, a nose, and a mouth with simple straight stitches, using the photos as a reference for placement. The nose is made by stacking horizontal stitches on top of each other over 1 to 2 stitches. Weave in all ends to the inside of the head.

The dark brown worsted weight scrap yarn is used for the hair. Cut different lengths of yarn for shaggy-looking hair. The sample has 14 "hairs" in lengths ranging from 4 to 6 in. / 10 to 15 cm each. Tack the strands down in the center of each length or use a small dab of fabric glue to secure in place. Untwist some of the plies on the hair for a shaggier look.

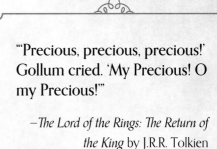

> "'Precious, precious, precious!' Gollum cried. 'My Precious! O my Precious!'"
>
> –*The Lord of the Rings: The Return of the King* by J.R.R. Tolkien

UNDYING LANDS THROW

DESIGNED BY TANIS GRAY

Separated from Middle-earth by the Belegaer Ocean, and also known as Valinor or Aman ("land that is not touched by evil"), the Undying Lands are home to immortal Elves or those given the gift of Valar. Mortal creatures are not welcome unless given rare permission. At the conclusion of the trilogy, Gandalf, Galadriel, Frodo, and Bilbo are given passage, followed many years later by Sam, Legolas, and Gimli because of their assistance in destroying Sauron. Though mortals are not granted immortality upon entering this mysterious realm, they are given the privilege of living out their days in peaceful paradise.

The perfect project to cozy up under while watching the trilogy or reading the books, this large throw is worked flat back and forth in rows. Beginning with a garter border, an alternating garter and stockinette lace leaf motif runs vertically, creating a waved edge on all sides. Knit with squishy yarn on large needles, this throw is as snuggly as mithril is strong.

SIZES
One size

FINISHED MEASUREMENTS
Width: 44 in. / 112 cm

Length: 62 in. / 157.5 cm

YARN
Bulky weight yarn, shown in Rowan *Brushed Fleece* (65% wool, 30% alpaca, 5% polyamide; approx. 125 yd. / 115 m per 1¾ oz. / 50 g ball) in color #270 Hush, 11 balls

NEEDLES
US 8 / 5.00 mm, 60 in. / 152 cm long circular needle

US 10 / 6.00 mm, 60 in. / 152 cm long circular needle or size needed to obtain gauge

NOTIONS
Stitch markers (optional)

Tapestry needle

GAUGE
12½ sts and 17 rows = 4 in. / 10 cm over Leaf Lace Pattern on larger needle, taken after blocking

Make sure to check your gauge.

PATTERN NOTES
The blanket is worked flat, back and forth in rows, from the bottom up.

It may be helpful to place a marker between each chart repeat.

PATTERN STITCHES
Leaf Lace Pattern (worked over a multiple of 32 + 8 sts)

Row 1 (RS): P3, (p2, k1, p12, k1, p2, k14) to last 5 sts, p5.

Row 2 (and all WS rows): Purl.

Row 3: P3, (p2, yo, k1, yo, s2kp, p9, k1, p2, yo, k1, yo, s2kp, k10) to last 5 sts, p5.

Row 5: P3, [p2, (k1, yo) twice, k1, s2kp, p7, k1, p2, (k1, yo) twice, p1, s2kp, k8] to last 5 sts, p5.

Row 7: P3, (p2, k2, yo, k1, yo, k2, s2kp, p5, k1, p2, k1, p1, yo, k1, yo, p2, s2kp, k6) to last 5 sts, p5.

Row 9: P3, [p2, k3, yo, k1, yo, k3, s2kp, p3, (k1, p2) twice, yo, k1, yo, p3, s2kp, k4] to last 5 sts, p5.

Row 11: P3, (p2, k4, yo, k1, yo, k4, s2kp, p1, k1, p2, k1, p3, yo, k1, yo, p4, s2kp, k2) to last 5 sts, p5.

Row 13: P3, (p2, k5, yo, k1, yo, k5, s2kp, p2, k1, p4, yo, k1, yo, p5, s2kp) to last 5 sts, p5.

Row 15: P3, (p2, k14, p2, k1, p5, k1, p6, k1) to last 5 sts, p5.

Row 17: P3, (p2, k14, p2, k1, p12, k1) to last 5 sts, p5.

Row 19: P3, (p2, k10, k3tog, yo, k1, yo, p2, k1, p9, k3tog, yo, k1, yo) to last 5 sts, p5.

Row 21: P3, [p2, k8, k3tog, p1, (yo, k1) twice, p2, k1, p7, k3tog, (k1, yo) twice, k1] to last 5 sts, p5.

Row 23: P3, (p2, k6, k3tog, p2, yo, k1, yo, p1, k1, p2, k1, p5, k3tog, k2, yo, k1, yo, k2) to last 5 sts, p5.

Row 25: P3, [p2, k4, k3tog, p3, yo, k1, yo, (p2, k1) twice, p3, k3tog, k3, yo, k1, yo, k3] to last 5 sts, p5.

Row 27: P3, (p2, k2, k3tog, p4, yo, k1, yo, p3, k1, p2, k1, p1, k3tog, k4, yo, k1, yo, k4) to last 5 sts, p5.

Row 29: P3, (p2, k3tog, p5, yo, k1, yo, p4, k1, p2, k3tog, k5, yo, k1, yo, k5) to last 5 sts, p5.

Row 31: P3, (p2, k1, p6, k1, p5, k1, p2, k14) to last 5 sts, p5.

Row 32: Purl.

Rep Rows 1–32 for patt.

PATTERN INSTRUCTIONS

CAST ON & BOTTOM EDGING

Using smaller needle, CO 136 sts using the Long Tail cast on method. Do not join to work in the rnd.
Knit 5 rows.

BODY OF BLANKET

Switch to larger needles.
Begin working from Leaf Lace Pattern chart or written instructions.
Work [Rows 1–32] 8 times, or until blanket is approx. 1 in. / 2.5 cm short of the desired total length, ending with Row 32. The patt rep is worked 4 times across each row.

TOP EDGING & BIND OFF

Switch to smaller needles.
Knit 5 rows.
With WS facing, BO all sts knitwise.

FINISHING

Weave in all loose ends to the WS with tapestry needle. Wet block the blanket to allow the sts to relax. Once dry, trim all ends.

KEY

LEAF LACE PATTERN

- ☐ Knit on RS, purl on WS
- − Purl on RS, knit on WS
- ○ yo
- ⋀ s2kp
- ⊼ k3tog
- ☐ Pattern repeat

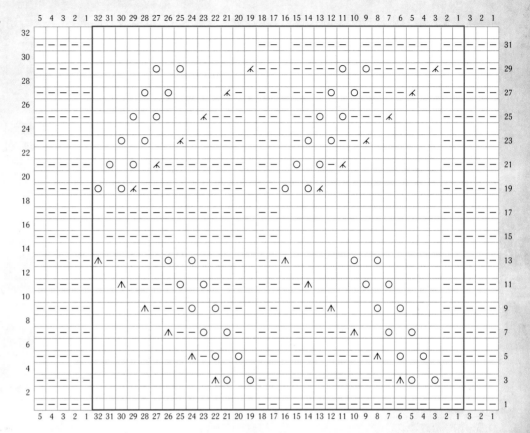

Pippin: "I didn't think it would end this way."

Gandalf: "End? No, the journey doesn't end here. Death is just another path, one that we all must take. The grey rain-curtain of this world rolls back, and all turns to silver glass, and then you see it."

Pippin: "What? Gandalf? See what?"

Gandalf: "White shores, and beyond, a far green country under a swift sunrise."

— *The Lord of the Rings: The Return of the King* film

GLOSSARY

CAST ONS

BACKWARD LOOP CAST ON

*Holding the yarn over your left thumb with the end coming from the ball held by your last three fingers and at the outside of the thumb, insert the needle up under the yarn next to the outside of your thumb. Remove your thumb from the loop, and pull the end to tighten the yarn slightly to snug the yarn up on the needle.

Repeat from * until the required number of stitches have been cast on.

CABLE CAST ON

TO START A PROJECT:

Make a slipknot and place it on the needle. Holding the needle with the slipknot in your left hand, insert the right needle into the stitch. Knit but do not slip stitch from the left needle. Place this new stitch on the left needle.

*Insert right needle between the first two stitches on the left needle and knit; place the new stitch on the left needle.

Repeat from * until the required number of stitches are on the needle.

MID-ROW:

*Insert right needle between the first two stitches on the left needle and knit; place the new stitch on the left needle.

Repeat from * until the required number of stitches are on the needle.

KNITTED CAST ON

TO BEGIN A PROJECT:

Place a slipknot onto the left-hand needle (this will be the first stitch cast on).

*Insert right-hand needle into the first stitch on the left-hand needle and knit; place the new stitch on the left needle.

Repeat from * until the required number of stitches are on the needle.

MID-ROW:

With the wrong side facing, holding the needle with the live stitches in your left hand, *insert the right needle into the first stitch. Knit but do not slip stitch from the left needle. Place this new stitch on the left needle.

Repeat from * until the required number of stitches are on the needle.

AT END OF ROW:

After completing the previous row, turn the work so the opposite side of the work is facing. Holding the needle with the live stitches in your left hand, *insert the right needle into the first stitch. Knit but do not slip stitch from the left needle. Place this new stitch on the left needle.

Repeat from * until the required number of stitches are on the needle.

LONG TAIL CAST ON

Make a slipknot with the yarn, leaving a tail long enough to cast on the required number of stitches (usually about 1 in. / 2.5 cm per stitch), and place the slipknot onto the needle. Holding the needle in your right hand, clasp both strands in your lower three fingers with the long tail over your thumb and the end coming from the ball over your index finger.

*Spread your thumb and index finger apart to form a V. Insert the needle tip up between the two strands on your thumb. Bring the needle tip over the top of the first strand around your index finger, then down to draw a loop between the strands on your thumb. Remove your thumb and tighten the stitch on the needle—1 stitch cast on. Place your thumb and index finger between the strands of yarn again.

Repeat from * until the required number of stitches have been cast on.

TWISTED GERMAN CAST ON

Make a slipknot with the yarn, leaving a tail long enough to cast on the required number of stitches (usually about 1 in. / 2.5 cm per stitch), and place the slipknot onto the needle.

*Holding the needle and yarn as for a Long Tail cast on, bring the needle toward you, under both strands around your thumb. Swing the tip up and toward you again, then down into the loop on your thumb, then up in front of the loop on your thumb. Then swing it over the top of the loops and over the first strand on your index finger, catch that strand, and bring the needle back down through the thumb loop and to the front, turning your thumb as needed to make room for the needle to pass through. Remove your thumb from the loop, then pull the strands to tighten the stitch.

Repeat from * until the required number of stitches have been cast on.

CROCHET CAST ON (NON-PROVISIONAL)

This is an end-of-row cast on method that doesn't leave gaps in the work and mimics a Long Tail cast on edge.

With the WS of the work facing, and the working yarn on the back side (i.e., the right side of the work), insert the crochet hook purlwise in the last stitch on the needle and slip the stitch onto the hook, removing it from the knitting needle.

With the working yarn behind the knitting needle, *wrap the working yarn around the crochet hook from left to right and pull the yarn through the stitch on the hook. This creates one new stitch on the knitting needle (1 stitch remains on the crochet hook).

Move the working yarn behind the knitting needle.

Repeat from * until the required number of stitches are cast on (1 stitch remains on the crochet hook).

Chain 1 stitch into this remaining loop on the crochet hook and transfer this new loop back to the knitting needle (this replaces the original stitch removed from the knitting needle at the start of the method). The cast on is now complete.

TWO-COLOR ITALIAN CAST ON

Also known as the Two-Color Tubular cast on, this method provides a stretchy but stable cast on edge that flows seamlessly into 1x1 ribbed fabric. The following instructions cast on a purl stitch first, followed by a knit stitch. To cast on a knit stitch first, reverse the order of Steps 3 and 4.

Step 1: Using LC and DC held together, create a slipknot and place the slipknot onto the working needle. The two loops of the slipknot will count as extra stitches and will be removed before any work begins. Hold the needle with the slipknot in your right hand, with the tip pointing to the left (as if ready to knit). Secure this slipknot onto the working needle by placing your index finger on top of the knot (to prevent it from sliding off the needle).

Step 2: With your index finger and thumb of your left hand positioned to an L shape, drape the DC yarn over your index finger and the LC yarn over your thumb. Secure both tails to the palm of your left hand by holding them with your lower 3 fingers. This provides tension for the cast on. The yarn now appears to create a triangle shape—the right tip of the triangle is the slipknot secured to the knitting

needle in your right hand and the two lower points of the triangle are where the yarns drape over your index finger and thumb. The yarn over the thumb will be used to add stitches purlwise, and the yarn over the index finger will be used to add stitches knitwise.

Step 3: Create a purl stitch—swing the knitting needle away from you, over the top of the DC yarn on your index finger; then point the needle tip down and toward you, catching the DC yarn. Swing the needle toward you, over the top of the LC yarn on your thumb; then point the needle tip down and away from you, catching the LC yarn. Continue the motion of moving the needle tip away from you, under the DC yarn, then back into the original position. One purl stitch has been created with the LC yarn.

Step 4: Create a knit stitch—swing the needle point toward you, over the top of the LC yarn on your thumb; then point the needle tip down and away from you, catching the LC yarn. Swing the needle upward between the LC and DC yarns, away from you, over the top of the DC yarn on your index finger; then point the needle tip down and toward you, catching the DC yarn. Continue the motion of moving the needle toward you, under the LC yarn,

then back into the original position. One knit stitch has been created with the DC yarn.

Repeat Steps 3 and 4 until the required number of stitches have been cast on (be sure not to count the slipknot in your total stitches).

Work the final 2 setup rows 1 time before beginning work (reverse the order of the slipped and knit/purl stitches if you reversed Steps 3 and 4 during the cast on).

Setup Row 1 (RS): With LC, (sl1 wyif, k1tbl) to end. Drop slipknot off the needle. Slide.

Setup Row 2 (RS): With DC, (p1, sl1 wyib) to end of row. Do not turn.

PROVISIONAL CAST ONS

CROCHET PROVISIONAL CAST ON—AROUND KNITTING NEEDLE

With waste yarn, make a slipknot and place on the crochet hook. Hold the needle in your left hand, the waste yarn over your left index finger, and the crochet hook in your right hand.

*Hold the needle above the yarn coming from the hook. With the crochet hook, reach over the top of the needle and make a chain, making sure the yarn goes around the needle—1 stitch cast on.

Repeat from * until the required number of stitches have been cast on. Cut the yarn and fasten off the last chain, being careful not to tighten the stitch.

Change to the working yarn, ready to work across the cast on stitches per pattern.

To finish the edge or pick up the stitches to continue working in the other direction, pull the waste yarn tail out of the last stitch cast on, and pull carefully to unzip the edge, placing the resulting stitches onto the needle as you go.

CROCHET PROVISIONAL CAST ON—CHAIN METHOD

With waste yarn and a crochet hook, place a slipknot on the crochet hook. This will serve as the first stitch. Chain the required number of stitches, plus a few extra. Cut the waste yarn and pull the tail through the last stitch to secure.

Using the bumps on the back side of the crochet chain as indicators, *insert your knitting needle under a bump, wrap the working yarn around the needle, and pull through to make a live stitch with the working yarn.

Repeat from * until the required number of stitches are on the knitting needle.

Proceed to pattern directions.

To finish the edge or pick up stitches to continue work in the opposite direction, remove the crochet chain by undoing the end where you pulled the tail through the final stitch. Gently unravel the chain and place the resulting stitches onto the needle as you go.

BIND OFFS

I-CORD BIND OFF

The I-Cord bind off is a lovely way to prevent rolling while providing a clean finished edge. The combination of always knitting on the right side and sliding stitches (rather than turning the work) creates the tube.

With the RS facing, and using the Cable or Knitted cast on method, cast on the required number of stitches.

*K3, k2tog, slip 4 stitches purlwise back to the left-hand needle; repeat from * until all 4 stitches remain.

Bind off the remaining 4 stitches knitwise or break the yarn and pull the tail through the live stitches to secure.

SEWN TUBULAR BIND OFF

Also known simply as the Tubular bind off, this method creates a seamless yet stretchy edge to ribbed fabric. This method uses 2 working needles and a

THREE-NEEDLE BIND OFF

The Three-Needle bind off is a way of joining two sets of live stitches in a bound-off edge, creating a firm seam. This method of seaming is ideal for seams that need the firmness to support the weight of the body and sleeves of a garment.

Place each set of stitches to be joined on separate needles, making sure the needle tips are at the right-hand edge of the sts to be bound off.

Hold both needles in your left hand with needle tips pointing to the right.

Insert the right needle knitwise into the first stitch on both needles, then knit them together—1 stitch from each needle has been joined. *Knit the next stitch on both needles together; lift the first stitch worked over the stitch just worked and off the needle—1 stitch bound off.

Repeat from * until all stitches have been worked and 1 stitch remains on the right needle. Cut yarn and fasten off the remaining stitch.

tapestry needle to graft the live stitches together.

Tubular Setup Round 1: *K1, sl1 wyif; rep from * to end of rnd.

Tubular Setup Round 2: *Sl1 wyib, p1; rep from * to end of rnd.

Slipped Stitch Round: Without knitting any stitches, slip all the stitches purlwise onto 2 needles, placing all the knit stitches on the original working needle, and all the purl stitches on a second circular needle that will be inside/behind the working needle. Each needle will now hold half the stitches.

Cut a tail of working yarn that is 4 times the length of the stitches to be bound off.

Thread a tapestry needle with the tail and using Kitchener stitch, graft all the stitches between the two needles.

KITCHENER STITCH

Very often referred to as grafting, Kitchener stitch joins two sets of live stitches without a visible seam. This seaming method is not well suited for joining shoulder seams, which need to support the weight of the body and sleeves of the garment. It should be used for smaller seamed areas or for joining sections of a cowl or the toe of a sock that is expected to be stretched.

Work a few stitches at a time, pulling the yarn loosely, then adjust the length of each stitch to match the tension on each side of the join.

Place each set of stitches to be joined onto two separate needles, making sure the needle tips are at the right-hand edge of the stitches to be joined.

Hold both needles in your left hand, parallel, with needle tips pointing to the right.

Step 1: Insert tapestry needle purlwise through first stitch on front needle and pull the yarn through, leaving stitch on front needle.

Step 2: Insert tapestry needle knitwise through first stitch on back needle and pull the yarn through, leaving stitch on back needle.

Step 3: Insert tapestry needle knitwise through first stitch on front needle, slip stitch off front needle, and pull the yarn through.

Step 4: Insert tapestry needle purlwise through next stitch on front needle and pull the yarn through, leaving stitch on front needle.

Step 5: Insert tapestry needle purlwise through first stitch on back needle, slip stitch off back needle, and pull yarn through.

Step 6: Insert tapestry needle knitwise through next stitch on back needle and pull the yarn through, leaving stitch on back needle.

Repeat Steps 3–6 until the yarn has been threaded through the last stitch of each needle once. Insert tapestry needle knitwise into last stitch on front needle, slip stitch off front needle, and pull yarn through. Then insert tapestry needle purlwise into last stitch on back needle, slip stitch from needle, and pull yarn through. Weave in ends on the wrong side to secure.

HORIZONTAL INVISIBLE SEAMING

A method of seaming two horizontal pieces of knit fabric together, such as a cast on edge to a bind off edge (or two cast on / two bind off edges).

Align the two edges to be seamed so that they are lined up, stitch by stitch, with the right side facing up.

With a threaded tapestry needle with a length of yarn approximately 3 times the length of the seamed edges, insert the needle under both legs of the first stitch of one piece and pull the yarn through (leaving a tail for weaving in).

Insert the needle under both legs of the lined-up stitch on the opposite edge (the piece you are joining to) and pull the yarn through.

Repeat these two steps (without leaving a tail for weaving in on each subsequent stitch) until all the stitches are seamed. Once the seaming is complete, you may adjust the tension of the seaming yarn so it lies flat and the stitches appear the same size as the joined edges. Trim ends and weave in.

DOUBLE KNITTING

Double knitting is a method of creating two-sided fabric, such as for a scarf or a coaster, without having an exposed wrong side. The front and back of the fabric are created simultaneously, knitting every other stitch with one color and purling the adjacent stitches with the opposite color so that the front and back of the project are mirrors of one another. As such, double knitting is done in multiples of two stitches. The colorwork charts provided for double knitting indicate the color of the stitch that will be knit; the opposite color will be worked on all purl stitches and is not charted.

To Work in the Round:

*Move both yarns to the back between the needles as if to knit (if not already in position) and knit 1 stitch using the color indicated in the chart square. After completing the knit stitch, move both yarns to the front between the needles as if to purl and purl the next stitch with the opposite color as what is indicated for the knit stitch. Repeat from * to end of round.

To Work Flat:

With the RS facing: *Move both yarns to the back between the needles as if to knit (if not already in position) and knit 1 stitch using the color indicated in the chart square. After completing the knit stitch, move both yarns to the front between the needles as if to purl and purl the next stitch with the opposite color as what is indicated for the knit stitch. Repeat from * to end of row.

With the WS facing: *Move both yarns to the back between the needles as if to knit (if not already in position) and knit 1 stitch using the opposite color indicated in the chart square. After completing the knit stitch, move both yarns to the front between the needles as if to purl and purl the next stitch with the color indicated in the chart square. Repeat from * to end of row.

APPLYING/ PLACING BEADS

CROCHET HOOK METHOD

Using abbreviated letters to indicate the color of bead (i.e., G for green, R for red, or Y for yellow), AB-X indicates to apply a bead to the fabric.

Using a crochet or bead hook appropriate for the size of bead being used, insert the hook through the bead and leave the bead on the hook. Pick up the loop of the stitch over which you want to place the bead with the crochet hook and let it drop off your knitting needle. Pull this loop through the bead and place the loop back onto the left-hand needle and remove the crochet hook. Knit this stitch in pattern to secure the bead.

DUPLICATE STITCH

Duplicate stitch is a way of adding sections of color to a knitted piece without having to work stranded knitting or intarsia. The technique covers each stitch completely. Large areas can become thick and stiff, so it's best used in small areas.

With the color to be stitched threaded into a tapestry needle, insert the needle from wrong side to right side in the stitch below the first stitch to be covered.

*Insert the tapestry needle under both legs of the stitch in the row above the stitch to be covered, and pull the yarn through, being careful not to pull the yarn too tightly. Insert the needle back into the same spot where you initially brought it to the right side, and pull the yarn through to completely cover the first stitch. Bring the needle up through the stitch below the next stitch to be covered.

Repeat from * to continue covering stitches.

BOBBLES

SB (make a 5-stitch small bobble): Into 1 stitch: Kfbfbf—4 stitches increased. Without turning the work, slip 5 sts back to the left-hand needle purlwise. Pulling the yarn behind, knit across the same 5 stitches.

Without turning the work, leaving the 5 stitches on the right-hand needle, *pass the second stitch over the first and off the needle; repeat from * 3 more times—1 stitch remains.

LB (make a 5-stitch large bobble): Into 1 stitch: Kfbfbf—4 stitches increased. *Without turning the work, slip 5 sts back to the left-hand needle purlwise. Pulling the yarn behind, knit across the same 5 stitches; repeat from * 1 more time.

Without turning the work, leaving the 5 stitches on the right-hand needle, *pass the second stitch over the first and off the needle; repeat from * 3 more times—1 stitch remains.

MB3 (make a 3-stitch bobble): Into 1 stitch: Kfbf—2 stitches increased. Turn to the WS and purl 3 stitches. Turn back to the RS and sk2p over the 3 stitches—1 stitch remains.

REVERSE YARN OVER

Worked in the opposite direction as a standard yarn over, this method twists the yarn over stitch.

To make a reverse yarn over before a purl stitch after a knit stitch: Move the working yarn to the front over the top of the right-hand needle (not between the needles) from back to front, purl the next stitch.

TWISTED DECREASES

Twisted cdd (twisted center double decrease)—slip 1 stitch purlwise, slip second stitch as if to purl through the back loop, move these 2 stitches back to left-hand needle purlwise (the second stitch is twisted); slip 2 stitches knitwise, knit 1, pass slipped stitches over (2 stitches decreased).

Twisted k2tog—slip 1 stitch purlwise, slip second stitch as if to purl through the back loop, move these 2 stitches back to left-hand needle purlwise (the second stitch is twisted); knit 2 stitches together (1 stitch decreased).

Twisted ssk (twisted slip, slip knit)—slip 1 stitch purlwise, slip second stitch knitwise, move these 2 stitches back to the left-hand needle purlwise, and knit 2 together through the back loop (1 stitch decreased).

STRANDED COLORWORK

Sometimes referred to as Fair Isle knitting, stranded colorwork uses two (or more) colors per round, with the color not currently being used being stranded, or carried, loosely across the wrong side of the work. Both yarns can be held in either the right or left hand, however you prefer to knit, or with one color in each hand. Whichever method you use, make sure to maintain even tension and keep the position vertically to maintain color dominance. The bottom strand carried will have more dominance than the top; it's best practice to carry the contrast colors as the dominant (or bottom) yarn.

When rounds of stranded colorwork are placed between rounds of stockinette, make sure to check both gauges before you begin; most knitters will work the stranded colorwork section more tightly than plain stockinette. Adjust your needle size when switching to the stranded section as needed to match gauge and remember to change back to the smaller needle(s) when beginning the next section of plain stockinette.

As you work across a round of the pattern, spread the stitches just worked apart slightly before knitting the next stitch with the color that has been carried across the wrong side. The float across the back should be relaxed, not sagging, but should also not be tight, so as to avoid puckering of the fabric.

If floats between color changes will be more than ½ to ¾ in. / 1 to 2 cm long, it's a good idea to catch the unused/floating color to reduce the risk of snagging the float later. The easiest way to do this is to hold the color to be "caught" in your left hand and the working color in your right hand. Insert the right needle into the next stitch and under the floated yarn, then knit as usual, allowing the floated yarn to come back down behind the needles so the working yarn will lie over the top of it on the next stitch. Catching floats more regularly than is necessary uses more yarn and can create a stiffer fabric.

SHORT ROWS

WRAP AND TURN (W&T) SHORT ROWS

Slip all stitches purlwise in the following sequences.

On knit rows: Knit to instructed turning point. With the yarn in back, slip the next st to the right needle, move the yarn to the front between needles, slip the stitch back to the left needle, and move the yarn to the back between needles to the purl side. Turn work.

On purl rows: Purl to the instructed turning point. With the yarn in front, slip the next stitch to the right needle, move the yarn to the back between needles, slip the stitch back to the left needle, and move the yarn to the front between needles to the purl side. Turn work.

To process the wrap on a subsequent row: Work to the wrapped stitch, pick up the wrap from front to back for a knit stitch (and from back to front for a purl stitch), and place the wrap on the left needle. Work the wrap together with the stitch as a k2tog or p2tog.

GERMAN SHORT ROWS

Double stitches are created by distorting the stitch at the end of the previously turned row.

On knit rows (following a turn): Move the working yarn to the front between the needles. Slip the first stitch purlwise to the right-hand needle. To create the double stitch (DS), pull the working yarn up and over the right-hand needle so the stitch now looks like an upside-down V, with 2 legs. Keep the yarn in back, ready to knit the next stitch, and work across the row in pattern.

On purl rows (following a turn): With the working yarn still in front, slip the first stitch purlwise to the right-hand needle. To create the double stitch (DS), pull the working yarn up and over the right-hand needle so the stitch now looks like an upside-down V, with 2 legs. Move the working yarn to the front between the needles, ready to purl the next stitch, and work across the row in pattern.

To process a double stitch on a subsequent row: Work to the double stitch and knit (or purl) the two legs together as if it were one stitch as a k2tog (kDS) or p2tog (pDS).

ABBREVIATIONS

1/1 LC—slip 1 stitch to cable needle and hold to front, knit 1; knit 1 from cable needle

1/1 RC—slip 1 stitch to cable needle and hold to back, knit 1; knit 1 from cable needle

1/1 LPC—slip 1 stitch to cable needle and hold to front, purl 1; knit 1 from cable needle

1/1 RPC—slip 1 stitch to cable needle and hold to back, knit 1; purl 1 from cable needle

1/1 LPT—slip 1 stitch to cable needle and hold to front, purl 1; knit 1 through back loop from cable needle

1/1 LT—slip 1 stitch to cable needle and hold to front, knit 1 through back loop; knit 1 through back loop from cable needle

1/1 RPT—slip 1 stitch to cable needle and hold to back, knit 1 through back loop; purl 1

1/1 RT—slip 1 stitch to cable needle and hold to back, knit 1 through back loop; knit 1 through back loop from cable needle

1/2 LPT—slip 1 stitch to cable needle and hold to front, purl 2; knit 1 through back loop from cable needle

1/2 LT—slip 1 stitch to cable needle and hold to front, knit 2 through back loop; knit 1 through back loop from cable needle

1/2 RPT—slip 2 stitches to cable needle and hold to back, knit 1 through back loop; purl 2 from cable needle

1/2 RT—slip 2 stitches to cable needle and hold to back, knit 1 through back loop; knit 2 through back loop from cable needle

2/1 LC—slip 2 stitches to cable needle and hold to front, knit 1; knit 2 from cable needle

2/1 LPC—slip 2 stitches to cable needle and hold to front, purl 1; knit 2 from cable needle

2/1 RC—slip 1 stitch to cable needle and hold to back, knit 2; knit 1 from cable needle

2/1 RPC—slip 1 stitch to cable needle and hold to back, knit 2; purl 1 from cable needle

2/2 LPC—slip 2 stitches to cable needle and hold to front, purl 2; knit 2 from cable needle

2/2 RPC—slip 2 stitches to cable needle and hold to back, knit 2; purl 2 from cable needle

2/2 LC—slip 2 stitches to cable needle and hold to front, knit 2; knit 2 from cable needle

2/2 RC—slip 2 stitches to cable needle and hold to back, knit 2; knit 2 from cable needle

2/3 LC—slip 2 stitches to cable needle and hold to front, knit 3; knit 2 from cable needle

2/3 LPC—slip 2 stitches to cable needle and hold to front, purl 3; knit 2 from cable needle

2/3 LPCDEC—slip 3 stitches to cable needle and hold to front, knit 1 through back loop, purl 1; knit 3 stitches together through the back loop from cable needle (2 stitches decreased; 3 stitches remain)

2/3 RC—slip 3 stitches to cable needle and hold to back, knit 2; knit 3 from cable needle

2/3 RPC—slip 3 stitches to cable needle and hold to back, knit 2; purl 3 from cable needle

2/3 RPCDEC—slip 2 stitches to cable needle and hold to back, knit 3 stitches together; purl 1, knit 1 through the back loop from cable needle (2 stitches decreased; 3 stitches remain)

3-to-2 (uses 3 stitches, nets 2)—knit 3 stitches together without dropping original stitches from left-hand needle, knit into the first stitch of the left-hand needle, and then drop all 3 original stitches from the left-hand needle (1 stitch decreased)

3-to-3 (uses 3 stitches, nets 3)—knit 3 stitches together without dropping original stitches from left-hand needle, yo, knit the same 3 stitches together, and then drop all 3 original stitches from the left-hand needle

3-to-9 (uses 3 stitches, nets 9)—knit 3 stitches together without dropping original stitches from left-hand needle, [yo, knit the same 3 stitches together] 4 times, and then drop all 3 original stitches from the left-hand needle (6 stitches increased)

5-to-3 (uses 5 stitches, nets 3)—knit 5 stitches together without dropping original stitches from left-hand needle, yo, knit the same 5 stitches together, and then drop all 5 original stitches from the left-hand needle (2 stitches decreased)

5-to-5 (uses 5 stitches, nets 5)—knit 5 stitches together without dropping original stitches from the left-hand needle, [yo, knit the same 5 stitches together] 2 times, and then drop all 5 original stitches from the left-hand needle

approx.—approximately

beg—begin/beginning

BN—back needle

BO—bind off

BOR—beginning of round

br4st dec (brioche 4-stitch decrease)—worked over 5 stitches: slip first brioche stitch knitwise, slip second stitch knitwise, place third brioche stitch (with its wrap) onto locking stitch marker and hold in front of work, knit fourth stitch on left-hand needle, pass second slipped stitch on right-hand needle over, move stitch to left-hand

purlwise, pass fifth brioche stitch (with its wrap) over, move stitch to right-hand needle purlwise, pass first slipped brioche stitch (with its wrap) over, move third stitch from marker to left-hand needle, move stitch on right-hand needle to left-hand needle purlwise and pass the third stitch over, move remaining stitch back to right-hand needle purlwise (4 stitches decreased)

br4st inc (brioche 4-stitch increase)—[(brk1, yo) 2 times, brk1] into the same stitch (4 stitches increased)

brk (brioche knit)—knit the stitch together with its wrap

brkyobrk (brioche 2-stitch increase)—(brk1, yo, brk1) into the same stitch (2 stitches increased)

brLsl dec (brioche left slant decrease)—worked over 3 stitches: slip first brioche stitch knitwise, brioche knit next 2 stitches together, pass slipped brioche stitch (with its wrap) over (2 stitches decreased)

brp (brioche purl)—purl the stitch together with its wrap

brRsl dec (brioche right slant decrease)—worked over 3 stitches: slip first brioche stitch knitwise, knit next stitch, pass first slipped brioche stitch (with its wrap) over, move stitch on right-hand needle to left-hand needle purlwise, pass next (third) brioche stitch (with its wrap)

over, move remaining stitch back to right-hand needle purlwise (2 stitches decreased)

CC—contrast color

cdd—slip 2 stitches together knitwise, knit 1, pass slipped stitches over (2 stitches decreased)

cm—centimeter(s)

CN—cable needle

CO—cast on

cont—continue

DC—dark color

dec—decrease(s/d)

dpn(s)—double-pointed needle(s)

DS—double stitch (used in German short rows)

EOR—end of row/round

est—established

FN—front needle

g—gram(s)

in.—inch(es)

inc—increase(s/d)

incl—include/including

k—knit

k2tog—knit 2 stitches together (1 stitch decreased)

k3tog—knit 3 stitches together (2 stitches decreased)

k5tog—knit 5 stitches together (4 stitches decreased)

kDS—knit double stitch (used in German short rows)

kfb—knit into front and back of same stitch (1 stitch increased)

kfbf—knit into front, back, and front of same stitch (2 stitches increased)

kfbfbf—knit into front, back, front, back, and front of same stitch (4 stitches increased)

kfbS—knit into front of the st, then without dropping the original st off the left-hand needle, insert the right-hand needle into the back of the same stitch, and slip it purlwise without knitting it (1 stitch increased)

ktbl—knit through the back loop

kyok—(knit 1, yarn over, knit 1) into the same stitch (2 stitches increased)

LB—make large bobble

LC—light color

LHN—left-hand needle

LR1 (Lifted Right Increase)—using the right-hand needle, pick up the right leg of the stitch 1 row below the last stitch worked and place it on the left-hand needle; knit this new stitch (1 stitch increased)

m—meter(s)

M—marker

M-A (B, C, etc.)—marker A (B, C, etc.)

M1L—insert the left-hand needle under the running thread from front to back, knit this new loop through the back loop (1 stitch increased)

M1LP—insert the left-hand needle under the running thread from front to back, purl this new loop through the back loop (1 stitch increased)

M1R—insert the left-hand needle under the running thread from back to front, knit this new loop (1 stitch increased)

M1RP—insert the left-hand needle under the running thread from back to front, purl this new loop (1 stitch increased)

MB3—make 3-stitch bobble

MC—main color

mm—millimeter(s)

N1 (2, 3, etc.)—Needle 1 (2, 3, etc.)

oz.—ounce(s)

p—purl

p2tog—purl 2 stitches together (1 stitch decreased)

patt—pattern

pDS—purl double stitch (used in German short rows)

pfb—purl into front and back of same stitch (1 stitch increased)

pm—place marker

prev—previous(ly)

psso—pass slipped stitch(es) over

ptbl—purl through the back loop

rem—remain(s/ing)

rep—repeat

RHN—right-hand needle

rm—remove marker

rnd(s)—round(s)

RS—right side

ryo—reverse yarn over

s2kp—slip 2 stitches together knitwise, knit 1, pass slipped stitches over (2 stitches decreased)

SB—make small bobble

sc—single crochet

sk2p—slip 1 stitch knitwise, knit 2 stitches together, pass slipped stitch over (2 stitches decreased)

skp—slip 1 stitch knitwise, knit 1, pass slipped stitch over (1 stitch decreased)

sl—slip stitch purlwise (unless otherwise noted)

sl1yo—with yarn in front, slip 1 stitch purlwise, then move working yarn into position over the right-hand needle to work next stitch (creating yarn over)

slide—slide stitches from one end of the needle to the other

sm—slip marker

ssk—slip, slip, knit: slip 1 stitch knitwise, slip second stitch knitwise, move these 2 stitches back to left-hand needle purlwise, and knit 2 together through the back loop (1 stitch decreased)

SSM—side seam marker

ssp—slip, slip, purl: slip 1 stitch knitwise, slip second stitch knitwise, move these 2 stitches back to left-hand needle purlwise, and purl 2 together through the back loop (1 stitch decreased)

sssk—slip, slip, slip knit: slip 1 stitch knitwise, slip second stitch knitwise, slip third stitch knitwise, move these 3 stitches back to left-hand needle purlwise, and knit 3 together through the back loop (2 stitches decreased)

St st—stockinette stitch

st(s)—stitch(es)

tbl—through back loop(s)

turn—turn work so opposite side of work is facing

twisted cdd—slip 1 stitch purlwise, slip second stitch as if to purl through the back loop, move these 2 stitches back to left-hand needle purlwise (the second stitch is twisted); slip 2 stitches together knitwise, knit 1, pass slipped stitches over (2 stitches decreased)

twisted k2tog—slip 1 stitch purlwise, slip second stitch as if to purl through the back loop, move these 2 stitches back to left-hand needle purlwise (the second stitch is twisted); knit 2 stitches together (1 stitch decreased)

twisted ssk—slip 1 stitch purlwise, slip second stitch knitwise, move these 2 stitches back to the left-hand needle purlwise, and knit 2 together through the back loop (1 stitch decreased)

w&t—wrap and turn (short row method)

WS—wrong side

wyib—with yarn in back

wyif—with yarn in front

yd.—yard(s)

yo—yarn over (1 stitch increased)

slash (/)—used to separate US units from metric measurements, with additional sizes in parentheses, brackets, and/or braces

asterisk (*)—used to indicate the beginning of a length of instructions to be repeated

parentheses ( ), brackets [ ], or braces { }—used to indicate a set of instructions to be repeated or to differentiate between sizes

YARN RESOURCES GUIDE

BERROCO
Berroco.com

**BLUE MOON
FIBER ARTS**
Bluemoonfiberarts.com

BLUE SKY FIBERS
Blueskyfibers.com

BROOKLYN TWEED
Brooklyntweed.com

CASCADE YARNS
Cascadeyarns.com

DRAGON HOARD YARN
Dragonhoardyarnco.com

EMMA'S YARN
Emmasyarn.com

EWE EWE YARNS
Eweewe.com

**FREIA FINE
HANDPAINT YARNS**
Freiafibers.com

HAZEL KNITS
Hazelknits.com

**JAMIESON'S OF
SHETLAND**
Jamiesonsofshetland.co.uk

KIM DYES YARN
Kimdyesyarn.com

KNITCIRCUS YARNS
Knitcircus.com

**LEADING MEN FIBER
ARTS**
Leadingmenfiberarts.com

**MISS BABS HAND-DYED
YARNS**
Missbabs.com

OINK PIGMENTS
Oinkpigments.com

QUEEN CITY YARN
Queencityyarn.com

**ROBIN'S PROMISE
YARN CO.**
Robinspromiseyarn.com

ROWAN
Knitrowan.com

SPINDRIFT FIBERS
Spindriftouray.com

SPUN RIGHT ROUND
Spunrightround.com

SWEETGEORGIA YARNS
Sweetgeorgiayarns.com

THE PLUCKY KNITTER
Thepluckyknitter.com

URBAN GIRL YARNS
urbangirlyarns.com

URTH YARNS
Urthyarns.com

YARN CAFÉ CREATIONS
Yarncafecreations.com

FOR BROOKS HOLMES, WHO TAUGHT ME HOW TO PLAY
CHESS, INSISTED I MEMORIZE ROBERT FROST, AND
INSTILLED IN ME AN APPRECIATION FOR TOLKIEN

ACKNOWLEDGMENTS

Every author has a strong Fellowship behind them, and I am no exception.

Thank you to my Gandalf, my Editor Anna Wostenberg, for your wizardly wisdom. You may not wear a pointy hat, but I'd follow you through Khazad-dûm without question.

As always, deepest gratitude to my clan—Roger, Callum, and Astrid—you mean more to me than all the treasure stashed beneath the Lonely Mountain. Thank you for pulling me back to reality after each day spent in Middle-earth, for making our home as cozy as any Hobbit hole, for the steady flow of cappuccino and snuggles, and your tolerance of my constant Tolkien chatter. I'd be nothing without the three of you behind me. Tolkien stated, "Not all those who wander are lost," but I cannot think of anyone else I'd rather get lost with than the three of you.

For Mom and Dad, I am grateful you taught me to stay true to myself, and that you constantly encouraged knowledge and reading growing up. I so appreciate your enthusiasm for each project I work on. You're my best and loudest cheerleaders!

Sincere thanks to my 5th grade teacher, Brooks Holmes. You read us *The Hobbit* each day out loud with such charisma and whimsy that I felt like I was part of Middle-earth. For your introduction of Tolkien to my 10-year-old self, I am forever thankful.

Infinite gratitude to keen-eyed Technical Editor, Meaghan Schmaltz. Making a book is like embarking on an adventure, and there's no one else I'd want watching my back on a journey than you. Sam and Frodo have nothing on us!

Many thanks to the brilliant group of designers who shared their talents within these pages. You're a big part of our Fellowship, and we went on this journey together. Thank you for your care, your genius, your talent, and your companionship. I'm always up for Second Breakfast, Elevensies, or any adventure with you.

Thank you to wonderful sample knitters Drew Harder and Beth Leith. Your hands are as swift and magical as the Elves.

I am much obliged to the very talented dyers who offered yarn support. Thank you for your trust in me and for geeking out with me over this project. Your talent knows no bounds!

To my second family at Insight Editions, "Someone else always has to carry on the story." Thank you for letting me carry on this one.

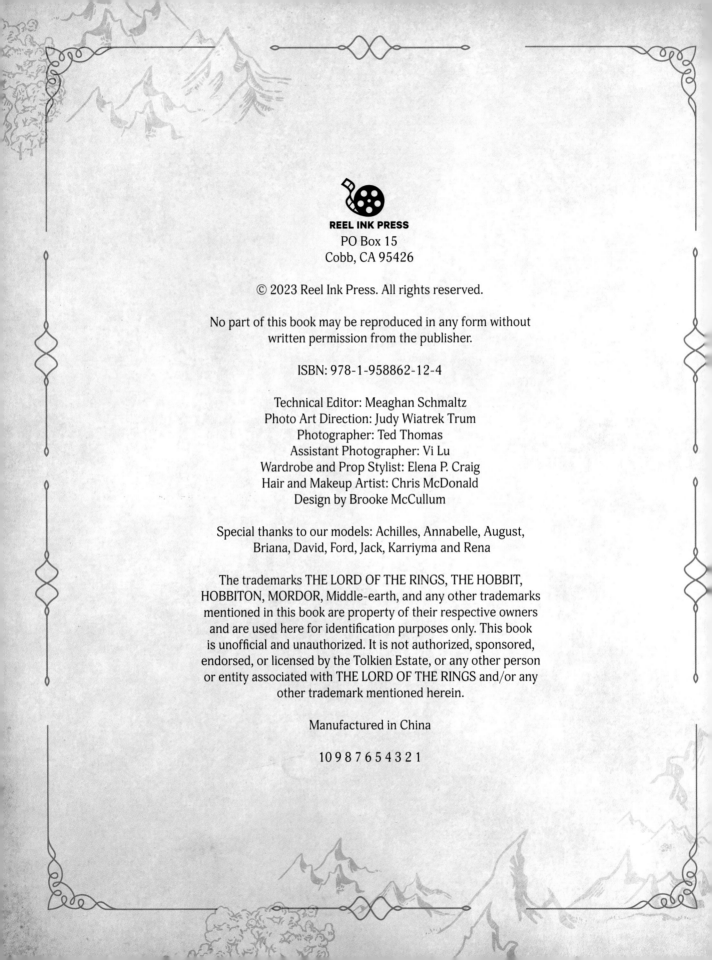

REEL INK PRESS
PO Box 15
Cobb, CA 95426

ISBN: 978-1-958862-12-4

Technical Editor: Meaghan Schmaltz
Photo Art Direction: Judy Wiatrek Trum
Photographer: Ted Thomas
Assistant Photographer: Vi Lu
Wardrobe and Prop Stylist: Elena P. Craig
Hair and Makeup Artist: Chris McDonald
Design by Brooke McCullum

Special thanks to our models: Achilles, Annabelle, August,
Briana, David, Ford, Jack, Karriyma and Rena

Manufactured in China

10 9 8 7 6 5 4 3 2 1